THEY FOUGHT THE GOOD FIGHT:

ORESTES BROWNSON
AND
FATHER FEENEY

Rejoice O Virgin Mary, you alone have destroyed all the heresies in the whole world.

THEY FOUGHT THE GOOD FIGHT:

ORESTES BROWNSON
AND
FATHER FEENEY

edited
by
Thomas Mary Sennott

CATHOLIC TREASURES
Monrovia, California

Imprimi potest
+ *Timothy J. Harrington*
Bishop of Worcester
January 15, 1987

The *Imprimi potest* is an official declaration that a book or pamphlet is free of doctrinal or moral error. No implication is contained therein that he who has granted the *Imprimi potest* agrees with the contents, opinions or statements expressed.

Library of Congress Catalog Card Number: 88-71543
ISBN #0-9620994-0-6

"IF MY REQUESTS ARE NOT GRANTED...MANY WILL BE MARTYRED, THE HOLY FATHER WILL HAVE MUCH TO SUFFER, SEVERAL NATIONS WILL BE ANNIHILATED."
OUR LADY OF FATIMA
For More Information About The Blessed Virgin Mary's Requests Write:
THE FATIMA CRUSADE, SERVANTS OF JESUS AND MARY
NAZARETH HOMESTEAD, R.D. 1, BOX 258, CONSTABLE, NY 12926-9741

For
my
Mother and Father

GENERAL INTRODUCTION

"St. Benedict Center" is now an umbrella term for several, separate religious communities located in the Still River section of Harvard, Massachusetts. The Center buildings are strung out along the top of a long hill overlooking the Nashua Valley with Mount Wachusetts in the distance. Just a short way down the road on the same hill is "Fruitlands," one of the Utopian communities that grew out of the Transcendentalist movement of the last century.

Fruitlands was founded by Bronson Alcott, who was one of the leaders of Transcendentalism, along with Ralph Waldo Emerson, Henry David Thoreau, George Ripley, Orestes Brownson, and others. Orestes Brownson thought that he and Bronson Alcott were distant relatives. Alcott was from Connecticut, as was Brownson's father, and one branch of the Brownson family spelled the name, Bronson.

These men also sponsored the most famous of the Transcendentalist communities, Brook Farm in West Roxbury. Isaac Hecker who lived for a time at both Fruitlands and Brook Farm, said of Brook Farm: "It was the greatest, the noblest, the bravest dream of New England. Nothing greater has been produced. No greater sacrifice has been made for humanity than the movement that Brook Farm embodied...Brook Farm was the realization of the best dreams these men had of Christianity, it embodied them."*

Bronson Alcott, however, was not satisfied with Brook Farm and founded the more austere Fruitlands. If Brook Farm can be compared in many ways to a Benedictine monastery, Fruitlands is its more Trappist counterpart. The little Utopian community tried to live on fruit and vegetables, hence its name.

It is usually beautiful on our hill overlooking the Nashua Valley, but for about two months during the winter we really have to pay for it. It comes as no surprise then that our Transcendentalist neighbors of long ago, trying to live on potatoes and apples, were unable to make it through their first winter.

One of the old Yankee ladies who conducted tourists through Fruitlands, which is now a museum, used to wind up her little talk on the dreams of Bronson Alcott by saying: "And now, just down the road, Father Feeney is trying to do the same thing."

---

* An undated memorandum among the *Hecker Papers*, Paulist archives, New York City. Quoted in: Ryan, Fr. Thomas R., CSSP. *Orestes A. Brownson: A Definitive Biography*, Our Sunday Visitor Inc., Huntington, Indiana, 1976, p.214.

ACKNOWLEDGEMENTS

I would like to thank all my kind friends who read the manuscript of They Fought The Good Fight *for their suggestions and encouragement, especially Fr. Giles Dimock, O.P., Fr. Peter D. Fehlner, O.F.M.,Conv., Fr. James McCurry, O.F.M.,Conv, Fr. Richard J. Shmaruk, Fr. Dennis P. Smith, and Fr. Thomas M. Riley.*

I would also especially like to thank Thomas Syseskey of the Dinand Library, Holy Cross for his invaluable assistance, Fr. Laurence W. McGrath of St. John's Seminary Library, Brighton, and Fr. Walter E. Casey of St. Rose's Church, Chelsea.

I am also grateful to the following publishers for the use of copyrighted material, especially America Press Inc. for allowing me to reprint Leonard Feeney: In Memoriam *by Fr. Avery Dulles, S.J. which appeared in* America *on February 2, 1978, and for excerpts from* The Documents of Vatican Council II *edited by Fr. Walter M. Abbot, S.J. and Msgr. Joseph Gallagher, copyright © American Press Inc. New York, 1966; to Our Sunday Visitor Inc. for excerpts from* Orestes A. Brownson: A Definitive Biography *by Fr. Thomas R. Ryan, C.P.P.S., copyright © Our Sunday Visitor Inc., Huntington, Indiana, 1976; and to Macmillan Publishing Co. for excerpts from* Orestes Brownson: Yankee, Radical, Catholic, *by Theodore Maynard, copyright © Macmillan Publishing Co., New York, 1943.*

ORESTES BROWNSON (1850)

TABLE OF CONTENTS

Cover and photography by Bartholomew Sennott

INTRODUCTION

In the early nineteenth century Puritan New England experienced what Van Wyck Brooks has aptly described as a "flowering" in a literary, philosophic and social movement that was largely religious in inspiration, that is in Transcendental-Unitarianism. But only in Orestes Brownson, a prominent member of this school, did that "flowering" come into full bloom with his entrance into the Catholic Church in 1844. Brownson had actually delayed his conversion for over a year hoping to bring with him many of his friends and associates, George Ripley, Henry David Thoreau, Margaret Fuller, Bronson Alcott, Ralph Waldo Emerson, Theodore Parker, and many others. Fr. Isaac Hecker, the founder of the Paulist Fathers has said: "He once told me that he was like the general of an army born in rebellion, and it was his duty to carry as many back with him to the true standard as he could. This delusion he soon got rid of and went alone at last." [1]

Although this little study necessarily majors in Brownson's Catholicity, he was a uniquely American Catholic. As the historian Arthur M. Schlesinger Jr. has well said: "He belongs to all Americans, not simply Catholics. Perhaps an age more sympathetic with men who would not compromise and would not retreat will accord him his rightful place. He is part of the national heritage." [2]

1 "Dr. Brownson in Boston," *The Catholic World*, LV (July 1887), p.472; Quoted in Ryan, Fr. Thomas R., CSSP., *Orestes A. Brownson: A Definitive Biography*, Our Sunday Visitor Inc., Huntington, Indiana, 1976, p.276.
2 Schlesinger, Arthur M. Jr., *Orestes A. Brownson: A Pilgrim's Progress*, Little, Brown and Co., Boston, 1939, p.297.

AN OUTLINE OF
BROWNSON'S LIFE

INTRODUCTION

I thought it appropriate to begin this study of Orestes Brownson with a brief chronological outline of his life from birth to death. But rather than just the bare bones of facts and dates, I have added in their proper place brief accounts about the major events in his life by various authors, as well as some of my favorite Brownson anecdotes. The outline is followed by a picture gallery of some of Brownson's friends also arranged in chronological order with additional commentary and anecdotes.

1803   Orestes Augustus Brownson born September 16 in Stockbridge, Vermont; son of Sylvester Augustus Brownson and Relief Metcalf Brownson.

1809   Father dies; Orestes placed in care of elderly couple on small farm in Royalton, Vermont.

> The simple history of the Passion of our Lord, as I read it in the Evangelists, affected me deeply. I hung with delight on the mystery of Redemption, and my young heart often burned with love to our Blessed Lord, who had been so good as to come into the world, and to submit to the most cruel death of the cross that he might save us from our wicked dispositions, and make us happy for ever in heaven. I wanted to know every thing about him, and I used to think of him frequently in the day and the night. Sometimes I seemed to hold long familiar conversations with him, and was deeply pained when anything occurred to interrupt them. Sometimes, also, I seemed to hold a spiritual intercourse with the Blessed Mary, and with the holy Angel Gabriel, Who had announced to her that she was to be the mother of the Redeemer.[1]

1817   Rejoins mother, brothers and sisters in Ballston Spa, New York. Attends Ballston Academy; works in printer's shop.

1822   Joins Presbyterian Church.

[1] Brownson, Orestes A., *The Convert, or Leaves from My Experience, Works,* Volume V, p.5.

I must then, I continued, revoke the act of surrender which I make of my reason to authority on entering the Presbyterian Church; for it was an irrational, an unmanly act. I offered in it no reasonable obedience or submission to God. It was a blind submission, and really no submission of my reason at all. It was a cowardly act of an intellectual desperado, although the motive was good. I reclaim my reason, I reclaim my manhood, and henceforth I will, let come what may, be true to my reason, and preserve the rights and dignity of my human nature. This resolution, of course, separated me from Presbyterianism. The peculiar Presbyterian doctrines I had never believed or professed to believe, except on the authority of the Presbyterian Church. Grant her authority from God to teach, I was logician enough to understand that I must believe whatever she taught, whether I could or could not reconcile it with my own reason. That authority taken away, then I was not bound to believe her doctrines, unless I found reasons for doing so elsewhere.[2]

1824   Teaches school in Detroit, Michigan. Contracts malaria; while convalescing, studies Universalism.

1826   Ordained Universlist minister at Jaffrey, New Hampshire. Itinerant minister and school teacher in New York State.

1827   Marries Sally Healy, a former pupil at Elbridge, New York.

Brownson's wife was so patiently constituted that whatever she may have suffered from marital harshness, she was always affectionate and loving to husband and children, ever cheerful and devoted to their comfort and happiness. Of her it may be said, her dignity consisted in being unknown to the world; her glory was the esteem of her husband; her pleasure the happiness of her family. One of her greatest sorrows was the unchristian character which her husband's writing and speeches assumed a few years

[2] *The Convert,* p.18.

after their marriage. She had been taught the so-called Orthodox faith [Congregationalism] and was a devout believer in it; but she knew that it was hopeless to try to bring her husband to this belief by attempting to argue the matter out with him. She could only hope and pray, patiently and hopefully. The years passed by, and Brownson not only accepted all of Christianity which his wife believed, but went further and embraced all of Christianity which Christ taught. He often read his articles to his wife before publication, and attached great importance to her judgment; indeed, he often said that, intellectually , she was his superior.[3]

1828   Editor of Universalist journal, *Gospel Advocate and Impartial Investigator*; first son, Orestes Jr., born.

1829   Becomes associate of Fanny Wright and Workingman's Party. Leaves Universalist ministry and becomes an infidel (his own term). Corresponding editor of *Free Enquirer*. Son, John Healy, born.

1831   Returns to practice of religion and becomes an independent minister. Edits and publishes *The Philanthropist*.

1832   Pastor of Unitarian parish in Walpole, New Hampshire. Studies French philosophers and social reformers.

Somehow he still found time for study. It was remorseless study, late into the night varied only by writing and preaching. For stimulation he would visit Boston, and he would play chess for hours on end with his eldest son, a boy of six who was later to edit a chess magazine. In 1887 he was to write describing these games to his younger brother Henry. Their father would sometimes send for him at eight in the morning, and they would play until midnight without respite. "How our dear father loved a game of chess!"[30] The preacher's library was still small, but Ripley lent him books - Jouffroy and Saint Simon, all

[3] Brownson, Henry, *Early Life,* H.F. Brownson, Detroit, 1898, p.485.

of whom, put a stamp upon his mind.[4]

1834   Unitarian minister at Canton, Massachusetts. Writes *Charles Elwood, or the Infidel Converted.* Associates with Transcendentalists, Emerson, Thoreau, Ripley, etc. Third son, William Ignatius, born.

1835   Ursuline convent in Charlestown, Massachusetts burned by anti-Catholic mob. Fourth son, Henry Francis, born.

1836   Moves to Chelsea, Massachusetts. Establishes Society for Christian Union and Progress. Urges reunion of all Christian churches, "a new Catholicity without the Papacy"; calls for an ecumenical council to bring this about.

> He was in truth a rough and rustic figure among the fastidious and almost lady-like "liberal" Christians. On the ferry between Chelsea and Boston everyone knew the tall preacher in the swallow-tail coat who always carried a pile of books under his arm and a chaw of tobacco in his cheek. In his hearty way he used to get into conversation with strangers and, more likely than not, into a metaphysical argument. For the first time his astounded fellow-passengers would hear the outlandish names of Kant and Jouffroy and Constant and Saint-Simon and Cousin.[5]

1838   Appointed steward of the United States Marine Hospital in Chelsea by George Bancroft as reward for supporting Van Buren for President. Founds own journal, *The Boston Quarterly Review.*

1839   Only daughter, Sarah, born.

1840   Son George born.

1842   Associates with Brook Farm in West Roxbury.

[4] Maynard, Theodore, *Orestes Brownson: Yankee, Radical, Catholic* The Macmillan Co., New York, 1943, p.54; n.30 Letter in Notre Dame Archives, dated Feb. 22, 1887.
[5] Maynard, *Op. cit.,* p.67.

It is unfortunate that so few traditions remain of Brownson's contact with Brook Farm, for he went there at the most critical moment of his life, when as a Brook Farmer once said, "he walked backward into the Catholic Church." A few anecdotes indicate plainly that when Brownson turned up the road leading to the Hive he brought his disputatiousness with him, and that he was apt to veer conversation around to matters which interested him if nobody else. Mrs. Kirby says with her occasional tartness that "he was not the prince of gentlemen in debate." "Do you approve of the priests of the Inquistion roasting off the feet of children under fourteen?" Cornelia asked. "Certainly," he replied, according to the same authority. "It was better for them to have their feet roasted off in this world than their souls in the next."[6] (Fr. Ryan comments: "Who was having the most fun in this case?")[7]

1843   Edward ("Ned") Patrick born.

1844   Catholics killed and churches burned in Philadelphia and other cities by Nativist mobs. Entire Brownson family becomes Catholic. Establishes *Brownson's Quarterly Review* under Bishop Fitzpatrick.

Fortunately for Brownson, there were no domestic complications over his conversion. Sally, who had grieved deeply, if silently, during the early years of their marriage, at witnessing his growing unbelief, now encouraged him to become a Catholic, and her own candid heart readily accepted the faith to which he had attained only with so much struggle. As for the children, they were not only Brownsons but Brownsonians, and they prattled around the meal-table of the *me* and the *not-me*, and *das reine Seyn*

[6] Swift, Lindsay, *Brook Farm,* The Macmillan Co., New York, 1900, p.248.
[7] Ryan, Fr. Thomas R., CSSP., *Orestes A. Brownson: A Definitive Biography,* Our Sunday Visitor Inc., Huntington, Indiana, 1976, p.329.

and *das Ding-an-sich*.[8] All except Orestes Junior, who was living his jolly life on the ocean wave and who knew nothing of what was happening at home until it was all over and he was back from Calcutta. Then he was at first so shocked that he left home and went to live with some relations in Ohio. But he, too, after a while entered the Jesuit college at Cincinnati to complete his interrupted education, and there he was baptized by Bishop Purcell. All the other members of the family entered the Church together.[8]

*   *   *

His theological essays in the *Review* for 1845, and the following nine years, were submitted to Bishop Fitzpatrick before publication. To many writers it might have been burdensome to undergo ecclessiastical censorship; but the editor took a brighter view of the matter, and was glad to read his articles to one who could both protect him from doctrinal error, and discuss with him intelligently the subject treated of. For years he had been in the habit of reading his more important articles to his wife before they were sent to the printers, and felt that he had derived benefit from her good sense and calm, clear judgment. By this submission of his theological essays to Fitzpatrick, he was saved from falling into erroneous statements of Catholic doctrine, which the neophyte may so easily fall into, and had the satisfaction and confidence resulting from a consciousness of entire conformity to the orthodox faith. In fact, if it was a burden to any one, it must have been so to the Bishop, whose time was so needed for the duties of his office, that it was no small matter for him to hear and discuss, one or two or more long articles every three months for nine or ten years. Nor did Brownson view it differently, as the frequent expressions of his gratitude and reverence towards the great Bishop expressed in his writ-

---

[8] Maynard, *Op. cit.,* pp.146,147;n.89 Brownson, Henry, *Early Life,* H.F. Brownson, Detroit, 1898, pp.98,99.

ings on every opportunity bear witness.[9]

*　　　*　　　*

Tufts College, College Hill, Mass.,
January 30, 1890

My Dear Mr. Brownson:

I wish I could help you in your good work; but my acquaintance with your father was very slight. I was young when he lived in Chelsea – too young every way to come in the range of such a man. Dr. Langworthy and Rev. Samuel Robbins knew him well. Both of these men (who might have given you help) are dead.

I can only tell you how awed I used to be by the "man of power," as some of us used to call him, and how I longed to know him.

One thing I may tell you – one of those slight things that show a man, and a man's faith in things. He was the center of little gatherings on the ferry-boats in the early days when the ferry-boats were the only means of conveyance to and from Boston. Dr. Brownson was full of the motive of the Catholic faith, and loved to talk of it to the persons – twenty or more – who were sure to gather about him of a summer morning on the deck of the ferry-boat.[10]

*　　　*　　　*

Like most New England ministers, Brownson had been very lean in his Protestant days; but soon after he became a Catholic, he began to put on flesh, till his weight increased to two hundred and fifty pounds. One day he was walking towards his publishers on Washington Street with one of his sons, and he met two Reverend Doctors of Divinity, Salter and Woods, who were both as lean as Brownson had ever been. They turned and walked with him. One of them said: "How is it, Brother Brownson, that you, who used to

[9] Brownson, Henry, *Middle Life,* H.F. Brownson, Detroit, 1899, pp.98,99.
[10] *Middle Life,* pp.639,640.

be as lean as we are, have grown so big? Tell us the secret."

"It is very simple," he answered, "all you have to do is to become Catholics, go to confession and get your sins off your conscience, and you will grow fat and laugh."[11]

*   *   *

One day a man named Hoover, from Charleston, S.C. was abusing Brownson to his publisher, the Rev. Benjamin H. Greene. As Brownson entered the bookstore, Greene said, "There is Mr. Brownson now, talk to him." Hoover thereupon turned to Brownson and violently abused him for becoming a Catholic. Brownson interrupted him, saying, "Another word, and I will throw you over that stove-pipe." As the man defiantly went on, Brownson took hold of his coat-collar with one hand and the seat of his trousers with the other, and pitched him over the pipe, which ran from a stove in the front part of the shop to the wall in the rear.

Hoover commenced an action for assault and battery against Brownson; but it never came to trial, because the Masonic lodge to which Hoover had gained entrance by false representations, sent inquiries to Charleston concerning him; and learning that he had never been a Mason, but had been expelled from the Odd-Fellows there, gave Hoover to understand that it would be advisable for him to leave Boston without delay. The verb to *hooverize*, was added to the language on this occasion: though it has long since died out.[12]

1845   Eighth and last child, Charles Joseph Maria, born.

1846   Sixth Provincial Council of Baltimore dedicates United States to Immaculate Conception.

---

[11] *Middle Life,* p.634.
[12] *Middle Life,* pp.634,635.

Apparently the full explanation of his deep Catholic spirit is that it flowed from his own interior spiritual life. He always wrote with the crucifix before him, flanked by a statue of the Blessed Virgin Mary. He wore Our Lady's scapular and recited the rosary daily, usually at sundown.[13]

1847 Article entitled "The Great Question" appears in *Review*.

1849 Seventh Provincial Council of Baltimore sends Brownson letter of encouragement signed by all attending bishops. Article "Civil and Religious Toleration" appears in *Review*. Son George, age nine, dies of scarlet fever.

Dear Sir:

After the close of our Council I suggested to our venerable Metropolitan the propriety of our encouraging you by our approbation and influence to continue your literary labors in defence of the faith, of which you have proved an able and intrepid advocate. He received the suggestion most readily, and I take the liberty of communicating the fact to you, as a mark of my sincere esteem, and of the deep interest I feel in your excellent *Review*. I shall beg of him and the prelates who entertain the same views to subscribe their names in confirmation of my statement.

Your very devoted Friend
(signed) Francis Patrick Kenrick
Bishop of Philadelphia

† Samuel (Eccleston), Archbishop of Baltimore.
† Peter Richard (Kenrick), Archbishop of St. Louis.
† Michael (Portier), Bishop of Mobile.
† Ant. (Blanc), Bishop of New Orleans.
† John Joseph (Chance), Bishop of Natchez.
† John (Timon), Bishop of Buffalo.
† M. O'Connor, Bishop of Pittsburgh.

---

[13] Ryan, *Op. cit.,* p.329.

† Matthew (Loras), Bishop of Dubuque.
† John M. Odin, Bishop of Galveston.
† Martin John (Spalding), Bishop of Langone and Coadj., Louisville.
† M. de St. Palais, Bishop of Vincennes.
† Wm. Tyler, Bishop of Hartford.
† J. B. Fitzpatrick, Bishop of Boston.
† Richard Pius (Miles), Bishop of Nashville.
† John Baptist (Purcell), Bishop of Cincinnati.
† John Hughes, Bishop of New York.
† Richard Vincent (Whelan), Bishop of Richmond.
† James Oliver (Vandevelde), Bishop of Chicago.
† John M. Henni, Bishop of Milwaukee.
† John (McCloskey), Bishop of Albany.
† Amadeus (Rappe), Bishop of Cleveland.
† Peter Paul (Lefevre), Bishop of Zela, Coadj. Admr., Detroit.
† Andrew Byrne, Bishop of Little Rock.[14]

*   *   *

Planters House, St. Louis;
January 3, 1854

My dear wife:

I arrived through the protection of the Blessed Virgin and St. John, at this place, on Sunday between eleven and twelve o'clock. I had no serious accident until within eight miles of the city (I travelled all the way, except six miles, at Lake (name not legible), by RR to Alton, twenty miles from St. Louis), when our boat, Altona, ran on a sandbar. In getting off the sandbar, she struck upon a chain of rocks; from these she struck her bow upon a (word not legible) which knocked a hole in her bottom, and swung round and struck her stern upon another which broke six pins of her timbers.

She came across the channel, with a rapid current, and ice drifting against her with awful force. By means of pumps and buckets at which passengers as

[14] *Middle Life,* pp.116-118.

well as crew worked for some eighteen or twenty hours, till completely exhausted, we kept her afloat for a time; but the frigate sank to her guards. Sunday morning, about eight o'clock, the Ben West could not move; but after two hours detention, the Brunetta came along and took us off.

No lives were lost, and no passengers suffered otherwise than from apprehension, which the general disregard for life in these parts justified. For twenty hours, she was in imminent danger; for navigation is nearly closed, and the ice could have knocked us to pieces before a boat could save us. And we had no way of getting ashore; yesterday was mild; and today is as warm as a mild day in April.

I give my first lecture tomorrow evening, and my last in this city on Wednesday of next week. I hope to be in Louisville the week following. My friends received me cordially here, and have provided me with rooms in the Planters Hotel, the best in the city. Yesterday, I was out all day, making calls and paying the compliments of the season. I drank my quantity of eggnog, which with a cold bath last night has more than half cured the cold. I am a little hoarse; but not any more ill; and am as comfortable as I can be away from my home, my dear wife and children. I shall not expose myself on the river again, if the water remains as low as it is now. So do not suffer any apprehension. Let Father (name not legible) say a Mass of Thanksgiving for my preservation, and another for my protection.

I hope you are well, and that all goes well. Give my love to the boys, to Sarah, and believe me,

your own affectionate husband,
O. A. Brownson.[15]

1851   Charles Joseph Maria, age eight, dies of scarlet fever.

1854   Pope Pius IX defines dogma of Immaculate Conception. Brownson ceases submitting articles in *Review* to Bishop

[15] Ryan, *Op.cit.,* p.430; n.39 Microfilm of *Brownson Papers,* Roll 9, Notre Dame.

Fitzpatrick. Receives letter of encouragement from Pope Pius IX. Criticized by many Irish Americans, including a few bishops of Gallican tendencies, for his ultra-montane stand during Know-Nothing troubles.

October 8, 1855

Gentleman:

...You ask in your third question: "Do you believe, or did you ever assert in your *Review* that Catholics in the United States owed (owe) temporal allegiance to the Pope of Rome?" I answer, *Never*. I owe obedience to the Pope only as the spiritual head of my Church, and I assert for him as such only a spiritual authority. Nevertheless, I have maintained and maintain that this spiritual authority extends to the morality of temporal things, in so far and only so far, as they are spiritually related or have a spiritual character; that is, so far as they have the right to pronounce for the Catholic conscience, whether they do or do not conform to the law of God; for the Pope as the head of the Church is the interpreter and judge for Catholics of the divine law, natural or revealed. To explain myself. The people of this country had on their gaining their independence the right to adopt such a form or constitution of government, not repugnant to natural justice or the law of God, as seemed to them good; this constitution, when adopted, is obligatory upon me as a Catholic citizen, and not being repugnant to the divine law, is obligatory on the Pope in his relations with us as upon us. Then every law made in conformity to it is obligatory on my conscience, and consequently on the conscience of the Pope; for what binds the conscience of the simple believer binds alike the conscience of bishop and Pope. The Pope has recognized the American constitution as compatible with the law of God. Suppose the supreme court decided the fugitive-slave law to be constitutional, then I am bound in conscience to obey. Suppose, however, the constitution or a law passed under it should command me to be an idolator, a Mormon, a

Mohammedan, or a Presbyterian, the Pope would have the right to forbid me to obey it, and to declare the law and the constitution in so far as it authorizes such a law, null and void for the Catholic conscience, because it is repugnant to the law of God. But in either case, you will perceive, gentlemen, that I assert no civil or temporal jurisdiction for the Supreme Pontiff, for I extend his authority only to the decision of the spiritual question involved in the temporal...[16]

*　　　*　　　*

Boston, August 25, 1855

My dear Sir:

...The course which some Catholic prelates who approved my doctrine to myself personally, have taken, has not given me so high an opinion of their Catholic honor as of their policy. I have dared, at the risk of my reputation and means of subsistence, of all I hold dear except the truth and the approbation of heaven, to bring out the only doctrine that can save society from ruin, and they who *agree* with me, misrepresent, banter, or denounce me, or remain silent. Is this what Catholic faith and honor demand?...

I have never been able to discover any difference between you and myself on the nativist question, except that I am *not* proud of my New England ancestors. I want precisely what you do, that influence must be Catholic, not foreign, because otherwise it will do harm instead of good. The whirlwind that is excited against us has been occasioned not by the cause or persons your St. Louis friends imagine, but by a premature attempt to organize the Catholic or Irish influence. I could, if I were with you, tell you what has been done, and show you that the Know-Nothing movement is nothing but a punishment

---

[16] *Middle Life*, pp.553-559. A perfect illustration of what Brownson means by the spiritual authority of the Holy Father extending to the morality of temporal things is the question of abortion.

upon us for our imprudence...I foresaw it during the late presidential canvass. I have only been trying to recover the ground we have lost, and nobody except Know-Nothings seems to understand me...[17]

*   *   *

Last December we gave to the Bishop of Boston, a set of the volumes of the *Review* from the commencement with the request that he would lay them at the feet of the Holy Father, as a public token of our filial devotion and unreserved submission to the Apostolic See, and of our profound veneration of the person of the reigning Pontiff. These volumes, together with a letter from us, the Bishop on his late visit to Rome was so kind as to present to the Holy Father, who has deigned to acknowledge their reception in the most gracious and benignant terms. We hope we shall be pardoned for laying his Brief, with a translation, before our readers...

"Beloved son, health and apostolical benediction. Our venerable brother, John Bishop of Boston, brought to us your letter of the 26th last December, in which you offered us several works written by you. He spoke to us with merited praise of these same books of yours, and therefore we are in a greater degree rejoiced and consoled by your sentiment of truly filial devotion, obedience, and piety towards us, and this Holy See, which your letter expresses throughout. With our suppliant vows and prayers we beseech the God of Mercies and Father of Lights that with his celestial protection he may cherish and guard these sentiments, which we trust you will always preserve. And as a token of our so great benignity, and as a pledge of our gratitude to you for the service you have done us, we add our apostolical benediction, which we lovingly impart, with the poured forth affection of our paternal heart, to you

[17] *Middle Life,* pp.601-606.

yourself, beloved son, and to your whole family.

"Given at St. Peter's at Rome, on the 29th day of
April, in the year of Our Lord 1854, and the eighth of
our Pontificate."

(Signed) Pius IX, Pope.

This is indeed no formal approbation of our *Review*,
and no such approbation was deserved or expected;
but it is more than a simple acknowledgement of the
reception of the volumes and accompanying letter. It
is a recognition and encouragement most dear to our
heart, and which it will be our study, as far as in us
lies, to justify.[18]

1855   Moves to New York City. Under influence of Fr. Isaac Hecker
and others, gradually adopts a more liberal tone for the sake of
the convert movement.

Just before leaving Boston, Brownson received
from Europe two communications that gave him
pause. In its houses of study for seminarians, the
Catholic Church was being benefited by the sort of
work he had been doing. His article against Kant and
against Gallicanism had been extremely useful. He
paced the floor of his room, at first slowly; and then
with such fire in his heels that Sally went upstairs to
find the cause for worry. Orestes asked her how much
of the furniture was sold and whether it were too late
to decide upon remaining in Chelsea. Was he being
saved from another blunder? Would New York be a
mistake?

Mrs. Brownson read the first letter. It was from
J.C. Shaw. In it was related the flattering reaction of
Father Glover, S.J. to the *Brownson Quarterly*. And
Shaw declared Glover to be, "the profoundest man I
ever met." The Jesuit had just completed the reading
of a half dozen issues.

"He took off his spectacles, and said with great
emphasis: 'This man astonishes me; he is clear and

---

[18] *Brownson's Quarterly Review,* (October 1854), pp.538,539.

strong beyond compare; that is the most masterly refutation of Kant I have ever read.' And again after reading several of the articles a second time, he returned to the attack. 'He pleases me more and more,' he said, 'I think God has raised him to hunt down and destroy the absurd principles now in vogue in politics, in philosophy, and in religion; but,' and he went on solemnly, 'but his very greatness makes me fear for him; for unless he be solidly grounded in humility, the success, which so great power applied to teaching the truth assures him, will turn his head, and make him forget that he has all from God, and none from himself. May he remember that there have been Origens and Tertullians as well as Augustines.'"

Hecker had once advised "any place but New York." But lately he had joined with Rev. J.F. Cummings and Father Manahan in advocating Brownson's moving to the metropolis immediately. Brownson had decided, at last, in the light of differences between diocesan heads. The editor owed no debt of gratitude to Archbishop Hughes and in case of dispute he would have to deal with him frankly, man to man.[19]

*   *   *

...While he remained in Boston he ever asserted the highest toned Catholicity. After his removal to New York, some of his clerical friends there, with the Reverend Isaac Hecker at their head, urged that the best way to make converts in this country was to present only so much of Catholic doctrine to those not Catholics as was absolutely necessary for them to accept in order to enter the Church; and that they would be repelled rather than attracted by doctrines and practices too much opposed to their habits of

[19] Whalen, Doran (Sr. Rose Gertrude Whalen, CSC.), *Granite for God's House,* Sheed and Ward, New York, 1941, pp.236,237; *Middle Life,* pp.64,65.

belief and of conduct. Brownson eventually gave into this policy...[20]

1856   Publicly criticized by Archbishop Hughes for "Americanizing" tendencies.

The archbishop once said to us, "I will suffer no man in my diocese that I cannot control. I will either put him down or he shall put me down." We do not object to the principle; no bishop should suffer, if able to prevent it, the rise within his jurisdiction of any power, in opposition to his authority, too strong for him to control. We suppose he regarded us not unlikely to become dangerous, and therefore felt it his duty, "to put us down," though we do not think we were ever powerful enough, however ill- disposed, to be dangerous, and we know that we were never capable of resisting legitimate authority. At no time had authority to do more than to speak in its own name to be obeyed, and obeyed cheerfully.[21]

1857   Moves to Elizabeth, New Jersey. Writes spiritual auto-biography, *The Convert; or Leaves from my Experience.*

About the time Brownson quit the New York diocese, in a letter to Bishop Fitzpatrick of Boston, dated May 12, 1857... Brownson concluded by remarking nostalgically:

"I take this occasion to renew my assurance of my grateful recollection of all your kindness to me, the invaluable service you have rendered, your steady friendship and support for years, and in confidence, my regret that I am no longer under your spiritual direction and that I ever removed from my only home. Think of me as well and kindly as you can and believe me with all my faults your grateful friend and

Dutiful and affectionate son in Christ
O. A. Brownson." [22]

---

[20] Brownson, Henry, *Latter Life,* H.F. Brownson, Detroit, 1900, p.262.
[21] *Latter Life,* p.491.
[22] Ryan, *Op. cit.,* p.547; n.61 Microfilm *Brownson Papers,* Roll 9, Notre Dame.

Some of the Irish were getting mighty tired by this time of the way in which Brownson had been jabbing them from various angles, as they saw it, and felt they had some old scores to square off with him. And out from their midst stepped their champion: Fr. John Boyce. Fr. Boyce was from Maynooth Seminary, Ireland, and was at this particular time pastor of the only Catholic church in Worcester, Massachusetts. He had also become a novelist. Brownson had already taken notice of his two novels, *Shandy McGuire* and the *Spaewife*. When Fr. Boyce published his latest novel, *Mary Lee or the Yankee in Ireland,* Brownson had a special reason for not overlooking it. In the novel as first published in the *Metropolitan Record*, Brownson was satyrized in the person of a certain Dr. Horseman, one of the main characters in the book. He was castigated for his indiscreet zeal as a convert, especially for his interpretation of the dogma that there is no salvation outside the Church, and the author, as Brownson said, "warned his countrymen (the Irish) against one whom he regarded as their enemy." It is true that the author did not mention Brownson by name, but there could be no doubt in the mind of the public who was meant. For all knowledgeable readers saw at once certain humorous resemblances between Brownson and Dr. Horseman – Dr. Horseman chewed tobacco, and so did Brownson chew "the weed"; Dr. Brownson wore gold-bowed spectacles, so did he; Dr. Horseman spoke in a gruff, harsh voice, and Brownson's voice was deep base, and not very musical. To clinch the identity, Dr. Horseman was given as a Yankee reviewer, and as Brownson pointed out, there was only one such in the whole wide world himself. It was Michael Earls, S.J., who explained more recently in the *Commonweal* that it was Bishop Fitzpatrick of Boston who prevailed upon Fr. Boyce to tone down the severities of Dr. Horseman's character, and when the novel came out in book form, Dr. Horseman had been metamorphosed into the banal Dr. Henshaw, a Scotch reviewer. While acknowledging the implied apology,

Brownson did not appreciate this, saying the change had really marred the artistic merits of the book. Admirably pachydermatous in the matter, he assured Fr. Boyce that he had not been offended by the personalities indulged in his regard, and that he loved a joke as much as any of his Irish friends. "So here is our hand Fr. John," he said, "only give us back our friend Dr. Horseman and remember for the future that Jonathan can bear with good humor a joke, even at his own expense, if it lack not the seasoning of genuine wit."[23]

1858   Son John, age 29, killed in accident.

Elizabeth, New Jersey,
July 17, 1860

Dear wife:

We are all well and get along well, except myself. I am about as fidgety when you are gone as they say you are when I am gone, and though my health is well enough, I shall not be worth much till your return. I really did not know before, how necessary you are to me, and that I am really nothing without you. Yet I wish you to stay where you are as long as you continue to improve, or you and Sarah find it agreeable. Edward will go after you some time next week, and you can regulate his stay. He must be at St. John's [Fordham University] the first week in September, and I suppose you will want a little time to get his things in order. But you must take your own time.

Margaret [the cook] is quite well, and does so-so; though like myself a little lonesome.

In coming home by Troy. The boats are not quite as elegant as the Albany boats; but you will have no shifting of cars or baggage. Take your tickets at Ballston, and checks for baggage to New York. Take

[23] Ryan, *Op. Cit.*, p.555; n.21 "Mary Lee or the Yankee in Ireland," *Brownson's Quarterly Review*, (January 1860), pp.118- 130; n.22 "Greek Meets Greek," *Commonweal*, XX, 1934, pp.40-42; n.23 "Mary Lee," p.127.

the last train from the Springs, about 7 P.M. The boat waits for it, and arrives in New York in season for the 8 o'clock, or at the latest the 9 o'clock train to Elizabeth. You may be coming so late as not to get so good a stateroom as you might wish, but you must run your chance like other folk.

Patrick has done nothing to keep out the water, and I presume will not. Even my refusal to pay rent does not stir him up. The garden prospers. I have had two roses from my bush; and Sarah's pinks blossomed finely.

I hope mother is getting better. I am sure you will find her a dear old lady, and Thorina a dear good sister. My love to both of them, and to my own dear daughter. Take all the comfort you can, and get some flesh on your bones, and let me see you hale and hearty when you get home... Write to me, and believe me your

Savage but affectionate husband
Orestes A. Brownson[24]

1861   Campaigned strenuously during the Civil War for the emancipation of slaves as a war measure. Denounced to Rome by Archbishop Hughes and others for liberalism.

(Excerpt from letter of Archbishop Hughes to Cardinal Barnabò, Prefect of the Propaganda Fide, dated September 30, 1861.)

...I have already pointed out to your Eminence that apart from the personal spiritual good of Dr. Brownson, the Catholic Church has never drawn much profit from his conversion. From the first minute of his submission to the church, the Boston clergy has admitted him to too great familiarity. He was almost always at the Bishop's table, where he laid down the law and taught philosophy as if he were an oracle.

[24] Ryan, *Op. cit.,* pp.582,583; n.19 Microfilm, *Brownson Papers,* Roll 9, Notre Dame.

When he came to live in New York, he wanted to submit to me manuscripts of all articles that were going to appear in his *Review*, so that I might change, correct, or disapprove them as I saw fit. I excused myself for several very good and excellent reasons. I treated him with a lot of consideration, not allowing him either too much intimacy or too much familiarity, but leaving him a little bit off to one side in his aloofness. However he made the acquaintance of several of my priests, particularly of a class of young priests who had the advantage of studing theology in Europe and who had literary and philosophical pretensions. Of this number, four had studied in Europe and two or three others, although priests, were converts. They kept up the practice of meeting just to make conversation – and everything that pertained to the Church all the way from the general administration of affairs by the Supreme Pontiff down to the way of acting of one of our insignificant sacristans, all this was then discussed, criticized, approved or disapproved according to the wise and discreet views of Dr. Brownson and his associates. They were impatient for the moment when they could illuminate the Church of this country with a new light and communicate to it the spirit of the century in which we live. I was the first and principal obstacle to the execution of their plans. They know very well that if they did or said anything that was contrary to religion or that displeased the archbishop of New York, they would draw down upon themselves the contempt of the faithful.[25]

*   *   *

(Excerpt of letter to Cardinal Barnabò by Brownson dated July 24, 1861. H.E. stands for His Eminence.)

...I wish to assure H.E. that in nothing I have written on the temporal Principality of the Supreme Pontiff

[25] Ryan, *Op. cit.,* p.594; Microfilm, *Brownson Papers,* Roll 9.

have I had any intention of opposing that Principality or of siding with its enemies. My design has been simply to guard against the erroneous and injurious inference which might be drawn from the statements of many Catholic journals, that the retention of the Principality is *essential* to the maintenance of the Church and to show that its loss, which I regard as possible, and even probable, would still leave the spiritual power of the Pope untouched and by no means involve the downfall of the Catholic Church.

My language has been on this subject the less guarded because having been so long and so well known for my devotion to the Holy See and for my uncompromising defense of the rights and prerogatives of the Chair of Peter, having so earnestly and so repeatedly battled against Gallicanism and for what is here called Ultramontanism, I thought I was free from all danger of being misapprehended or misconstrued, and H.E. will permit me to say that I do not think I should have been seriously complained of had it not been for political and national susceptibilities which my course as a Reviewer had offended and armed against me.

Though the staunch advocate of all legitimate authority however constituted, I am an American citizen and, for my own country, a Republican accustomed from my youth up to free thought and free speech; but the prelates of the Church in the United States have only to signify to me under their own name the questions which they wish me not to discuss, or to give me frankly the directions they wish me to follow, to find me avoiding everything that could be offensive or disagreeable to them or inconsistent with their views of Catholic interests. I am and will be docile to authority, but I do not and cannot recognize the voice of authority in anonymous newspaper articles.

I wish to say in conclusion that all the articles in my *Review* written by myself which have been complained of, excepting the last number, have been submitted to Episcopal or theological revision and approval before being printed; and the very articles touching the temporal power of the Supreme Pontiff were revised and approved by a theologian designated by Episcopal authority. This indeed excused not my errors and relieved me from no personal responsibility, but is perhaps an evidence of my Catholic aims and docility. My wish is in all things to conform strictly to the teachings and wishes of the Church, and I am and always will be ready and even anxious to correct and avoid any and every error which the Holy See may point out to me. Err I may, but a heretic I am not and never will be. I wish to save my soul, and I believe that, for me at least there is no salvation out of the Catholic Chuch.[26]

*   *   *

New York City,
October 9, 1861.

Dear Doctor:

Your letter of explanations, dated August 12th, was received and read with pleasure at the Propaganda. Had it been received sooner the Cardinal Prefect would not have forwarded the subsequent document dated August 31st, which they now desire to be considered *non avenu*. Rome is satisfied with your explanations and with your disposition to submit all you write to the judgment of the Church. By the mail of August (September?) 12th, the Propaganda wrote to the Archbishop of New York to inform him of Mr. Brownson's *éclairissements* and to tranquilize his mind in reference to that writer's "disposition."

...They notice the closing expression of your letter, "There is no salvation at least for me, outside of the Catholic Church," and do not suppose that you believe that there is salvation under the circumstances indicated for anybody else. I am, in fine,

[26] Ryan, *Op. cit.,* p.592; n.18 Microfilm, *Brownson Papers,* Roll 9.

exhorted to comfort the Reviewer especially under the various afflictions which God has permitted to befall him at the present time...

I am, Dear Doctor, very truly yours
(Signed) J.W. Cummings[27]

1863   Henry wounded at battle of Chancellorsville.

At Chancellorsville, in May, 1863, two of Brownson's sons were in the battles; one was wounded and captured (Henry), but the other (Edward), who was in a different staff of the army, wrote his father that it was reported that he with other wounded soldiers had been cremated in the fire which consumed the woods. It was several days before the truth was known; but as soon as Brownson learned that his son was in the hands of the enemy, he set to work to secure his freedom. He went at once to the Commissary General of Prisoners at Washington, who promised to have him exchanged as speedily as possible, and May 21, sent him a note saying: "I have this moment learned that your son, Capt. Brownson has not yet been delivered, but he will leave Fort Monroe for City Point tomorrow." Brownson proceeded to Fort Monroe, where his friend, General Dix, was in command, who detained the boat coming down from City Point with Brownson's son till he had put the father aboard. Arriving at Annapolis, where there was a "Parole Camp," his son was detained with all others that had been released, and on telegraphing to Colonel Hoffman, the Commissary General of Prisoners, was told that he must apply in the usual form for leave of absence, enclosing a surgeon's certificate of disability. Brownson thought that so much red-tape was out of place where his son was in need of careful treatment to save him from the necessity of suffering amputation, and having telegraphed the Secretary of

[27] *Latter Life,* pp.255,256.

War without receiving an answer, he took his son home with him. About an hour after he left Annapolis, the secretary's dispatch, giving his son leave, arrived at the camp. Brownson wrote Stanton from his home in Elizabeth, explaining what he had done and why. This is Stanton's answer:

War Department, Washington City, D.C.
May 28, 1863

Dear Sir:

On the receipt of the intelligence that your son was at Annapolis immediate orders were given that he should be furloughed home. No condition of any kind was directed, and no one had any right to impose a condition upon my order. There is no impropriety in your having taken him home, that being in conformity with my own wishes. The order giving him a leave of absence will be repeated and a copy of it forwarded to him. His leave is for thirty days, at the expiration of which he ought to report the condition of his health, and it will be continued from time to time as his health may require.

Yours truly,
(signed) Edwin M. Stanton
Secretary of War[28]

1864 Son, William Ignatius, an officer in the Union Army, accidentally killed on way to join his unit. Son, Edward Patrick, killed in action at Ream's Station in Virginia. Ceases publication of *Review*.

Headquarters 2nd Army Corps
August 29, 1864

Dear Sir:

The undersigned officers of the staff of Major Gen-

[28] *Latter Life,* pp.434-436.

eral Hancock, and comrades of your lamented son, who fell in the battle of Ream's Station on the 25th inst., feel that some expression of their appreciation of his many admirable qualities will be neither inappropriate in itself nor unacceptable to you.

Long and intimately associated with him as we were we had learned to love and esteem him in no ordinary degree.

He was a brave and faithful soldier, who fell in the very act of rallying our broken ranks. He was as pure-minded and modest as a girl. He was a scholarly gentleman. He was a model of method as to his business. He was a genial companion, a devoted friend, a true patriot, a sincere Christian, a fond brother, a filial son.

These are certainly ample claims to the regard friends greatly felt for him, and, now that he is gone forever, are eager to acknowledge.

The loss of such a son and brother is indeed an inconsolable affliction. Allow us in our measure to share in your sacred grief. At the same time, may we all find some alleviation in the reflection that he had died with so many more noble and gallant men in the holy cause of our country, whose approaching rehabilitation and regeneration his precious blood will have helped to secure.

His is one more name inscribed on the long roll of our martyrs. You, his family, and we, his comrades, have a right to be proud of it, to value it as a precious legacy which Time, *edax rerum*, can only enhance.

> "How sleep the brave who sink to rest
> By all their country's wishes blest!"

We have the honor to be, dear Sir, cordially and respectfully your friends,

Officers of the staff of Major General Hancock.[29]

---

[29] Ryan, *Op. cit.*, p.641; n.79 Microfilm, *Brownson Papers*, Roll 8.

1864 Pope Pius IX issues encyclical *Quanta Cura* and *Syllabus of Errors* condemning indifferentism and liberalism.

1865 Death of Archbishop Hughes.

1866 Contributes articles to Father Isaac Hecker's *Catholic World* and at request of Fr. Edward Sorin, CSC, submits series of articles on Our Lady to *Ave Maria*.

> Father Sorin wrote in January, 1867: "With regard to your course in the *Ave Maria*, of which by the bye, the Most Reverend Archbishop of St. Louis was good enough to say that he considered it was the best paper in the States, I wish to say that you must consider yourself the representative of the American Catholics, speaking to his own people of the Mother of God, as you think that they should be talked to. It cannot be without a design that our New World has been dedicated to the Blessed Virgin by Columbus, and lately by our American hierarchy. Were Americans once convinced that she is the Mother of God and not only the Mother of Christ, even Protestants would acknowledge that it is right to honor her. It seems to me that no one better than yourself could tell the American people what our country has to gain by spreading such a devotion, were it only for the atmosphere of purity in which it will enable the present generation, which is bad enough, to raise the succeeding one, which I trust will be better. Shall I tell you, and why not? that the beautiful statue we erected last May, on the dome of our new college, is doing wonders among our 400 students? Would to God such a type of modesty and pure love would meet the eye of our youth everywhere! Ah, if pains were taken it might be soon effected to a great extent, and wherever it will be properly explained it will be loved by Americans as readily (and more efficiently, perhaps,) as by any other nation in the world. I never saw either in France or in Italy warmer feelings of devotion towards the Mother of God than here among our American converts. I thought at a time that I loved

her; they literally shame me, and my confusion helps
me in my little task. I would get on my knees before
anyone who can speak to those honest-minded people
whose misfortune is their ignorance of the truth, to
aid me to open their eyes to the light and to reveal to
them the grace, the beauties and the perfection of her
who is the Gate of Heaven for them as well as for
ourselves. Americans, as a nation, are a sensible one,
they cannot remain long blind to their interests. They
will bless the hand that tore off, however much
against their wishes, the veil that hid the light from
their sight. As a nation, they cannot remain much
longer estranged from a mother so lovely and so
loving. My dear Doctor, I do not know either for
yourself or for me, any subject more worthy of our
efforts on the decline of our life, or anything that will
give us as much consolation on our death-bed, as to
have tried our best to make her known, to represent
her as she is, and give her the place she ought to
occupy among us.[30]

1870   Vatican Council I condemns Gallicanism and defines Papal
        infallibility.

What he considered of the most vital importance as
bearing on the controversies of the day was the Council's utter condemnation of the first‘three Gallican
articles, which controverted the supremacy of the
vicar of Christ, both in relation to the civil power and
in relation to a general council, and the assertion of
the primacy of jurisdiction of the successor of Peter in
relation to both. The Vatican proclamation of the
papal prerogatives leveled, he said, "a death-blow at
the wretched Gallicanism and political atheism
which enfeebles and kills the life of every nation." He
felt free now for the first time in his life to defend the
Catholic Church unhampered by a mutilated
orthodoxy. He could now bring out and insist on the
very truths needed to combat the dominant heresies

[30] *Latter Life,* pp.499,500.

of the age. And with renewed energy and assurance he returned once more to a promulgation of his high-toned ultramontanism as the only medicament that could heal the wounds of a well-nigh moribund society.[31]

1871   Wife Sally dies. At her request he revives *Review*.

She had been for a long time failing; but in spite of increasing feebleness, kept up her practice of attending Mass daily. The distance was considerable for her to walk, especially in wintry weather. A cold caught in a January storm settled on her lungs, which had been weak for twenty years or more, and she expired early in April, 1872, aged 68 years.

In a prepared introduction to the *Last Series* of the *Review,* Brownson wrote, but did not publish, the following paragraphs:

"One of the last requests made to me by my dear wife before her recent peaceful and happy death in the Lord, as I cannot doubt, and for whom my tears are yet fresh, was that I should revive my *Review,* which I suspended eight years ago. She insisted that I owed it to the vindication of my own honor as a Catholic, to my surviving children who must suffer from any stain of my reputation for orthodoxy and devotion to the Holy See, and in fine I owed it to the Church in this her hour of affliction, when her enemies seem to have gained a victory over her." [32]

*   *   *

...I willingly admit that I made many mistakes; but I regard as the greatest of all the mistakes into which I fell during the last three or four years that I published my *Review,* that of holding back the stronger points of the Catholic faith, on which I had previously

[31] Ryan, *Op. cit.,* pp.452,453; n.58 "Gallicanism and Ultramontanism," *Brownson's Quarterly Review,* (July 1874), p.323; *Works,* XIII, p.470.
[32] *Latter Life,* p.580

insisted; of laboring to present Catholicity in a form as little repulsive to my non-Catholic countrymen as possible; and of insisting on only the minimum of Catholicity, or what had been expressly defined by the Holy See or a general council.

I am not likely to fall into that mistake again. My experiment was not very successful; and besides, the *Syllabus* and the decrees of the Council of the Vatican, published since, would protect me from it, if nothing else would. I have no ambition to be regarded as a *liberal* Catholic. A *liberal* Catholic I am not, never was, save in appearance for a brief moment, and never can be. I have no element of liberal Catholicity in my nature or in my convictions, and the times, if I read them aright, demand Catholicity in its strength, not in its weakness; in its supernatural authority and power, not as reduced to pure rationalism or mere human sentimentality.

What is most needed in these times – perhaps in all times – is the truth that condemns, point-blank, the spirit of the age, and gives no quarter to its dominant errors; and nothing can be more fatal than to seek to affect a compromise with them or to form an alliance with what is called Liberalism, – a polite name for sedition, rebellion, and revolution...Time was when I paraded my Americanism, in order to repel the charge that an American cannot become a convert to the Church without ceasing to feel and act as an American patriot. I have lived long enough to snap my fingers at all charges of that sort. I love my country, and, in her hour of trial, I and my sons, Catholics like myself, did our best to preserve her integrity, and save her Constitution; and there is no sacrifice in my power that I would not make to bring "my kinsmen after the flesh" to Christ; but, after all, the Church is my true country, and the faithful are my real countrymen. Let the American people become truly Catholic and submissive children of the Holy Father, and their republic is safe; let them refuse and seek safety for the secular order in sectarianism or secularism, and nothing can save it from destruction.[33]

1872   Discontinues *Review*. Moves to Detroit with son Henry.

It was pleasant basking in the kindly household. Fifine, his daughter-in-law, had always been a special favorite of his. Being accustomed to manage a difficult husband, she understood the Brownson temperament; and he was charmed by his small granchildren. One day five-year-old Sally [60] happened to mention that she would like to have a statue of the Blessed Virgin she had seen in a store, but that her mother had told her it cost too much. At once the old man's hand went into his pocket and pulled out a few crumpled dollar bills. This child too showed herself a true Brownson by telling him, "Oh, but you can't afford it."

"Why not, young lady?" he wanted to know.

"Because you don't go to an office or do any work or earn any money. If father can't afford to buy it —"

The huge paw took the tiny hand and pressed the bills into it. "Never mind about that. Go and buy your statue." If she had wanted a doll he might have given it to her; as it was a statue of Mary she wanted, he simply could not refuse it.[34]

1876   Dies in Detroit April 17, age seventy three.

It was in no sense incongruous that Orestes Brownson was to near his end on an argument. From the day when as a mere lad of only nine years he had accompanied an older boy "to the middle of the town" to witness a muster of the local militia, and had actually wedged his way into the discussion of two old men about free will and election, and had stoutly maintained against Jonathan Edwards the freedom

[33] *Brownson's Quarterly Review,* January 1873, pp.2,3; *Works,* Vol. XX, pp.382,383.
[34] Maynard, *Op. cit.,* p.425; n.60 She is now Mother Brownson, a Religious of the Sacred Heart.

of the will,[35] he had been arguing strenuously all his life though – always of course on the side of truth and justice as he saw it. And so it happened on Good Friday he and son Henry fell into an argument after lunch about the precise nature of the unforgivable sin (the sin against the Holy Spirit). So engrossed in the subject did they become that the discussion dragged into the afternoon hours. Finally the old philosopher felt that he had had enough. Henry seemed strangely obtuse, he did not grasp the point he was making. Rising suddenly from his chair, he shuffled across the room with the aid of his cane and the supporting balustrade, he pulled his huge bulk up the stairs to his room. Hours later when Fifine knocked at his door, carrying the evening tray, he called out: "If that is Henry, I'm too tired to make it plainer tonight." He was sinking into his last illness. By midnight he was critically ill.

The next day Holy Saturday, the vicar general of the diocese, Father Hennaert, known for his learning and virtue, who was also his Father Confessor, heard his confession. On Easter Sunday he was brought Holy Communion and was given the Last Anointing, or the Anointing of the Sick, as it is now called. Shortly before dawn on Easter Monday morning, the soul of Orestes Brownson went forth to meet the God of all Truth and Goodness. It is recorded that at the moment of death he heaved a great sigh. It was a fit signal that a life of enormous labors had come to an end.[35]

1886   Body moved to Brownson Memorial Chapel at Notre Dame University. His epitaph reads:

Here lies Orestes A. Brownson, who humbly acknowledged the true faith, lived a full life, and by writing and speaking bravely defended his Church and country, and granted that his body may have

[35] Ryan, *Op. cit.,* p.721.

been broken by death, the labors of his mind remain immortal monuments of his genius.[36]

---

[36] Translation from the Latin by Americo D. Lapati; Lapati, Americo D., *Orestes A. Brownson,* Twayne Publishers, New York, 1965, p.137; n.106.

A PICTURE GALLERY OF BROWNSON AND SOME OF HIS FRIENDS

Brownson's personal appearance as a Protestant minister was very different from what he became in later life. Two inches over six feet in height, with broad shoulders and a large frame, his weight was less than 170 pounds. His bodily strength was unusually great, and his vigor was kept up by habitual exercise, both in walking and working in the garden. His hair was black and brushed straight back from his forehead without parting; around his mouth he was shaved, and in the upper part of his cheeks; his eyes seemed black, but were of mixed grey and hazel; his upper lip long, his hands long and broad. His dress at this time and until he gave up preaching, was broadcloth; he wore a dress coat, what is sometimes called a swallow-tail, at all hours of the day, even in his studies, and a large square white handerchief folded to a width of three or four inches in front of his neck, crossed behind and tied in front. He slept little, but sat up writing or studying till 2 or 3 o'clock or later. His diet was sparing, his abstinence from wine and spirits total, though he drank strong coffee morning and evening. His total abstinence from alcohol was as much due to taste as to principle, and indeed he never heartily took up the total abstinence fanaticism, though he often addressed temperance societies.[1]

[1] Brownson, Henry, *Early Life,* H.F. Brownson, Detroit 1898, p.98.

1) Orestes Augustus Brownson (1803-1876).

In Brownson's semi-autobiographical novel *The Spirit Rapper* Francis Wright appears as "Priscilla":

> "I cannot say that the difference I found among these excellent people when it concerned their philanthropic projects or their various schemes of world-reform, edified me much, but I was charmed with their disinterestedness, with their zeal, and their superiority to the restraints of popular prejudice, and what they stigmatized as conventionalism. I was above all delighted to observe the new importance assumed in behalf of women; and it was a real pleasure to hear a charming young lady, whose face a painter might have chosen for his model, in a sweet musical voice, and gentle loving look, which made you all unconsciously take her hand in yours, defend our great grandmother Eve, and maintain that her act, which an ungrateful world had held to have been the source of all the vice, the crime, the sin and misery of mankind, was an act of lofty heroism, of noble daring, of pure disinterested love for man. Adam, but for her, would never have known how to distinguish between good and evil. How, with the sweet young lady – I see and hear her now – sitting on a stool near me, laying her hand in the fervor of her argument on mine, and looking up with all the witchery of her eyes into my face, how could I fail to be convinced that man is cold, calculating, selfish, and cowardly, and that the world cannot be reformed without the destruction of the male (it might be called the *mal*) organization of society, the elevation of woman to her proper sphere, and the infusion into the government and management of public and private affairs, some portion of the love, the daring, the enthusiasm, and disinterestedness of woman's heart? There was nothing to be said in reply." [2]

[2] Brownson, Orestes, *The Spirit Rapper, Works,* Vol. IX, Thorndike Nourse, Detroit, 1882-1887, p.46. The theme of Eve as heroine and God as villain is found in many early Gnostic writings. Cf. Nag Hammadi Scrolls: *The Nature of the Archons,* and *On the Origin of the World.*

2) *Frances Wright D'Arusmont (1795-1852), World-Reformer, Philanthropist, Feminist.*

There was a moment when I looked to Dr. Channing, the foremost man among the Unitarians, as the one who was to take the lead in this work of reorganization. His reputation in 1834 was high, and he loomed up at a distance in my eyes as the great man of the age; but a closer view, an intimate personal acquaintance with him, soon disabused me. Dr. Channing had done me a great service in the beginning of my efforts to rise from the abyss of unbelief into which I had fallen; he was my warm, considerate and steady friend ever after to the day of his death. He consoled me, encouraged me, aided me in various ways; and I can never forget my personal obligations to him. I hold, and always shall hold, his memory in grateful respect. But he was not the great man many supposed him to be. He was benevolent, philanthropic, and anxious to do all in his power for the good of mankind, especially for the relief of the poorer and more numerous classes. He had a just horror of Calvinistic theology, and warred to the last against the Calvinistic view of human nature. He rejected with indignation the doctrine of total depravity, asserted in eloquent terms the dignity of human nature, and entertained the loftiest conceptions of the greatness and capacity of the human soul. He asserted so frequently and so strongly the dignity of man, that one of his brother ministers said of him, with more point than truth, however: "Dr. Channing makes man a great God, and God a little man." He certainly, in revolting against the Calvinistic doctrine, which so unduly depresses the human to make way, as it supposes, for sovereign grace, ran to the opposite extreme, and unduly depressed the divine and exaggerated the human. He is answerable for no small portion of the soul-worship, which was for a time the fashionable idolatry of the metropolis of New England.[3]

[3] *The Convert, Works* V, p.77.

3) William Ellery Channing (1780-1842), Unitarian.

...One man, and one man only, shared my entire confidence, and knew my most secret thought. Him, from motives of delicacy, I do not name; but, in the formation of my mind, in systematizing my ideas, and in general development and culture, I owe more to him than to any other man among Protestants. We have since taken divergent courses, but I loved him as I have loved no other man, and shall so love and esteem him as long as I live. He encouraged me, and through him chiefly I was enabled to remove to Boston and commence operations.[4]*

[4] *The Convert, Works* V, p.81. This is George Ripley, the founder of Brook Farm (Cf. Ryan, *Op. cit.*, pp.98,99).

Brownson's son Henry claimed that his father was "the main instrument" in bringing about the conversion to the Catholic faith of at least three rather prominent persons at Brook Farm: two ministers, Rev. William J. Davis and Rev. George Leach, and the third person was Mrs. Ripley, the wife of the founder of Brook Farm...Miss Sarah Stearns of Brook Farm, a niece of Mrs. Ripley, also became a Catholic, and eventually a nun. Charles Summer's brother and Isaac Hecker, the future founder of the Congregation of the Missionary Priests of St. Paul the Apostle, also became converts. Ripley himself, as is well known, never became a Catholic. Brownson's last effort to convert him was made after Ripley had been for some time one of the editors of the New York *Tribune*. Ripley put off the idea saying that he would ask to be received into the Catholic Church as soon as he had a sufficient amount laid aside to support himself when his job was gone, as it would be he claimed, when he became a Catholic.[31] When Fr. Isaac Hecker returned from Europe a Redemptorist, he went to see Ripley at the *Tribune* office. Ripley asked the newly ordained: "Can you do all that any Catholic priest can do?" When Fr. Hecker replied "yes," Ripley said: "Then I will send for you when I am drawing near my end." When the end did come, Ripley sent for him, but the message was not delivered. Finally hearing of Ripley's illness, Fr. Hecker hastened to his bedside, but it was too late. Ripley's mind was gone, and he could do little for him.[32]*

* Ryan, *Op. cit.,* pp.212,213; n.31 Brownson's repeated efforts to convert Ripley reminds one of John H. Newman's persistent efforts to convert his dear friend Edward B. Pusey, but with no better results...n.32 Fr. Walter Elliott, *The Life of Father Hecker,* 2nd ed. Columbia Press, New York, 1894, p.90.

*4) George Ripley (1802-1880), Transcendentalist, Founder
of Brook Farm.*

Brownson remained for two years in Canton, where he became a very useful member of the community. He organized a Lyceum, and he started a small library. One summer (1835) he was called upon to examine a Harvard sophomore who wanted to teach the town school. "The two sat up talking till midnight," as Ellery Channing described it later, "and Mr. Brownson informed the school committee that Mr. Thoreau was examined, and would do, and would board with him." Thoreau and Brownson spent a stimulating summer, reading German together and walking the shady banks of the cool Neponset River. These six weeks gave young Thoreau his first continuous association with a mature and provocative intelligence. "They were an era in my life," he wrote Brownson, "the morning of a new *Lebenstag*. They are to me as a dream that is dreamt, but which returns from time to time in all its original freshness." [5]

---

[5] Schlesinger, Arthur Jr., *Orestes A. Brownson: A Pilgrim's Progress,* Little, Brown and Co., Boston, 1939, pp.31,32; n.1 Thoreau to Brownson, December 30, 1887, *Early Life,* p.204.

5) *Henry David Thoreau (1817-1862), Transcendentalist, Naturalist.*

We know Mr. Emerson; we have shared his generous hospitality, and enjoyed the charms of his conversation; as friend and neighbor, in all the ordinary relations of social and domestic life, he is one it is not easy to help loving and admiring; and we confess we are loath to say aught severe against him or his works; but his volume of poems is the saddest book we ever read. The author tries to cheer up, tries to smile, but the smile is cold and transitory; it plays an instant round the mouth, but does not come from the heart, or lighten the eyes. He talks of music and flowers, and would fain persuade us that he is weaving garlands of joy; but beneath them is always to be seen the ghastly and grinning skeleton of death. There is an appearance of calm, of quiet, of repose, and at first sight one may half fancy his soul is as placid, as peaceful, as the unruffled lakes sleeping sweetly beneath the summer moonbeams; but it is the calm, the quiet, the repose of despair. Down below are the troubled waters. The world is no joyous world for him. It is void and without form, and darkness broods over it. True, he bears up against it; but because he is too proud to complain, and because he believes his lot is that of all men and inevitable. Why break thy head against the massive walls of necessity. Call thy darkness light, and it will be as light – to thee. Look the fiend in the face, and he is thy friend, – at least, as much of a friend as thou canst have. Why complain? Poor brother, thou art nothing, or thou art all. Crouch and whine, and thou art nothing; stand up erect on thy own two feet, and scorn to ask for aught beyond thyself, and thou art all. Yet this stoical pride and resolve require a violent effort, and bring no peace, no consolation, to the soul. In an evil hour, the author overheard what the serpent said to Eve, and believed it; and from that time it would seem, he became unable to believe aught else.[6]

[6] "R.W. Emerson's Poems," *Works*, Vol. XIX, pp.191,192; *Brownson's Quarterly Review*, April 1847, pp.264.

Ralph Waldo Emerson (1803-1882), Transcendentalist.

When Emerson invited Brownson to attend a meeting at his home for the purpose of discussing the Fruitlands project with Bronson Alcott and his backers he replied:

Chelsea, Massachusetts,
November 9, 1842

Dear Sir:

It grieves me that a previous engagement must prevent me from meeting at your home tomorrow agreeably to your invitation, I am engaged to address tomorrow evening the good people of Nantucket. Be so obliging as to make my respects to Messers. Lane, Alcott and Wright, and assure them from me that I should listen with great interest and respect to their exposition, anxious as I always am to be enlightened as to the means of ameliorating man's social condition, though I must say that I have long ceased to have any faith in any actual or possible schemes of world-reform. The world jogs very much in its own way, and with or without our cooperation. The perfect social state these men seem to be dreaming of, I look upon as perfectly chimerical. A perfect state is incompatible with the imperfection of individuals; and imperfect individuals must be, till they cease to be finite. All that remains for us, it seems, is to do what our hands find to do, but advancing toward a better state, by trying to make the best of our present.

Forgive me, I did not intend to philosophize in this way, but simply to acknowledge your note, and my inability to accept your invitation. I have worn out the best part of my life devising schemes of world-reform. And as far as I am concerned to no purpose...[7]

---

[7] Microfilm *Brownson Papers*, Roll 9, Notre Dame; quoted in Ryan, Fr. Thomas R., CSSP., *Orestes A. Brownson: A Definitive Biography*, Our Sunday Visitor Inc., Huntington, Indiana, 1976, p.210.

*Amos Bronson Alcott (1799-1888), Teacher, Transcendentalist,
Founder of Fruitlands.*

To many Miss Fuller (once the editor of *The Dial*) was the modern Aspasia of Boston, if not of the country. She was probably not wholly unconscious of her remarkable gifts. Whatever the merits of her famous *Conversations*, she is perhaps best remembered for her remark which Emerson repeated to Carlyle, namely, "I accept the world." To which Carlyle replied: "Gad, she'd better."[36] Although Brownson acknowledged that Margaret exhibited certain gifts of a very high order, he plainly could not take her seriously. He mourned the great harm she was doing in substituting art for religion, and adopting exotic principles for the stern morality of the Gospel. To him her memoir was a sad book he could not commend...

"We are able, we trust to distinguish between persons and doctrines. For persons, however far gone in error, or even sin, we trust we have the charity our holy religion commands, and which the recollection of our own errors and sins, equal to any we may have to deplore in others, requires us to exercise. But for erroneous doctrines we have no charity, no tolerance. Error is never harmless, and in no instances to be countenanced." [47] [8]

---

[8] Ryan, *Op. cit.*, pp.340,341; n.47 "Miss Fuller and the Reformers," *Brownson's Quarterly Review*, April, 1845, p.257; *Works*, Vol. VI, p.229.

Margaret Fuller Ossoli (1810-1850), Transcendentalist, Feminist.

Mr. Parker at that time was one of my highly prized personal friends, a young man, full of life and promise. There was no young man of my acquaintance for whom I had a higher regard, or from whom I hoped so much. He had a very respectable intellectual ability, was learned, witty, and eloquent. His ideas were perhaps a little crude, and his taste needed a little chastening, but his fancy was lively, his imagination brilliant, and his rhetorical powers were of the first order. He had devoured an immense number of all sorts of books, and could discourse not badly on almost any subject. He was more brilliant than solid, less erudite than he appeared or was thought to be, and in translating a work from the German of De Wette, made some sad blunders; but he was still young and his attainments were unquestionably above the average standard of American scholarship. His powers as a reasoner, and his attachment to his own opinions was stronger than his love of truth. His greatest defect was lack of inherent loyalty. He would, perhaps, walk boldly to the dungeon, the scaffold, or the stake, in defense of the cause he had espoused, or an opinion he had once emitted, but he closed resolutely his mind, his heart, and his eyes to the reception of any light which might require him to revise and modify views to which he had once committed himself. He might be a fanatic, and die in defense of his opinions, but never a martyr to the truth, even in case it and his opinions should happen to coincide. He had the pride of the Stoic, but not the humility of the Christian. His boldness, firmness, courage, and independence were striking, and would have deserved very high reverence, if they had been exhibited in the cause of truth, not simply in the cause of Mr. Theodore Parker. Nevertheless, he has not belied his early promise, and is undeniably one of the most distinguished Protestant ministers in the United States.[9]

[9] *The Convert, Works* V, pp. 151, 152.

Theodore Parker (1810-1860), Unitarian,
Transcendentalist, Abolitionist.

Mt. Bellingham
June 6, 1844

My dear Isaac:

...You cannot gain this victory alone, not by mere private meditation and prayer. You can obtain it only through the grace of God, and the grace of God through its appointed channels. You are wrong. You do not begin right. Do you really believe the Gospel? Do you really believe the Holy Catholic Church? If so you must put yourself under the direction of the Church. I do not as yet belong to the family of Christ. I feel it. I can be an alien no longer, and without the Church I know by my own past experience that I cannot attain to purity and sanctity of life. I need the counsels, the aids, the chastisements and the consolations of the Church. It is the appointed medium of salvation, and how can we hope for any grace except through it? Our first business is to submit to it, that we may receive a maternal blessing. Then we may start fair...

I want you to come and see our good bishop. He is an excellent man, learned, polite, easy, affable, affectionate and exceedingly warm hearted. I spent two hours with him immediately after parting with you in Washington Street, and a couple of hours yesterday. I like him very much.

I have made up my mind, and I shall enter the Church if she will receive me. There is no use in resisting, you cannot be an Anglican, you must be a Catholic or a Mystic. There is nothing else. So let me beg you, my dear Isaac, to begin by owning the Church and receiving her blessing.[10]

[10] Holden, Fr. Vincent, CSP., *The Yankee Paul: Isaac Thomas Hecker,* Bruce Publishing Co., Milwaukee, 1958, pp.90,91; n.24 *Hecker Papers,* Archives of Paulist Fathers, New York City.

10) Isaac Thomas Hecker (1819-1888)
Founder of the Paulist Fathers.

What most impressed us in this second interview with Bishop Fenwick was the firm and uncompromising character of his Catholicity. He used not a single unkind word, in speaking of Protestants; but with all our art, – and we did our best, – we could not extract from him the least conceivable concession. He saw clearly what held us back, and that we believed we were prepared to join the Church, if we could only have some assurance that individuals dying out of the pale of her communion need not necessarily be despaired of; but neither by word nor tone did he indicate that he had any assurance to give. He was a Catholic, heart and soul; he had learned the Church as the way of salvation, but he had learned no other. What he had received, that he could give; but nothing else. He was not the author of the conditions of salvation, and he would not take the responsibility of enlarging or contracting them. It was well for us that he was thus stern and uncompromising in his Catholicity. A man brought up a Protestant is apt to distrust the sincerity of another's faith, and, in general, looks upon a well educated and intelligent Catholic priest or bishop as acting a part, or merely speaking from his brief, without any firm conviction of what he professes. He also understands, in advance, that Catholicity is exclusive and boldly asserts that salvation out of the pale of the Church is not possible. If, then, we had found him less uncompromising; if we perceived in him the least disposition to soften what seemed to us the severity of the Catholic doctrine, or to conceal or explain it away, we should have distrusted the sincerity of his faith, have failed to give him our confidence, and lost what we had in his Church.[11]

[11] "The Right Reverend Benedict Joseph Fenwick, Second Bishop of Boston," *Brownson's Quarterly Review,* October 1846, p.522; *Works,* Vol. XIV, pp.474,475.

11) Benedict Joseph Fenwick (1772-1846)
Second Bishop of Boston,
Founder of Holy Cross College.

Delicacy and his own retiring character prevent me from speaking of his successor, the present Bishop of Boston, in the terms which naturally present themselves. He was my instructor, my confessor, my spititual director, and my personal friend, for eleven years; my intercourse with him was intimate, cordial, and affectionate, and I owe him more than it is possible for me to owe any other man. I have met men of more various erudition and higher scientific attainments; I have met men of bolder fancy and more creative imaginations; but I have never met a man of a clearer head, a firmer intellectual grasp, a sounder judgment, or a warmer heart. He taught me my catechism and my theology; and, though I have found men who made a far greater display of theological erudition, I have never met an abler or sounder theologian. However for a moment I may have been attracted by one or another theological school, I have invariably found myself obliged to come back at last to the views he taught me. If my *Review* has any theological merit, if it has earned any reputation as a staunch and uncompromising defender of the Catholic faith, that merit is principally due, under God, to him, to his instructions, to his advice, to his encouragement, and his uniform support. Its faults, its shortcomings, or its demerits are my own. I know that, in saying this, I offend his modesty, his unaffected Christian humility; but less I could not say without violence to my own feelings, the deep reverence, the warm love, and profound gratitude with which I always recall, and trust I always shall recall his name and his services to me.[12]

[12] *The Convert, Works* V, pp.164,165.

12) John Bernard Fitzpatrick (1822-1866)
Third Bishop of Boston.

Brownson was now moving along in his forty-second year. His giant muscular six-feet-two-inch frame, just beginning to put on weight, was becoming even more formidable in appearance. His great shock of hair, brushed straight back from his high sloping forehead, balanced by a full spreading beard, giving him something of the appearance of a biblical prophet, was already streaked with gray. Under shaggy brows his eyes looked out through his small gold-rimmed spectacles that rested on a slightly beaked nose. Ruddy of complexion, his whole appearance was leonine. And like the lion he was ready for any battle. The battles he had passed through had only served to prepare him for those ahead, and his greatest battles by far lay in the future. He had fed on battles, and seemed to bid Armageddon welcome. His sword was the pen he held in his long graceful fingers. His countenance wore the mein of a no-nonsense man. And he was utterly without fear. As Arthur M. Schlesinger Jr. has said: "He was not a man to be intimidated by all the devils in hell when he thought he was right." [13]

---

[13] Ryan, *Op. cit.,* p.315; n.5 Schlesinger, *Op. cit.,* p.107.

13) Orestes Augustus Brownson (1803-1876).

...Yet certain it is, that Archbishop Hughes was one of the most remarkable and efficient prelates the Church in the United States has ever had. He was a prelate of large views, great firmness and decision of character, ceaseless activity, and untiring industry. We will not say he never made any mistakes, or misjudged the time for raising and discussing certain great questions; nor will we say the contrary. Time and events have proved that he was right in many things in which we thought him wrong, or at least injudicious, at the time, and it is not for us to say that he was not always right, wise and judicious. We are laymen, and not judges of episcopal administration.[14]

[14] "The Most Reverend John Hughes, D.D., *Brownson's Quarterly Review,* January, 1874, p.88; *Works,* Vol. XIV, p.495.

14) John Joseph Hughes (1797-1864)
Fourth Bishop of New York,
Founder of Fordham University.

...During one of these visits, – perhaps in '63, – His Eminence alluded incidentally to rude criticisms that had been levelled at certain principles broached by your Father, presumably in his *Review*. What precisely the subject was to which the Cardinal referred, I have not now, well nigh forty years afterwards, any very clear definite recollection; especially as it was rather of the *rough manner* in which these critics had dealt with what they regarded as Dr. Brownson's short-comings, than of the *merits of the case* itself that His Eminence spoke; but, unless my memory plays me false, it was in some way linked with the matter of eternal punishment. Be that as it may, I do distinctly remember how strongly the straightforward Cardinal deprecated the fierceness of the attack which had been made on a man whose lofty spirit and fearless character was not unlike his own. Plainly it annoyed him. What serves to fix the visit in my memory, was the dramatic manner in which His Eminence showed how an old Dreadnaught like Dr. Brownson would act, if threatened with the fire of a whole fleet of popular pamphleteers. But that Cardinal Barnabò was a very small man, and your Father a man of Daniel Webster's build, but taller by some inches, I could have fancied the Doctor stood before me. Rising from his chair and dropping his scarlet biretum on the floor, His Eminence put himself in an attitude of defence, as if to say: Come one; come all! intimating, for that I remember well, that if critics had dealt gently with him, and pointed out his error, if error there was, no man was more ready to humbly acknowledge it, than that great champion of the faith, who for us was what Newman was for England. Each in his day put Catholicism fifty years ahead in their respective countries; and it is now, when people see there are none to take the places of those two intellectual giants, that they are beginning to appreciate both the one and the other.

I remain yours faithfully,
(Signed) W. G. McCloskey,
Bishop of Louisville.[15]

---

[15] Brownson, Henry, *Latter Life,* H.F. Brownson, Detroit, 1900, pp.259,260.

*15) Alessandro Cardinal Barnabò (1801-1874)
Prefect of the Propaganda Fide.*

On an occasion when he ("Ned") returned home, Sarah's friend, Miss White, was her guest; and she gives us a vivid picture of the close-knit union of the family. Sarah had taken her friend to her room, and had remained for a time chatting before going down to her own. Miss White remembered that she had left a book below on the table; and she slipped down, quietly to get it. There was only the light of the fireplace in the room, and no sound. In the glow of the logs, had been drawn the two chairs occupied by Orestes and Sally; and their youngest proud in his army uniform, but still a little boy, sat on the floor with his head in his mother's lap. The desire to read left Miss White. She went back without the book.[16]

[16] Whalen, Doran (Sr. Rose Gertrude Whalen, CSC.), *Granite for God's House,* Sheed and Ward, New York, 1941, p.331.

16) Edward Patrick Brownson (1843-1864).

A little later Brownson writes to his son: "The only trouble I have grows out of the fact that Father Hewit is not sound on the question of original sin, and does not believe that it is necessary to be in communion with the Church in order to be saved. He holds that Protestants may be saved by invincible ignorance, and that original sin was no sin at all except the individual sin of Adam, and that our nature was not wounded at all by it. Father Hecker agrees with him on these points, and is in fact a semi-Pelagian without knowing it. So I am obliged to abstain from bringing out what I regard as the orthodox doctrine of original sin and of exclusive salvation. But in all other respects I am unrestrained.[17]

---

[17]*Latter Life,* pp.565,566.

17) Augustine Francis Hewit (1820-1897)
Second Superior of Paulists.

A little girl who was visiting the house at Elizabeth during these last years gazed, astonished at the huge shaggy old man she saw there and whispered to her mother. "Is he not just like a great lion!" Father Hewit, who tells the story, adds that the description hit him off even better than Bishop Bayley's *Ursa Major*. But Hewit continues: "The marks of infirmity which time had imprinted upon him, with the expression of loneliness and childlike longing for sympathy added a touch of the pathetic to the picture, fitted to awaken a sentiment of compassion, tempering to a more gentle mood and awe and admiration excited by his venerable appearance." [1] [18]

[18] Maynard, *Op. cit.,* p.442; n.1 *Catholic World,* Vol. XXIII, No. 135, June 1876.

18) Orestes Augustus Brownson (1803-1876).

...With the awful conviction that she would not live a year, Sarah wrote Henry and insisted that he take their father to Detroit.

Brownson did not wish to go; but when "Francis" came on for him, he yielded; and he placed a note in Sarah's hand as he said goodbye:

"Thursday.

"I am very sorry, my dear Sarah, that I showed so much resistance to the arrangement that you and Henry thought best. I am now perfectly satisfied that you were right. And I want you to feel that I am perfectly convinced of it, and am perfectly reconciled to the arrangement.

"You need and must have, a change of scene, and a change of air; and the sooner the better. This is absolutely necessary for you. I shall do well enough, and shall not be unhappy. You need feel no uneasiness on my account.

Your loving Father." * [19]

---

[19] Whalen, *Op. cit.,* p.361; * Microfilm of *Brownson Papers,* Roll 9 (Ryan).

19) Sarah Brownson Tenney (1839-1876).

Of all Brownson's grown children, Henry alone met his hopes in a goodly measure, or, if he had disappointed him a bit, it was on the score that he had not gone on to the priesthood. He had been with the Jesuits at Frederick, Maryland, when he was fourteen,[9] and had again been in the seminary at Issy, France. If Henry did not continue in the way of a priestly vocation, his father could scarcely have foreseen how kind Providence was being to him personally. Later as a lawyer Henry was to have sufficient leisure to give the world the twenty-volume set of his father's writings, and leave behind also the three-volume biography of his father which is still by all odds the best source of undoctored facts in Brownson's life. With the passing of the years Henry was to become the apple of his father's eye. On July 9, 1863 the father wrote him: ... "Should you survive me, I wish you to understand that my library goes to you, and all my papers are to pass into your hands. I charge you with my honor and fame." [10] [20]

[20] Ryan, *Op. cit.,* p.712; n.9 *Brownson Papers,* Roll 3, n.10 *Brownson Papers,* Roll 9.

20) Henry Francis Brownson (1835-1913).

In St. Rose's Church in Chelsea, Massachusetts there is a stained glass window dedicated in honor of Orestes A. Brownson, and commemorating the fact that the first Mass said in Chelsea was celebrated in Brownson's home. The following excerpt is from "An Historical Sketch of the Parish of St. Rose, Chelsea, Massachusetts" written by the pastor, Rev. Michael J. Scanlan in 1927.

> The year 1924 marked the seventy-fifth anniversary of the founding of the Parish of St. Rose, Chelsea, Massachusetts; that is to say, in 1849, the first permanent Pastor of the Catholic community in Chelsea, the Reverend Charles Smith, took up his residence here. It is very definitely established, however, that Catholic services had been provided for the people of this section now and then, but with no regularity, for at least five years prior to 1849. Although there was for a while some question as to the exact place where the Holy Sacrifice of the Mass had been offered up for the first time publicly in Chelsea, it seems now that this great privilege was vouchsafed to the Bellingham Hill home of the great Catholic philosopher and reviewer, Orestes Augustus Brownson, sometime in the fall of 1844. According to one account, there were present at the first Mass about fourteen worshippers, while another account says there were more nearly thirty present, exclusive of children.

*21) Brownson Memorial Window, St. Rose's Church,
Chelsea, Massachusetts.*

THE GREAT QUESTION

(*Brownson's Quarterly Review,* October 1847)

INTRODUCTION

Brownson was received into the Catholic Church in 1844 at the height of the Native American and Know-Nothing persecutions. Churches and convents had been burned, and Catholics killed by mobs in Philadelphia, Louisville, Boston and other cities. As a result Catholics had become extremely timid and apolgetic concerning their religion. Bishop Fitzpatrick urged Brownson to go over to the offensive. Henry Brownson gives us an example of his father's militant Catholicity:

> Brownson in traveling, and he traveled much, took every occasion to turn the conversation with his companions to the question of the true faith. Even on the ferry boat between Chelsea and Boston, and if he met persons at his barber's or butcher's, he commenced a religious discussion. It is not to be supposed that Brownson expected to make converts by these casual arguments; nor will it do to attribute his fondness for them to the idle wish to parade his skill in arguing, or in turning others into ridicule or contempt. The real motive must be sought in the desire strongly expressed by the Bishop of Boston, and entertained by Brownson, to do all in his power to elevate the tone of Catholics in the United States. Two things the Bishop particularly lamented, the timid tone of Catholics and their liberalism. To counteract the former, Brownson everywhere asserted his Catholicity publicly. At one time, he was lecturing in Andover, Lawrence, Haverhill, and places in that vicinty. At the hotel in Andover, one Friday morning at breakfast, which all the guests of the house ate in common, Brownson commanded a waiter in a loud voice to send the landlord to him, and when the landlord came, Brownson inquired in a tone heard throughout the room, "Why don't you have something in your house that a Christian can eat?" The other said he had beefsteak and other meats which he mentioned; but his guest interrupted him by asking, "Why don't you have fish? No Christian eats meat on Friday." Fish was soon procured, and the matter ended: but it is very clear that Brownson aimed solely at asserting his

Catholicity in the very hot-bed of Puritanism.[1]

But it was mainly in the pages of his Review *that Brownson sought "to elevate the tone of Catholics in the United States." Probably the best example of this new spirit in American Catholicism is found in the article entitled* The Great Question (*"What must one do to be saved?"*), *which appeared in the* Review *for October of 1847 and which was supervised and actually revised by Bishop Fitzpatrick.*

[1] *Middle Life,* pp. 97,98.

THE GREAT QUESTION*

Mr. Penny is a convert from Anglicanism, and a young man of great worth and promise. The little work he has given us here was for the most part written while he was passing into the Church, and retains some traces of his transition state; but it indicates learning, ability, and a turn for scholastic theology not common in Oxford students. It is written in a free, pure, earnest spirit, mild but firm, and, though not always exact in thought or expression, is a very valuable controversial tract, and may, with slight reservations, be cheerfully recommended to all who are willing to seek for the truth, and to embrace it when they find it.

The recent converts from the Anglican Establishment are making large contributions to our English Catholic literature. We give their productions a cordial welcome, for, though they are in some respects immature, and not always critically exact, they breathe a free and earnest spirit, and are marked by a docile dispostion, and a deep and tender piety. Nevertheless, the greater part of them are, perhaps, too local and temporary in their character to be of any general or permanent utility. They are almost exclusively confined to the controversy between their authors and their former high-church associates. Where that controversy is the only or principal one remaining between Catholics and Protestants, they are no doubt not only valuable, but all we could desire. Yet, after all, that controversy is not the important one; it affects, in reality, only a small portion of the English people, and the works specially adapted to it are far from meeting the wants of the great body of English Evangelicals and Dissenters. Still less do they meet the wants of the various sects in our own country. The great body even of Episcopalians here are low-church, and as far from conceding the premises from which the Oxford converts reason as they are from accepting their conclusions.

---

* *The Exercise of Faith Impossible except in the Catholic Church,* by W.G. Penny, late student of Christ's Church Oxford, Philadelphia, 1847. (Brownson's footnotes are indicated by an asterisk or dagger, my own are numbered. T.M.S.)

Protestant Episcopalians, whether high-church or low-church, though respectable for their social standing, do not constitute with us a leading sect. We are pleased, rather than otherwise, to see the tendency of a very considerable number of persons to unite themselves with them, because we cannot doubt, that, if the American people go far enough from their present position to become Episcopalians, they will soon go further, and attain to the reality of which Episcopalianism is only a faint and mutilated shadow. But the sect has no firm hold on the American mind and heart, and does and can exert no commanding influence. It is an exotic, and no labor or pains can naturalize it. The grand current of American life and nationality flows on, saving a few ripples on the surface, undisturbed by its presence or its absence. Except, perhaps, in here and there a particular locality, it is Anglican rather than American, and is patronized chiefly, if not exclusively, by those who are affected by English rather than American tendencies, – as a fashionable religion, which serves to distinguish its professors from the vulgar. Works, therefore, which seek primarily its refutation, and confine themselves to the points specially in debate between it and us, however useful they may be to a few individuals, can make no deep impression on the national mind, and will contribute very little towards the conversion of the country. The Catholic makes no secret of his earnest wish to convert the country. He of course is not contented to reside here simply as one of a number of sects extending a certain degree of religious fellowship one to another and asking only not to have his property confiscated or his throat cut. He would not only be Catholic himself, but he would extend the unspeakable benefits of his holy religion to all, and, by all the *Christian* means in his power, he must seek to convert the whole population to Catholicity. He would be wanting in the blessed charity of the Gospel, if he aimed at anything less. But in order to effect this glorious result, he must strive to reach the heart of the peculiarly American people, through which flows the mighty current of the peculiarly national life; he must labor to make an impression on that portion of the American population which is an especial sense the repositry of peculiarly American thought, principles, passions, affections, traditions, and tendencies, – the indigenous portion, the least affected by foreign culture and influences; and it is only in proportion as he reaches and gains the attention of these, that he can flatter himself that he is advancing in the work of converting the country.

These are not Episcopalians, nor distinguished individuals, whatever the sect to which they may appertain. The conversion of a considerable number of distinguished individuals may take place with scarcely a perceptible effect on the great body of the American people; because these individuals do not represent the general thought and tendency of the country; because their example has little weight with the people at large; and because they are, for the most part, under foreign rather than native influences. The peculiarly American people are democratic and generally distrust whatever rises above the common level. Distinguished individuals count for less here than in any other country of the globe. With us the individual loses himself in the crowd only by sharing their passions and consenting to be their organ. It is, therefore, on the crowd that we must operate, if we would effect anything. The multitude govern, and it is their views and feelings, their tastes and tendencies, that decide the fate or determine the character of the country. These are now all either not for us or strongly against us; and our great and pressing work is to turn them into the Catholic channel. Hence, the important thing for us to study and address is the views and feelings, tastes and tendencies, not of distinguished individuals who may seem to be leaders, but of the great body of the common people. When we hear of the conversion of a distinguished individual, we rejoice for his sake, for he has a soul to save, and his conversion places him in the way of salvation; but when we hear of the conversion of large numbers from the middle and lower classes, we give thanks and rejoice for our country's sake, for we see in it a token that God himself is at work in the heart of the people, and preparing the conversion of the nation itself, – that our holy religion is penetrating the living mass of American society, and subjecting it to the truth, beauty, and sanctity of the Gospel. We hope even the conversion of England, not so much from the large numbers of individuals eminent for their rank, talents, and acquirements, who have recently been converted, as from the hundreds of undistinguished individuals who have been gathered in, and whose names have not been gazetted. If we may say this of England, where distinguished individuals still count for something, much more may we say it of our own beloved country. When and where the people yield readily to the influence and example of their social chiefs, true wisdom may be to penetrate first of all into the palace and the castle, and labor to convert royalty and nobility; but by no means can it be here in this country, where princes and nobles are at a discount, and the chiefs of the people are their chiefs only by being their slaves, consulting and exaggerating their tendencies. The controlling influences of modern society are in the lower instead of the higher ranks, – perhaps, in a religious point of view, with few exceptions, it has always been so. In seeking to restore an unbelieving or heretical country to the faith or the unity of the Church, if we may rely on the lessons of history, the true policy in general, and especially now and here, is to begin at the base of society, and seek first to convert the common people.

Believing therefore, as we do, that the Church has been divinely commissioned to teach all nations, and wishing, as we are bound in charity to wish, to add this nation as another rich gem to her crown, it becomes our duty to study and ascertain the religious state and tendencies of the great body of the American people, properly so called. This may be a difficult and even delicate task. It is not every one who can comprehend his own age and country, and there are not many who can do it all, unless they have shared their passions, unless their own hearts have beaten in unison with theirs, and they have been raised by divine grace above them to a position from which they can overlook the *mêlée*, and calmly survey all the movements and evolutions going on below. The Catholic who has lived apart and studied only works written for other times and countries, as well as the Protestant whose vision has all his life-time been contracted to his own petty sect, is very likely to mistake the true object of vision, or to see it only through a disturbing medium.

Catholicity is immovable and inflexible, one and the same always and everywhere; for the truth never varies. He who knows it in one age or country knows it all. But with the sects it is far otherwise. They must needs obey the natural laws of development, strengthened and intensified by demonical influence. Their spirit and tendency, indeed, are always and everywhere the same, but their forms change under the very eye of the spectator, and are rarely the same for any two successive moments. Strike where Protestantism is, and it is not there. It is in perpetual motion, and exemplifies, so far as itself is concerned, the old heathen doctrine that all things are in a perpetual flux. You can never count on its remaining stationary long enough for you to bring your piece to a rest and take deliberate aim. You must shoot it on the wing; and if you are not marksman enough to hit it flying, you will have, however well charged and well aimed your shot, only your labor for your pains. It is never enough to take note either of its past or its present position; but we must always regard the direction in which it is moving, and the celerity with which it moves, and if we wish our shot to tell, we must aim, not at the point where it was, or where it now is, but at the point where it will be when a ball now fired may reach it. To ascertain this point requires either long practice or exact science. Yet it is less difficult than it may seem at first sight. We as Catholics, know perfectly well that the point to which all the sects are moving, with greater or less celerity, is the denial of God in the order of grace, and therefore of all supernatural revelation and religion. To this tends the inevitable and necessary development of Protestantism. This development may be hastened or retarded by circumstances, but it must sooner or later reach this fatal termination, if suffered to follow its natural course. There is an invincible logic in the human race, which pushes them on to the last consequences of their premises; and when, as in the Protestant rebellion, they have adopted premises which involve as their last consequence the rejection of the order of grace, and the assertion, if the word may be permitted us, of mere *naturism*, they will inevitably draw that consequence, and become theoretical and practical unbelievers, unless previously induced to change their premises.

The early Catholic controversialists clearly foresaw and distinctly announced that the Protestant premises involved the rejection of all revealed religion, and in every age since our divines have continued to reassert the same; but, unhappily, in no age or country has this been enough to arrest the mad career of the Protestant people; for in no age or country has it ever been true that the mass of them would not continue the development of their principles, at the risk of running into no-religion, sooner than return to the Church. The illustrious Bossuet, in the latter part of the seventeenth century, proved to the Protestants of his time, beyond the possibility of a rational doubt, that, if they continued their course, they must run into Socinianism,[1] – a polite name for incredulity; but this did not arrest them; and not many years elapsed before they became, to an alarming extent, avowed Socinians, and even avowed infidels. To a Catholic, a doctrine or principle is refuted, proved to be false, when it is shown to have an infidel or Socinian tendency; but not to a Protestant. Convince him that his principle has such a tendency, and he will become a Socinian or an infidel sooner than abandon it. The

---

[1] "According to the Racovian Catechism (1605), which reflected the views of Faustus Socinus and his followers in Poland and Transylvania, God had made Christ a perfect man, and had endowed him with special authority as prophet, priest and king. By the end of the eighteenth century, Socinianism in a modified form had generally supplanted Arianism among English Unitarians. The Socinian Christology in England was best articulated in the writings of Joseph Priestly."
Mendelsohn, Jack, *Channing, The Reluctant Radical,* Little, Brown and Co., Boston, 1971, footnote, p.140.

only effectual way of arresting Protestants is, not merely to show them whither they are tending, but to refute that to which they tend. They have an instinctive sense even now of what it is they tend to, but unhappily, they do not, or will not, see, that, when they have reached it, they will not have whereon to rest the sole of their foot.

Foreseeing the inevitable tendency of Protestantism may indeed produce, and unquestionably has produced, a reaction in favor of the Church in the minds of many excellent individuals at home and abroad; but the great majority of the people in all Protestant countries are far from recoiling, and are steadily moving onwards to the rejection of all supernatural religion. They reject the Church as a positive institution, Jesus Christ as the consubstantial Son of the Father, and Holy Scriptures as the inspired word of God, and place them in the category of mere human books, and class the Lord that bought us with Zoroaster, Socrates, Apollonius of Tyana, Mohammed, Wesley, and Swedenborg. Especially is this true in this country, where all the sects are left free to run their natural course. The mass are borne onward with resistless force towards the goal, and it is useless to expect a reaction by merely showing the infidel results towards which they are borne; – far more useless to flatter ourselves that any general reaction has commenced. In spite of a few appearances on the surface, the deep undercurrent is flowing on in the same direction it has been for the last three hundred years.

We shall deceive ourselves, if we suppose the question today is only between us and the Oxford party in the Anglican establishment, or between Catholicity and any form of dogmatic Protestantism. Protestantism, as including some elements of revealed truth from which we may reason in favor of the Church, is virtually defunct, and to argue against it is as idle as to belabor a dead ass. The real obstacle which we have to surmount is Protestant only inasmuch as it is the natural development of Protestantism. It is seldom that we meet men and women who expressly avow, that, if they could be Christians, they would be Catholics, that in their view Christianity and Catholicity are identical, and that, if we will convince them of the inspiration of the Scriptures, they will feel bound to accept and obey the Church. Such persons as these – dispute it who may – are the real representatives of the age and country, the earnest of what the mass of the people are to be tomorrow. They are the only really significant class out of the Church. The ministers and elders and their adherents around the defunct body of dogmatic Protestantism, trying, on the one hand, to galvanize it into life, and, on the other, to persuade the uneasy multitude that it is not dead, but only taking its after-dinner *siesta*, are not worth taking into account. They neither represent the present, nor announce the future. They belong to a generation that was. The empire of the world out of the Church has dropped from their hands, and however numerous they may be, and however powerful they may appear to the superficial glance, they are only the relics of a past which can never return. Leave them to bury their dead.

The only portion of the Protestant world worth studying is the progressive portion, who continue and carry on the Protestant movement. These impersonate the age and country. What Strauss or Parker writes is far more important and instructive to Catholics than what Hengstenberg, Beecher, Spring, or Woods may write. The spirit and tendency of the age and country are better learned from *The Boston Quarterly Review, The Dial, The Herald of Truth, The Harbinger, The New York Tribune,* than from *The New Englander, The Princeton Review, The True* (Protestant) *Catholic, The Churchman, The Courier and Enquirer.* The progressive minority are the only significant portion, because the only living portion, of the Protestant world, and because they are to be the majority tomorrow. They live the real Protestant life, if life that may be called which is not life, but death, and are in the minority today only because they are alone faithful to the principles common alike to them and the majority. Wherever the people are withdrawn from the law of grace, and abandoned to natural development, the progressive minority is the only portion worth studying, and the only portion against which it is necessary to direct our attacks.

All who know anything of Protestantism know full well that it subsists, and can subsist, only so long as it has free scope to develop itself. It retains its adherents never by what it gives them, but always by what it is *just a-going* to give them. Few, if any, of them are perfectly satisfied with it as it is; and they cling to it only because they are in hopes further developments and modifications may make it precisely the thing they need and crave. Our course, then, is to head it in the direction in which it is moving, and must move if it move at all, cut off its opportunity for further development, compel it to come to a standstill by showing that it is tending nowither, and that further progress carries it off into the dark and inane. When we have shown that what it is developing itself into is a mere space and vacuity, and have thus compelled it to remain motionless, it soon begins to putrefy, to send forth its stench, and all who value their health or their nostrils hasten to bury it from their sight, and to leave it to return to the elements from which it was taken.

That Protestantism in most countries, especially in this country, is developing into infidelity, irreligion, *naturism*, rejecting and losing even all reminiscences of the order of grace, is too obvious and too well known to be denied, or to demand any proof. It is stated in a recent number of the *American Almanac*, that over one half of the adult population of the United States makes no profession of religion, are connected with no real or pretended church, and therefore belong at best to the class expressively denominated *Nothingarians*. The majority, then, it is fair to presume, either believe that they have no souls, or that their souls are not worth saving, or that they can save them without religion; and the great mass of those who may nominally belong to the sects, we know, hold that salvation is attainable in every form of religion, and many that it is attainable without any form. The point, then, at which we are to aim cannot be doubtful. We are called specially to convince the American population that *they have souls, souls to be saved or lost, and which cannot be saved without Jesus Christ in His Church.* Controversial works which overlook this fact, and assume that Protestants still retain some elements of Christianity, can avail us but little. They do not lay the axe at the root of the tree; do not strike the heart of the evil; are not adapted to the questions of the day; and, however logical they may be, they fail to convince, because their premises are not conceded. It is of the greatest importance that we bear this in mind, and govern ourselves accordingly.

The work assigned us here and now is a great and painful work. We cannot address those out of the Church as men who err merely as to the form of Christianity, and are yet resolved not to part with the substance.Unhappily, we are required to present our Church, not merely under the relations of the true and the beautiful, but under the relations of the necessary and indispensable. We are compelled by the existing state of thought and feeling to present it, not merely to men who hold the truth in error, as the corrective of their intellectual aberrations, but to men under the wrath of God, as the grand and only medium of salvation. We must address the world around us, not merely as aliens from the Church, but as being therefore aliens from God, without faith, without hope, without charity, without the first and simplest elements of the

Christian life, as dead in trespasses and sins, and with no possible means of attaining eternal life, but in embracing heartily, and faithfully, and perseveringly the religion we offer them. We must show them that they have souls, that these souls will live forever, in eternal bliss or eternal woe; that they are now in sin, and in sin which deserves eternal wrath, and from which there is no deliverance save in being joined to our Church. In a word, we must address them, in regard to those matters, in the same language and tone in which we should if they were Turks or pagans. No account can be made of the Christianity they may nominally profess; no reliance can be placed on it, and no appeal can be safely made to it.

It was the conviction that they had souls to be saved, and that they could not save them out of the Church of Christ, and their earnest effort to make others feel the same, that enabled Froude, Newman, and others, to produce that remarkable movement in the Anglican establishment which has given so many choice spirits to the Church. It was by telling the people that they had immortal souls to save, and that they could not save them otherwise than through Christ in His Church, that the blessed apostles and their successors, aided by divine grace, converted the world to Christianity; it was by their stern and awful rebukes of heresy, by showing its disastrous effects upon the soul, by declaring in tones of fearful strength and startling energy, that all who were out of the ark perished, and that all who separate or are separated from unity are separated from God and in danger of eternal death, that the fathers guarded against or suppressed the earlier heresies, and kept the world for centuries united in the profession of the Catholic faith. It is only by following such examples, by convicting those out of the Church of sin, and convincing them of the fact, and of their need, of salvation, that we can recall them to the bosom of the Church, and persuade them to come into the way of salvation.

It will not do to shrink from this stern, bold, and awful manner of presenting the Church and her claims. There is no use in trying to persuade ourselves that strong and decided language is not called for, that we must speak to the world around us in soft and gentle accents, and not venture to arraign it for its unbelief, for its iniquity, and to tell it plainly that it is in the road to perdition. It is idle to suppose that we may win it to God, by telling it, expressly or by implication, that it is a very good world, a very candid and pious world, virtually a Catholic world, only suffering from inculpable error, only separated from us because it has had no opportunity of learning our holy faith. Undoubtedly, we are never to forget charity, without which a man is as sounding brass or a tinkling cymbal; undoubtedly, he who contends for the Gospel is bound to contend for it in the spirit of the Gospel; undoubtedly, vituperation and abuse are as impolitic as they are unchristian; but we must be careful not to mistake liberality for charity, the natural meekness or amiability of our own dispositions for the meekness and tenderness of religion. We must never really or apparently strike hands with iniquity, or encourage error in her work of destruction, through fear of offending the fastidiousness or of wounding the delicate sensibiblties of her votaries. No man who knows aught of the Gospel needs to be reminded of its exhaustless charity and infinite tenderness; and no one who knows anything of human nature is ignorant that the road to the understanding lies through the affections, and that in dealing with individuals we cannot show too much sweetness and gentleness of dispostion; but there is nothing incompatible with all this in setting forth in firm and even startling tones the solemn truths of our religion, let them convict whom they may. The prophet Nathan showed no uncharitableness, no want of tenderness, when he said to David, "Thou art the man:" nor did our Lord, when he called the Jews "hypocrites," a "race of vipers," and likened them to "whitened sepulchres, which outwardly appear to men beautiful, but within are full of dead men's bones and of all filthiness." Nor, again, are we uncharitable, if, when we see a man rushing blindfold into the flames, we tell him whither he is rushing, and at what peril. Love can and often must proclaim severe truths, use hard arguments, and speak in tones of fearful power; and the deeper, the truer, the more tender it is, the more firm and uncompromising, the more stern and unflinching it will prove itself, whenever occassion requires. Who calls the surgeon cruel and uncharitable, because he probes to the bottom or cuts to the quick? Who regards the director of consciences harsh and wanting in charity, because he fears not to characterize the mortal sin of his penitent, and to insist, whatever the pain or mortification, on its being abandoned? In moral surgery, we have as yet discovered no letheon, and to heal it is often necessary to inflict even excruciating pain. Often, often, it is necessary to wound, if we would heal. Our Lord himself was wounded. "He was bruised for our sins," and none can come to him or be brought to him, till wounded for his sake as he was for ours. It cannot be avoided in the nature of things. But the Christian who gives pain, though he give it with a steady hand an unflinching nerve, suffers more pain than he gives. It is not always safe to conclude that the man of a severe exterior, of firm and decided speech, who makes no compromise with sin, and yields nothing to error or her deluded votaries, is necessarily hard-hearted and stranger to the infinite tenderness of the Gospel; or that your pretty men with smiling faces, bland tones, gentle caresses, and ready condescensions are not sometimes cold and heartless, that they are generally men of warm and gushing hearts, large souls, and generous sympathies, prepared to sacrifice all they have and all they are for the love of God and their neighbor.

He who sacrifices the truth sacrifices charity, and he who withholds the truth needed – the precise truth needed – by his age or country does sacrifice it. If that truth be offensive, and he tells it, it will offend, whatever the soft phraseology in which he may tell it. If, in order to save its offensiveness, he wraps it in circumlocutions and a mass of verbiage which conceal it, he does not tell it, and his labor counts for nothing. If these do not conceal it, if in spite of them it is divined in its clearness, distinctness, and power, they take nothing from its offensiveness, and it might have been as well told in plain, direct, and appropriate terms. After all, the least offensive, because the only honest, way of speaking, is to call things by their proper, their *Christian* names. We gain nothing in the long run by the round-about, the soft, or supple phraseology which timid or politic people sometimes fancy it is necessary to use to wrap up their meaning, as we use jam, jelly, or molasses, to wrap up disagreeable medicine; nor is such phraseology so respectful or so conciliating as is often supposed. To adopt it is to treat those we address as mere children, to whom we must not speak in the strong masculine tones we use when speaking to full-grown men. Few people like to be so addressed. Even your most delicate and fastidious lady prefers the gentleman who always converses with her in his simple, natural tones, and with the strong, clear, manly sense with which he speaks to one of his own sex, to the exquisite who fancies that whenever he addresses her he must simper, and soften his words and tones. He who has the truth, and utters it boldly, without circumlocution or reticence, with freedom, firmness, dignity, and energy, proving that he speaks from no motive but the love of God and the salvation of souls, though he may be feared, though he may be resisted, and in some ages and countries gain the crown of martyrdom, may always count on being personally respected, and, what is far more to his purpose, on commanding respect for his cause.

We should never forget that there is that even in the most abandoned of our race which loathes the timid and cringing, and admires the strong, the manly, and the intrepid. The free, firm, consistent, and fearless utterance of great and awful truths goes home to the minds and hearts even of the unbelieving and the heretical, and makes them tremble as did Felix before the blessed Apostle St. Paul. It was not the phrase and the tone of the nursery that terrified the corrupt and hardened governor. It was no fear on the part of St. Paul, then a prisoner before him, to call things by their Christian names, no forebearance to characterize the deep-dyed sinner as he deserved; but it was the minister of God speaking to his conscience, in stern and awful majesty unrolling before him his guilt, convicting him of sin, showing him the justice of God, presenting him the last judgment, and ringing in his very soul the sentence, "Depart, ye cursed, into everlasting fire!" that made the seared reprobate quake with fear. It is only when the minister of God so speaks that he makes the guilty tremble; and whenever he so speaks, no matter how unbelieving or heretical the sinner may be, how often or how long he may have scoffed at the idea of death, judgment, heaven, and hell, he will tremble; for God is at the bottom of his heart to give efficacy to the word uttered. If you have God's truth, in God's name give it free utterance. Let it speak in its own deep and awful tones; let its voice sound out a voice of doom to the guilty, a voice of consolation and joy to the just. Stand behind it, and let it have free course. Dare never tamper with it. Earth and hell may rise up against it, but it is mightier than earth and hell. Stand erect in the dignity of humility and majesty of love, and God speaks through you, and the word that goes forth from you must go to the heart of the people, rive it as the thunderbolt rives the hoary oak, and all that is not depraved in man, all that is generous and noble in nature, and all that is true and mighty in heaven, shall work for you.*

* What event in modern times has so struck the imagination, gone so to the heart of mankind, and called forth such a loud burst of applause, or done so much to reveal the majesty of God's minister, and to command universal homage and respect for the papacy, as the stern and terrible rebuke of the autocrat of all the Russias by the late sovereign pontiff? You told us the papacy was dead. You mocked at the feeble old man in the Vatican. The most powerful monarch of the day presents himself before that feeble old man, that aged monk standing on the brink of the grave, and that monarch at a few bold words turns pale, weeps as a child, and the world thrills with joy to learn that there is still a power on earth that can make the tyrant look aghast, the knees of the mighty smite together, and with severe and awful majesty assert the cause of the poor and vindicate the just. You told us the papacy was dead. You heard it speak to Nicholas of Russia, not in the tone of a suppliant, not in the tone of a courtier, but as became the minister of God, before whom diadems and sceptres weigh not a feather, and power is but weakness, and you have eyes and ears only for the papacy, and you feel and speak as if the pope were the only

Who are they who command men, touch the human heart, and make the race work with them and for them, – who but the heroic? And what form of heroism is comparable to the Christian? What are your Alexanders, your Hannibals, your Caesars, your Napoleons, by the side of St. Peter, St. Paul, St. John, or St. Athanasius, St. Leo, St. Basil, St. Ambrose, St. Augustine, St. Gregory, St. Bernard, St. Dominic, St. Francis, St. Thomas, St. Ignatius, St. Vincent de Paul, and thousands of others, who rose above the world while in it, sanctified the earth, and exalted human nature to communion with the divine? It is the Christian hero, he who counts nothing dear, who holds his life in his hand, who fears not the wrath of man nor the rage of hell, that, under God overcomes the world, and wins all minds and hearts to the faith and love of Jesus Christ. He alone who fears God, who fears sin, but fears nothing else, is the world's master, and able to do whatever he pleases.

In this country the church is placed by the constitution and laws on as high ground as any one of the sects, while, by the appointment of Almighty God, she is placed infinitely above them all. Not here, then, most assuredly, is the Catholic to fear to speak above his breath; not here is he to crouch and hide. He is at home here, and no man has a better right to be here. Let him stand erect; let his tone be firm and manly; let his voice be clear and distinct, his speech strong and decided, as becomes the citizen of a free state, and a freeman of the commonwealth of God. Let him be just to himself, just to his fellow-citizens, just to his religion, – be what his religion commands him to be, and fear nothing. The American people may fear him, they may not love him; but if he bows and cringes, and whimpers and begs, or scrapes and palavers, they not only will not love him, but they will despise him; for though puerile, deluded, and perverse on religion, they are in most other things straightforward and honest, high-minded and honorable. They love plain speaking and plain dealing, and they never fail to do honor to the man who, from a sense of duty tells them in strong and direct terms the awful truths he is bound, or regards himself as bound by his church to proclaim, though by doing so he convicts them of unbelief and heresy, of deep and aggravated sinfulness before God.

power under God on earth. See what the minister of God may do, when he asserts the majesty of truth, and displays the awful grandeur of his mission. That living word of the pope to the tyrant, to the schismatic, the heretic, the persecutor of the saints, has revealed to the world the astounding fact, that today the papacy is not only living, not only not dead, but that it has a power even in the affairs of this world that it never had before.

"The road to the understanding lies through the affections." But the first affection we are to seek to win is that of respect for our church, and that we must win by first winning respect for ourselves as Catholics; for the sects are slow to distinguish between the church and her members. The spirit we manifest will be assumed to be approved and inspired by our church. Nothing tends more to give Protestants a mean opinion of us, than for us to be tame or apologetic in setting forth or in defending our faith. We once loaned a Protestant lady a pamphlet by an eminent Catholic divine. She read it, returned it with a note, stating that she could not endure it, for nothing was so disgusting to her as to find a Catholic apologizing for his church, or defending it in a Protestant spirit. "If he believes his church infallible, there can be nothing in her history which he can believe needs an apology; and if he believes himself divinely commissioned, why does he not speak as one having authority?" Protestants, of course, in general appear delighted, when they find us apologizing or seeming to apologize for our church, or apparently laboring to soften what they regard as the severity of her doctrines; but it is only because in so doing we seem to them to surrender her infallibility. All our gentle phraseology, all our conciliating manners, all our apparently liberal expositions in the sense of latitudinarians, appear to them only as so many departures from what the church once insisted on; and while they applaud us for our Protestant tendency, they can but ill disguise their contempt for us, since, in spite of such tendency, we pretend that our church is infallible and invariable; and they conclude from our conduct only that either we are not sincere in our concessions, or the church, like the sects modifies her doctrines to suit times and places.

Protestants generally believe that the church is not what she was formerly; that, in fact, she has greatly improved since the reformation; and this in consequence of finding in her so little that is to them unreasonable or offensive. They cannot understand, if she was in the sixteenth century what she now appears to be, how the reformers could have been so enraged against her, or why they should have judged it necessary to separate from her communion; and it is a common theory among them, on which they seek to justify the reformers, that their movement has done by its reaction perhaps more to reform the church than to reform those who separated or have remained separated. But this, though it may tend, in some measure, to diminish hostility to her as she now is, is to them an unanswerable argument against accepting her for what she claims to be; for it implies progress, improvement, which is incompatible with the claim of catholicity and infallibility. Whatever a

Catholic says which looks, or can be imagined to look, like a departure from the earlier formularies of the church, though it should render her doctrines less unpalatable to them, has a direct tendency to keep them out of her communion.

Hence there is no use in affecting a liberal tone, and in treating those outside as if we regarded them, upon the whole, as very good Christians, not far out of the way, meaning right, perfectly well disposed, in only inculpable error, and by no means necessarily out of the way of salvation; for it only tends, on the one hand, to make them distrust our church, or, on the other, our sincerity. It only goes to confirm them in one of their most dangerous and unjust prejudices against us. Surveying the strange, eventful history of our church, seeing her survive all attacks, gaining strength at every effort to crush her, and turning every apparent defeat into a victory, a triumph, Protestants say she must be a miracle of craft and cunning, and they attribute her preservation and triumphs to her wily and adroit policy. They, in general, hold us to be destitute of principle, but extremely cunning and politic. The popular, though erroneous, sense of the word *Jesuitical* is the popular Protestant sense of the word *Catholic*. If we adopt the liberal tone of modern times, speak in the modern spirit, show ourselves ready to conform to prevailing modes of thought, anxious to throw off whatever appears exclusive or rigorous, or disposed to apologize for past practices not exactly acceptable to our own age and country, and to excuse them on the ground that they originated in the ignorance or barbarism of the times, or in popular sentiments now obsolete, we gain no credit for our church, or if so, none for ourselves; but seem only to furnish proofs of her consummate policy and suppleness and of her want of fixed and unalterable principles, leaving her always at liberty to assume the shape and color of the time and place, be they what they may.

In a country like ours, where we are a feeble minority, even if principle permitted, the affection of a liberal and condescending spirit, of a dispostion to conform to the views and feelings of the majority, and studied forbearance to assert the claims of our church in all rigor and exclusiveness, would indicate a policy the very reverse of wise. Where Catholics are the immense majority, where place, fashion, wealth, and social influence are in their hands, moderation towards dissenters, a mild and condescending demeaner, and the disposition to yield to their ignorance all that can be yielded without giving up any portion of the sacred deposit of faith, may be wise, and even a duty; for it is the condescension of the superior, of the nobleman, to those below him, always welcome, and seldom failing to beget gratitude and to win confidence. But the condescension of the social inferior to the social superior is a different thing. Here, where the social and political influences, instead of being ours, are against us, where we are voted in advance suspicious persons, and where our very virtues are tortured into grounds of accusation against us, such a policy would be regarded as sychophantic, or as tame and cringing, as a proof of meanness, weakness, or suppleness, and would only excite contempt or distrust. Our liberal professions, our apparent sympathy with views and feelings Protestant rather than Catholic, would be supposed to be affected, – adopted to ward off hostility till we had gained a footing, and become strong enough to exhibit our rigor or exclusiveness. It is lawful to learn of an enemy; and we all know, or may know, that this is the precise view which Protestants very generally take of such a policy, wherever Catholics are in the minority, and silly enough to adopt it.

It is hard for innocence to conceive that she is suspected and when she does get some glimmering of the fact, she almost inevitably blunders, and in attempting measures to remove suspicions adopts the very measures most likely to confirm them. No man can have studied the history of Catholics living in a Protestant community without being often reminded of this fact. They judge Protestants too often by themselves, and transfer to them their own innocence, candor, and good faith. But this will not do. What we are to aim at is not to make our religion acceptable to them as they are, but to make them feel, that, so long as they are what they are, they are wrong, and in need of "a radical change of heart." Our deepest and truest policy is to have no policy at all. By the very fact that we are Catholics, we are freed from all dependence on mere human policy. We have the truth, and it will sustain us, instead of our being obliged to sustain it. It is the glory of our religion that she identifies the expedient and the right, the true and the politic. That is most expedient, most politic, which is most consonant with her spirit; and the most effectual way of subserving the interests of the church is for members to be Catholics and nothing else, – to throw themselves without reserve and with entire confidence on God, and to leave him to support them, instead of their officiously undertaking to support him. We shall best advance the Catholic cause by showing that we hold our religion true and sacred, complete and all-sufficient, that we live for it, and for it alone, and that we do and can regard none who do not so live as the friends of God. God made and gave us our religion, and we have nothing to do with molifying it to suit prevailing tastes and prejudices, contracting it here or expanding it there, now by our ingenious distinctions increasing its laxity, now its rigor. It is perfect as God gave it; and it is ours simply to receive and obey. If its rigor or its laxity prove an odor of death unto death to some, that is not our affair, and the less we meddle with it the better.

In censuring loose and latitudinarian views, in commending the free, firm, frank statement of Catholic truth in its awful severity as well as in its sweetness, in contending for a bold, manly, independent, straight-forward, and energetic, as well as affectionate mode of addressing those who are without, and the fearless and faithful proclamation of the precise truth needed to rebuke the reigning error or the reigning sin of the age or the country, we trust no one will be so foolish as to suppose that we are urging a low, vulgar, harsh, or vituperative method of presenting the claims of our religion, and of addressing those who unhappily reject them. Fidelity to the cause we advocate, and the bold and firm assertion of unpalatable truths, do by no means require us to lose command of ourselves, or to forget the meekness of the Christian, or the courtesy of the gentleman. Firm adherence to principle, strong masculine language, plain and energetic speech, and even bold and severe denunciations, when called for by the rigor of our faith, and justified by the facts or arguments we adduce, are no departure from good breeding, and are rarely, if ever, offensive. What is to be avoided is not the severity of reason, but the severity of passion. Loose and violent declamations, low wit, vulgar and opprobrious epithets applied in ill temper, sustained by no principle, warranted by no argument, and called for by no truth established in our essay or discourse, are wrong, offend, and justly offend, and we should be sorry to suppose that there is any Catholic capable either of recommending or of resorting to them. But the severity of authority exercising its clearly legitimate functions, of charity speaking out from the depth of her infinite concern for the salvation of souls, or of reason evidently deducing necessary conclusions from premises regarded as incontrovertible, is always allowable, and is never held to be abusive, or a transgression of good manners.

In direct personal addresses to Protestants, it is rarely necessary to call them heretics, and we may with propriety, after the illustrious Bossuet, call them "our separated or dissenting brethern," if we call them so only through conventual politeness. But if we avoid the term heretic, and call them our separated brethern for the purpose of imply-ing some sort of religious sympathy with them, to conceal from ourselves or from them the fact that all good Catholics presume them to be heretics, or so as to produce an impression on those within or those without that we do not look upon heresy and schism as deadly sins, we occasion scandal, and have nothing to plead in our justification. If, on the other hand, we call Protestants heretics in ill-humor, from the virulence of passion, for the sake of wounding their feelings and insulting them,we are also unjustifiable; for even the truth spoken for unlawful ends is libellous, and the greater the truth, not unfrequently, the greater the libel. But if, in addressing Catholics, or in reasoning against Protestant errors, we call Protestants heretics, because they are so in fact, and because we would call them by their *Christian* name, either for the sake of leading them to reflect on the danger to which they are exposed, or for the sake of guarding the unwary against their seductions and the contamination of their heresies, we give them no just cause for offence, and do only what by the truth and charity of the Gospel we are bound to do.

Undoubtedly the mass of the American people are deeply prejudiced against the Christian religion; undoubtedly they are at heart strongly opposed to Catholics; but the course we urge is not likely to render them more prejudiced or opposed. Touching the matter of religion, we have of course nothing to say in their favor, and this is, no doubt, in the estimation of Christians, to say the worst against them; but in the natural order, in the domestic and social virtues which have their reward in this life, in the natural strength of their understanding, acuteness of intellect, and honesty and energy of character, they by no means rank lowest in the scale of nations. Should we call them theives, robbers, liars, cowards, or in general hard-hearted and cruel, they would be offended at our injustice, or smile at our folly, and justly; for we should then address them in our own name, on the authority of our own reason, or from the ebullition of our own passions, as weak and sinful men addressing their equals, and we could offer no excuse or palliation of our conduct. But if we speak to them in relation to the supernatural order, not from ourselves, but from the word of God, and tell them in the spirit of ardent charity, plainly, directly, unreservedly, energetically, what our religion commands, and assure them in unequivocal terms and tones that they are out of the way, following the devices of their own hearts, under the wrath and condemnation of Almighty God, and that their only possible chance of escape is in humble submission to that very church against which their fathers wickedly rebelled, and which they themselves so haughtily rejected, though they may be pricked in their hearts, though they may be startled from their dreaming, or may even bid us go our way for this time, till they find a more convenient season, they will respect our principles, and acknowledge in their hearts the free, noble, lofty, and uncompromising spirit of our church, and the high worth of character she gives to her children. It was thus spoke the prince of the apostles on the day of Pentecost: – "Ye men of Israel, hear these words: Jesus of Nazareth, a man approved of God among you, by miracles and wonders, and signs, which God did by him in the midst of you, as you also know; this same, being delivered up by the determinate counsel and foreknowledge of God, *you have crucified and put to death* by the hands of wicked men...Therefore let all the house of Israel know most assuredly, that God hath made him to be lord and Christ, this same Jesus whom *you have crucified*. Now when they heard these things they had compunction in their heart: and they said to Peter and the rest of the apostles, Men and brethern, what shall we do? But Peter said to them, Do penance, and be baptized *every one of you,* in the name of Jesus Christ, for the remission of your sins." – Acts ii, 22-41.

Protestants, indeed, expect Catholics to speak in this way. They expect them to speak differently from their own scribes and elders, with whom they are wearied half to death, and whose doubt, and hesitation, and arrogance they find all but insupportable. They know the Catholic claims to speak with authority, as divinely commissioned to teach, and they wish him to speak in character. They are disgusted when he descends from the pulpit to the rostrum, or when the preacher sinks into the mere reasoner, taking their standpoint, and discoursing to them in their own spirit, as one of their own number. They demand of him what he professes to have, and which they know their own ministers have not; and if he gives it not, they conclude it is because he has it not to give. He is then, say they, with all his lofty pretentions to authority, no better than one of us; and they turn away in disappointment and disgust. Let him speak as one having authority, as the authorized minister of God, never forgetting that he is priest and doctor, and that it is not he that teaches, but God through him, and, cold, and unbelieving, and heretical as they may be, they cannot but listen with awe, and some of them with profit.*

___

* We are often reminded, when we insist on this, that St. Francis de Sales, whose labors restored over seventy thousand Protestants to the church, was wont to say that "more flies can be caught with honey than with vinegar." This is unquestionably true, but they who are familiar with the saint's works do not need to be told that in his

The great body of the American people are serious, plain, and practical, little addicted to mere intellectual speculations, and not easily moved by what does not promise some positive result. They are not averse to change, have no invincible attachment to old ways and usages, or to the sects in the bosom of which they have been reared, and can, for what appears to them a solid reason, abandon them without much reluctance; but no reason drawn from merely intellectual or aesthetic considerations will appear to them sufficient. The only reasons which can weigh much with them, indeed with any people, are such as are drawn from ethical sources. They may be shown the truth and beauty, the consistency, grandeur, and majesty of our religion, and remain untouched; for it is not as philosophy or as art that they need it. Individuals in particular localities, or of a peculiar temperament, may at first be induced to think of entering our communion, as they are led to pass from one sect to another, to satisfy some particular intellectual want, to please some special taste, or to indulge some specific social or devotional tendency; but the great body of the people will remain unmoved and be unaffected by our profound philosophy, our learned expositions, our conclusive arguments, our eloquent appeals, unless we succeed in presenting the question as one involving life and death. In vain we show the truth of our doctrine, in vain we set forth our pure and lofty morality, in vain we exhibit the solemn grandeur, imposing magnificence, pomp, and splendor of our ritual, in vain we charm them with the simple majesty and unction of our divine hymns, or entrance them with our heaven-inspired chants, if we do not bring the matter home to the conscience, make them feel that they have souls to be saved, that they are sold unto sin, are under the wrath of God, and have no possible means of escaping everlasting perdition but by coming into the church, and submitting to her authority and direction. So long as we leave their consciences at ease, so long as we address only the intellect or the sense of the beautiful, or leave them feel that it is not absolutely impossible to be safe where they are, we have given them no solid or intelligible reason for becoming Catholics.

own practice he gave considerable latitude to the meaning of the word *honey.*. Certainly we ask for no more bold and severe mode of presenting Catholic truth, or stronger or severer language against Protestants, than he was in the habit of adopting. Even the editor of his controversial works did not deem it advisable to publish them without softening some of their expressions. In fact, much of the *honey,* of the saints generally, especially of such saints as St. Athanasius, St. Hilary of Poitiers, and St. Jerome, would taste very much like vinegar, we suspect, to some of our modern delicate palates.

There is not the least sense or propriety in addressing the great mass of Protestants, especially in this country, as if they were already Christian, sincerely and honestly Christian, according to their understanding of Christianity, and only in intellectual error as to the true form of Christianity. We cannot repeat this too often, nor insist upon it too earnestly. The error is moral rather than intellectual. The question between them and us is a question, not of form, but of substance. The whole head is sick, the whole heart is sad. From the sole of the foot to the top of the head there is no soundness. The disease has penetrated the whole system, and reached even the seat of life itself. The remedy which shall restore them is not the mere exposition of the truth and beauty of our holy religion, in contrast with what they still nominally profess to believe. It is with them as it was with the unbelieving Jews in the days of our blessed Saviour. Now, as then, there is no beauty in him, or comeliness; they see him, and there is no sightliness in him that they should be desirous of him. Despised and the most abject of men, a man of sorrows, and acquainted with infirmity, his look is, as it were, hidden and despised and they esteem him not. Surely he hath borne their infirmities and carried their sorrows, and they have thought him, as it were, a leper, and as one struck by God and afflicted. – Isaias, liii, 2-4. They have eyes, but they do not see, ears, but they do not hear, hearts, but they do not understand. What is true, beautiful, pure, and salutary in our holy religion is to them a stumbling block, as it was to the Jews, or foolishness, as it was to the gentiles. Not to them is Christ crucified, whom we preach, the power of God and the wisdom of God. – 1 Cor. i, 23,24.

What is doubted, scorned, rejected, is not Catholicity as a form of Christianity, but Christianity itself. It is Christ crucified that is denied. The doubt goes to the bottom and strikes at all revealed religion, at the whole order of grace. Forms are easily got over. No small portion of the people even now have no doubt of the identity of Catholicity and Christianity, if Christianity means a positive religion, anything more than a form of natural religion. The active cause of the hostility to the church is the want of belief in all positive religion, in the doubt that God has spoken or made a revelation of his will to men, established a church for their salvation, which he loves, protects, and out of which he will save no one. No matter what they pretend, no matter what they say their old symbols and formularies which they retain as so many heirlooms, it is Christianity itself they doubt, whenever it is assumed to belong to the supernatural order, to be inflexible and unalterable, authoritative and supreme, or to be elevated at all above mere natural morality, with perhaps a few sanctions more distinct and solemn than natural reason unaided could of itself have discovered. It is simplicity, not charity, to question this. We cannot prudently address them as believers simply holding the truth in error, but, if we wish to arrest their attention, we must address them as sinners in rebellion against God, dead in trespasses and sins, under the wrath and condemnation of God, – reason with them of sin, of justice, of chastity, and the judgment to come, and compel them to cry out, Men and brethren, what shall we do to be saved? What shall we do to be saved? asked from the depths of the affrighted soul, in the breaking up of the whole moral nature, trembling before the awful judgment of God, is the question; and till men ask it in deep and terrible earnestness, they will never become real and true-hearted Catholics. When they have once been made to feel their sinfulness, their danger, their lost and perishing condition, out of Christ, we shall have little difficulty in convincing them that there is no safety for them out of the communion of the church. It is not so much of infidelity, or of heresy, that they need to be convicted, as of sin; not so much of Catholicity as the only true Christianity, as of Christianity itself, that they require to be convinced; not so much of this or that particular error, as of the grand mother error of all, that they are safe where they are, and may be saved in any religion or in none, that it is necessary to disabuse them.

We say nothing new or recondite. Our holy religion has from the first been addressed to sinners, and its grand assumption is that all men are sinners, dead in trespasses and sins, till made alive in Christ Jesus. The wages of sin is death, and death hath passed upon all men, for all have sinned. The church addresses herself to a world lying in wickedness, festering in its own iniquity, as the divinely provided means, and only means, of their restoration to spiritual life and health. Her mission is the revelation of the glory of God in the salvation of sinners. It is against sin, sin in all its forms, in all its disguises, in all its subterfuges, in high places or low places, that she is commissioned to carry on a fierce and exterminating war. She is here in this world the church militant. She fights and never ceases to fight sin, for she is holy, and she only can overcome it. Wherever she sends her missionary, the brave soldier of the cross, she sends him to a world dead in trespasses and sins, to carry to them the Gospel of life and immortality. She sends him, not to find the Gospel with them, to tell them that what he brings is preferable to what they have, but yet it is possible for them to be saved without it; but to tell them that they are dead, that they are strangers to eternal life, that he has eternal life to offer them, that he alone has it, and that they must receive it from his hands or not receive it at all. "How beautiful are the feet of them that preach the Gospel of peace, that bring glad tidings of good things!" He goes to sinners to proclaim, in the name of his Master, the glad tidings of eternal life, through a crucified, a risen Redeemer; and who but he has these glad tidings to proclaim? "Lord to whom shall we go? Thou has the words of eternal life." And where is Christ, he who is the resurrection and the life, who has come that we might have life, and have it more abundantly, to be found as the Saviour of sinners, and the giver of eternal life, but in his church, his mystical body, his spouse, his beloved? Assuredly nowhere else. The words of eternal life are with us, and not elsewhere, – in our church, and in her only. Need we, then, fear to say so? Need we, then, hesitate to tell the world lying in wickedness around us, that they are destitute of eternal life, that they are in sin, and to beseech them, as they love their own souls, to come into the ark where, and where alone there is safety?

There is no salvation out of the church. Men must come into her communion or be lost, and lost forever. If it be not so, why has God instituted his church, why has he given her authority, and commanded her to teach all nations until the consummation of the world? Why are we so attached to her, why does she hold so high a place in our affections, and why would we rather suffer a thousand deaths than swerve one iota from the faith she enjoins? Why do we strive to bring all men into her sacred enclosure? Why visit our missionaries every land, and in every land suffer privation, want, distress, persecution, and death, to bring men into the church, if salvation is possible without her agency, if the people who sit in the region and shadow of death, by following such light as they have, can be saved, though living and dying out of her communion, and in ignorance of her very existence? Concede the possibility, and the conduct of the apostles, the fathers, the saints and martyrs, of zealous Catholics in every age, is madness, folly, or fanaticism.

But, if it be true, and as sure as God exists, and can neither be deceived nor deceive it is true, that there is no salvation out of the church, what a fearful responsibility should we not incur, were we to forbear to proclaim it, or, by our mistimed or misplaced qualifications, to encourage the unbelieving, the heretical, or the indifferent to hope the contrary! And how much more fearful still, if we should go further, and attempt in our publications to prove that he who firmly insists on it is harsh, unjust, uncharitable, running in his rash zeal to an unauthorized extreme! No doubt, the truth is always and everywhere to be adhered to, let the consequences be what they may; no doubt he who errs by his rigor is to be rebuked, as well as he who errs by his laxity; but if, in our zeal to rebuke imaginary rigor, we should compel the missionary to prove the necessity of his church against his own friends before he can be at liberty to assert it against infidels and heretics, if we run before him and intercept his arrows winged at the sinner's conscience, or follow immediately after and bind up and assuage the wounds they may have inflicted, our zeal would but indifferently atone for the good we hinder, or the scandal we cause. These poor souls, for whom our Lord shed his precious blood, for whom bleed afresh the dear wounds in his hands, his feet, his side, bound in the chains of error and sin, suspended over the precipice, ready to drop into the abyss below, admonish all who have hearts of flesh or any bowels of compassion to speak out, to cry aloud in awful and piercing tones to warn them of their danger, rather than by ingenious distinctions or qualifications to flatter them, or to have the appearance of flattering them, with the hope that, after all, their condition is not perilous.[2]

We speak not now in relation to other ages or countries. We are discussing the question in its relation to our own countrymen, the great practical question of salvation, as it comes up here and now. We have no

---

[2] Fr. Thomas R. Ryan has an excellent comment on the point that Brownson is attempting to make here:

> "In approaching his first exposition of the Catholic Church's exclusive claim of salvation, he deeply deplored... latitudinarianism, the increasing tendency among authors of current popular literature to soften or explain away altogether the qualifications or restrictions which theologians attach to the dogma... Such a tendency was only aiding and abetting a fatal latitudinarianism already rampant and widespread. Against this tendency in popular literature Brownson entered his vigorous protest. In doing so, he was anticipating by more than a century the solemn protest of Pope Pius XII uttered in his encyclical, *Humani Generis,* against those who were reducing this dogma to "a meaningless formula," (Brownson, too, used the identical word used by His Holiness "meaningless.".)[1]

The passage to which Father Ryan is referring is found in an article entitled *Extra*

concern with distant or merely speculative cases, or with scholastic distinctions and qualifications which have and can have no practical application here. The question is, what are we authorized and bound by our religion to proclaim to all those of our countrymen whom our words can reach? Here are the great mass out of the church, unbelieving and heretical, careless and indifferent, and it is idle to expect to make any general impression upon them, unless we present the question of the church as a question of life and death, unless we can succeed in convincing them, that, if they live and die where they are, they can never see God. This is the doctrine and the precise doctrine needed. Is it true? Yes or no? Is it denied? By those out of the church, certainly, and hence the great reason why they are content to live and die out of the church. Is it denied by those in the church? What Catholic dare deny it? To what individual or class of individuals are authorized by our holy faith to promise even the bare possibility of salvation, without being joined to the visible communion of the church of God?

It is said that those without are simply bound to seek, and that we can deny them the possibility of salvation only on the condition that they do not seek? Be it so. But if they are bound to seek, it is because Almighty God commands them to seek, and gives them the grace which enables them to seek; and who is prepared to say, if they seek *cauta sollicitudine* [with careful solicitude], as St. Augustine makes it necessary for them to do, that they will not find? If God commands them to seek, they can find; for he never commands one to seek in vain. "Seek and ye shall find; knock and it shall be opened unto you...For everyone that seeketh findeth, and to every one that knocketh it shall be opened." – St. Matt. vii. 7,8. It is fair, then, to conclude, if there is one who does not find, to whom it is not opened, that he is one who does not seek; and if he does not

Ecclesiam Nulla Salus, which appeared in the *Review,* in April of 1874:

> "It is seldom we meet a Catholic, man or woman, priest or layman, who will permit us to say 'out of the Church no one can be saved,' without requiring us to qualify the assertion, or so to explain it as to make it <u>meaningless</u> to plain people who are ignorant of the subtleties, the nice distinctions, and refinements of the theologians." [2]

[1] Ryan, *Op. cit.,* p.572

[2] *Extra Ecclesiam Nulla Salus, Brownson's Quarterly Review,* (April 1874), p.221; *Works,* V, p.578.

seek, he is out of the church by his own fault. The grace of prayer is given unto every one, and every one can pray, and if he does, he shall receive; and it would impeach both the wisdom and the veracity of God to maintain the contrary.

Those of our countrymen not in the church may be divided into two classes, and each of these may be subdivided into two subordinate classes, – infidels and sectarians, – and each negative and positive; that is, infidels and sectarians who are such through ignorance. The first two subdivisions are formal infidels or heretics, and are condemned for their sin of infidelity or heresy. Of these, there can be no question; not one of them can be saved, unless he become a member, truly a member of the church. These know the will of God and do it not, and therefore "shall be beaten with many stripes." – St. Luke xii, 47. But what is to be said of them that are infidels or sectarians through ignorance? "The servant that knew not his master's will, but did things worthy of stripes," shall he not escape? Our Lord answers, not that he shall escape, but that "he shall be beaten with few stripes." The Holy Ghost represents the sinners in hell as saying, – "We have erred from the way of truth; and the light of justice hath not shined unto us, and the sun of understanding hath *not risen upon us.* We wearied ourselves in the way of iniquity and destruction, and have walked through hard ways; *but the way of the Lord we have not known."* - Wisdom v.6,7. It is clear, then, that ignorance does not always excuse, and that the servant who knoweth not his master's will, though he may be punished less than the one who does know it and doeth it not, will nevertheless be punished.

But they who are merely negative infidels, or unbelievers purely through ignorance, in consequence of never having heard about the Gospel, are not guilty of the sin of infidelity? Certainly not. Every Catholic is presumed to know that the 68th proposition of Baius, *Infidelus pure negativa in his, quibus Christus non est praedicatus, peccatum est* [purely negative infidelity in those to whom Christ has not been preached is sinful], is a condemned proposition, and therefore that purely negative infidelity in those to whom Christ has not yet been preached is inculpable, – as St. Augustine teaches, the penalty of sin, not sin itself. But who *therefore* concludes that they are in the way of salvation, or that they can be saved without becoming living members of the body of the Lord? "Infidels of this sort," says St. Thomas, "are damned, indeed, for other sins which without faith cannot be remitted, but they are not damned for the sin of infidelity. Whence the Lord says,

'If I had not come and spoken to them, they would not have sin;' that is, as St. Augustine explains it, would not have the sin of not believing in Christ."* There is a considerable distance between being free from a formal sin of infidelity, and being in the way of salvation. No infidel, positive or negative, in vincible or invincible ignorance, can be saved; "for without faith it is impossible to please God," and "he that believeth not shall be damned," and faith *in voto* [in desire], not *in re* [in fact] is inconceivable. – Heb. xi.6; St. Mark xvi.16. Neither of the subdivisions of the unbelieving class of our countrymen are, then, in the way of salvation.

But may it not prove better with sectarians? With those who are knowingly such, of course not, and nobody pretends that it can. But may not those who are baptized in heretical societies through ignorance, believing them to be in the church of Christ, be regarded as in the way of salvation? We will let the Brothers Walenburch answer for us from St. Augustine. They are speaking of *de excusationibus simpliciorum* [concerning the excuses of the simple] among Protestants. The first excuse they notice, the influence of tyrants, etc., is nothing to our present purpose, and we begin with the second.

"The second excuse they make is, That not they who are born and educated in Protestant churches have separated themselves from the unity of the Catholic Church, but their ancestors, Calvin, Luther, etc. Let St. Augustine reply: – *'But those who through ignorance* are baptized there (with heretics), judging the sect to be the church of Christ, sin less than these (who know it to be heretical); *nevertheless they are wounded by a sacrilege of schism,* and therefore sin not lightly, because others sin more gravely. For when it is said to certain persons, It shall be more tolerable for Sodom in the day of judgment than for you, it is not therefore said because the Sodomites will not be punished, but because the others will be more grievously punished.'

"The third excuse is, They say that they have been baptized, that they believe in Christ, apply themselves to good works, and therefore may

---

* Qui autem sic infideles, damnatur quidem propter alia peccata, quae sine fide remitti non possunt; non autem propter infidelitatis peccatum. Unde Dominus dicit, Joan. xv,22, – Si non venissem, et locutus eis fuissem, peccatum non haberet. Quod Augustinus (Tract. in Joan. Lxxix, ante med.) dicit, 'quod loquitur de illo peccato quo non crediderunt in Christum.'" [Summa, 2a 2ae, Q. 10, a. 1, in corp.]

hope for salvation, although they adhere to the party divided from the church. St. Augustine replies, – 'We are accustomed from these words (1 Cor. xiii. 1-8) to show men that it avails them nothing to have either the sacraments or the faith, if they have not charity, in order that, when you come to Catholic unity, you may understand what is conferred on you, and how great is that in which you were before deficient. *For Christian charity cannot be kept out of the unity of the church;* and thus you may see that without it you are nothing, even though you have baptism and the faith, and by your faith you are able to move mountains. If this is also your opinion, let us not detest and scorn either the sacraments which we acknowledge in you, or the faith itself, but let us maintain charity, without which we are nothing, even with the sacraments and the faith. But we maintain charity, if we embrace unity; and we embrace unity when our knowledge is in unity through the words of Christ, not when through our own words we form a partial sketch.'

"The fourth excuse is, Some say that God is to be believed according to the measure of grace received from him; Catholics, indeed, believe many things which Protestants do not, but the former have received the five talents, the latter the two or three. They do not condemn Catholics, but they hope to be saved in the small measure which they have themselves received. But here may avail what we have just adduced from St. Augustine; for if even baptism and faith profit nothing without indispensable charity, much less will profit a mere portion which is held in division and schism."*

This is high authority, and express to the purpose. It cuts off every possible excuse which our countrymen can allege, or which can be alleged for them. They who are brought up in the church, instructed in her faith, and admitted to her sacraments, if they break away from her, can be saved only by returning and doing penance; and all who knowingly resist her authority, or adhere to heretical and schismatical societies, knowing them to be such, are in the same category, and have no possible means of salvation without being reconciled to the church, and loosened by her from the bonds with which she has bound them. Thus far all is clear and undeniable. But even they who are in societies separated from the church through ignorance, believing them to be the church of Christ, according to the authorities adduced, are wounded by sacrilege, a most grievous sin, are destitute of charity, which cannot be

* *De Controversiis Tractatus Generales IX, De Unit. Eccl. et Schism,* cap. 15.

kept out of the unity of the church, and without which they are nothing, and therefore, whatever may be the comparative degree of their sinfulness, are in the road to perdition as well as the others, and no more than the others can be saved without being reconciled to the church. But these several classes include all of our countrymen not in the church, and therefore, as every one of these is exposed to the wrath and condemnation of God, we have the right, and are in duty bound to preach to them all, without exception, that, unless they come into the church, and humbly submit to her laws, and persevere in their love and obedience, they will inevitably be lost.†

† *Vide,* Bishop Hay, *Sincere Christian,* 2nd. American edition, Philadelphia, pp. 345-390. This is a work of high authority, second to none in our language. It has fallen into our hands for the first time since the present article was written, or we should have drawn largely from its pages. We have small space left for extracts, but we cannot resist the temptation to quote an authority which the Rt. Reverend author cites from St. Fulgentius. "St. Fulgentius in the sixth century speaks thus : 'Hold most firmly, and without any doubt, that no one who is baptized out of the Catholic church can partake of eternal life, if before the end of this life he be not restored to the Catholic church and incorporated therein.' – *Lib. de Fid.,* cap. 37." To the same effect we may cite St. Augustine, *Tract. 45 in Joan,* . n.15. "Non autem potest quisque per ostium, id est per Christum, egredi ad vitam aeternam, quae erit in specie, nisi per ipsum ostium, hoc est per eumdem Christum in Ecclesiam ejus quod est ovile ejus, intraverit ad vitam temporalem, quae est in Fide." This, taken in connection with its context and the scope of the general argument of the *Tract,* can not possibly be understood otherwise than in the sense of St. Fulgentius; and it is worthy of especial notice, that those recent theologians who seem unwilling to assent to this doctrine cite no authority from a single father or medieval doctor of the church, not strictly compatible with it.

Unquestionably, authorities in any number may be cited to prove – what nobody disputes – that pertinacity in rejecting the authority of the church is essential to formal or culpable heresy, that persons may be in heretical societies without being culpable heretics, and therefore that we cannot say of all who live and die in such societies, that they are damned precisely for the sin of heresy. Father Perrone, and our own distinguished theologian, the erudite Bishop of Philadelphia, whose contributions have so often enriched our pages, cite passages in abundance to this effect, which as Suarez asserts, is the uniform doctrine of all the theologians of the church; but they cite not a single authority of an earlier date than the seventeenth century, which even hints anything more than this. But this by no means militates against St. Augustine, St. Fulgentius, the Brothers Walenburch, or Bishop Hay; because it by no means follows from the fact that one is not a formal heretic, that he is, so long as in a society alien to the church, in the way of salvation. A man may, indeed, not be damned for his erroneous faith, and yet be damned for sins not remissible without the true faith, and for the want of virtues impracticable out of the communion of the church. Father Perrone very properly distinguishes *material,* heretics from *formal,* heretics; but when treating the question *ex professo,* he by no means pronounces the former in the way of salvation; he simply remits them to the judgement of God, who, he assures us, – what nobody questions, – will consign no man to endless tortures, unless for a crime of which he is voluntarily guilty. *Tract. de Vera Relig. advers. Heterdox,* . Prop. xi.

Moreover, Father Perrone, when refuting those who contend that salvation would be attainable if the visible church should fail, that is, by internal means, by being joined in spirit to the true church, maintains that in such case there would be no *ordinary,* means of salvation; that when Christ founded his church, he intended to offer men an ordinary means, or rather a collection of means, which all indiscriminately, and at all times, might use for procuring salvation; that if God had been willing to operate our salvation by the assistance of internal means, there would have been no reason for instituting the church; that what is said of being joined to the church through the spirit, and of invincible ignorance, or of *material,* heretics, could be admitted only on the hypothesis that God should provide no other means; that since it is certain that God has willed to save men by other means, namely, by the institution of the church visible and external, which is at all times easily distinguished from every sect, it is evident that the subterfuge imagined by non-Catholics is altogether unavailable. *"Obj. Quae a Catholicis proferuntur ad indefectibilitatem Ecclesiae adstruendam nihili prorus pendenda sunt. Etenim quamvis vera Ecclesia deficeret vel ex toto vel ex aliqua sua parte, non propterea sequeretur homines omni destituti salutis medio; posset enin Deus supplere mediis internis, possent homines spiritu saltem conjungi cum vera Christi ecclesia: praesertim error est omnino involuntarius et ineluctabilis; tunc enim nocere non potest, ut constat ex haeretecis materialibus nuncupatis... Resp. Non sequeretur nomines omni destituti salutis medio extraordinario, Tr. vel O. Ordinario, N. Jam vero quando Christus condidit Ecclesiam suam, intendit praebere hominibus medium ordinarium, seu potius collectionem mediorum, quibus omnes indiscriminatim uti quovis tempore possent ad salutem sibi comparandam. Si Deus voluisset ope interiorem mediorum nostram operari salutem, nulla fuisset Ecclesiae instituendae ratio. Mediis internis, tum extraordinaria ratione nobis prospicit Deus, quando nulla alia suppetit via, neque nostra culpa factum est, ut media nobis ordinaria defuerint. Deus etiam posset hoc universum regere absque causis secundis, quod tamen non praestat, si excipias casus extraordinarios, cum nempe prodigia operatur. Quod vero adjiciunt adversarii de conjunctione per spiritum cum vera Ecclesia, de errore ineluctabili, aut de haereticis materialibus, locum pariter habere tantum posset in hypothesi quod Deus nullum aliud medium suppeditaret: cum vero constet Deum alia ratione voluisse hominum saluti consulere, per institutionem videlicet Ecclesiae visibilis atque externae, quaeque ab omni secta facile semper discerni possit, patet inutile prorus esse ejusmodi effugium ab acatholicis excogitatum, qui nolunt veram Ecclesiam agnoscere." – De Loc. Theologic,* . p. l, cap. 4, art. 1.

This says all we wish to say; for we are not discussing what is possible by a miracle of grace, but what is possible in the *order of grace. Nor does the admission of an extraordinary interposition for our salvation, when the ordinary means, through no fault of ours, fail us, necessarily imply the possibility of salvation without the medium ordinarium;* for it may be to bring us to it, or it to us, so that we may be saved by it, and not without it. That there may be persons in heretical and schismatical societies, invincibly ignorant of the church, who so perfectly correspond to the grace they receive, that Almighty God will by extraordinary means bring them to the church, is believable and perfectly compatible with

Into the church, unquestionably; but not necessarily into the visible church, some may answer. We must distinguish between the body or exterior communion of the church, and the soul or interior communion. The dogma of faith simply says, out of the church there is no salvation, and you have no right to go further and add the word *visible or exterior.*

We add the word *exterior* or *visible* to distinguish the church out of which there is no salvation from the invisible church contended for by Protestants, and which no Catholic does or can admit. Without it the dogma of faith contains no meaning, which even a Socinian or a transcendentalist has any urgent occasion to reject. Unquestionably, as our Lord in his humanity had two parts, his body and his soul, so we may regard the church, his spouse, as having two parts, the one exterior and

the known order of his grace, as is envinced by the case of the eunuch of Queen Candace, that of Cornelius, the captain of the Italian band, and hundreds of others recorded by our missionaries, especially the missionaries of the Society of Jesus. In all the instances of extraordinary or miraculous intervention of Almighty God, whether in the order of nature, or in the order of grace, known to us, he has intervened *ad ecclesiam,* and there is not a shadow of authority for supposing that he ever has miraculously intervened or ever will intervene otherwise. To assume that he will, under any circumstances, intervene to save men without the *medium ordinarium,* is perfectly gratuitous, to say the least. To bring men in an extraordinary manner to the church is easily admissable, because it does not dispense with the revealed economy of salvation, nor imply its inadequacy; but to intervene to save them without it appears to us to dispense with it, and to imply that it is not adequate to the salvation of all whom God's goodness leads him to save.

That those in societies alien to the church, invincibly ignorant of the church, if they correspond to the graces they receive, and persevere, will be saved, we do not doubt, but not where they are, or without being brought to the church. They are sheep, in the prescience of God Catholics, but sheep not yet gathered into the fold. "Other sheep I have," says our blessed Lord, "that are not of this fold; THEM ALSO I MUST BRING; THEY SHALL HEAR MY VOICE; and there shall be made one fold and one shepherd." This is conclusive; and that these must be brought, and enter the fold, which is the church, in this life, St. Augustine expressly teaches in the words cited in the beginning of this note. See also *Sincere Christian,* p. 366. Almighty God can be at no loss to save by the *medium ordinarium,* all who are willing to be saved, and that, too, without contradicting himself, departing from, or superseding the order of his grace; and, till better informed, we must believe it sounder theology to trust to his extraordinary grace to bring men to the church than it is to invincible ignorance to save them out of it; "*quia et ipsa ignorantia in eis qui intelligere noluerunt, sine dubitatione peccatum est; in eis autem qui non potuerunt, poena peccati. Ergo in utriusque non est justa excusatio, sed justa damnatio."* St. Aug. Epist. 194 ad Sixtum, n. 27. Those who think otherwise we hope will not go so far as to say with Rousseau, − "Quiconque ose dire, '*hors de l'Eglise point de salut,* ' doit etre chasse de l'etat!" *Du Contr. Soc., liv. iv. ch. 8.*

visible, the other interior and visible, or visible only by the exterior, as the soul of man is visible by his face; but to contend that the two parts are separable, or that the interior exists disconnected from the exterior, and is sufficient independently of it, is to assert, in so many words, the prevailing doctrine of Protestants, and, so far as relates to the indispensable conditions of salvation, to yield them, at least in their understanding, the whole question. In the present state of the controversy with Protestants, we cannot save the integrity of the faith, unless we add the epithet *visible* or *external*.

But it is not true that by so doing we add to the dogma of faith. The sense of the epithet is necessarily contained in the simple word *Church* itself, and the only necessity there is of adding it at all is in the fact that heretics have mutilated the meaning of the word *Church,* so that to them it no longer has its full and proper meaning. Whenever the word *Church* is used generally, without any specific qualification, expressed or necessarily implied, it means, by its own force, the visible as well as the invisible church, the body no less than the soul; for the body, the visible or external communion, is not a mere accident, but is essential to the church. The church by her very definition is "the congregation of men called by God through the evangelical doctrine, and professing the true Christian faith under the regimen of their legitimate pastors."*

This definition may, perhaps, not be complete, but it certainly takes in nothing not essential to the very idea of the church. The church, then, is always essentially visible as well as invisible, exterior as well as interior; and to exclude from our conception of it the conception of visibility would be as objectionable as to exclude the conception of body from the conception of MAN. Man is essentially body and soul; and whosoever speaks of him – as *living* man – must, by all the laws of language, logic, and morals, be understood to speak of him in that sense in which he includes both. So in speaking of the church, if the analogy is admissable at all. Consequently, when faith teaches that out of the church there is no salvation, and adds herself no qualification, we are bound to understand the church in her integrity, as body no less than as soul, visible no less than invisible, external no less than internal. Indeed, if either were to be included rather than the other, it would be the body; for the body, the congregation or society, is what the word

---

* *F.F. Walenburch, de Controv. Tract. IX, cap. 1, . Vide, Bellarmin. IV, Controv. Gen. Lib. 3, de Eccl. Milit. cap. 2.,*

primarily and properly designates; and it designates the soul only for the reason that the living body necessarily connotes the soul by which it is a living body, not a corpse. We have, then, the right, nay, are bound by the force of the word itself, to understand by the church, out of which there is no salvation, the visible or external as well as the invisible or internal communion. Hence the Brothers Walenburch begin their Treatise on Unity and Schism by assuming, – "1. Ecclesiam vocatorum esse visibilem; 2. Extra communionem *externam* cum vera Jesu Christi Ecclesia, non esse salutem; Extare hoc tempore visibilem Ecclesiam Jesu Christi, cui se fideles debeant conjugere."* ["1. The Church of those called is visible; 2. Outside external communion with the true Church of Jesus Christ, there is no salvation; There exists in this time a visible Church of Jesus Christ, to which the faithful must be joined."]

What Bellarmine, Billuart, Perrone, and others say of persons pertaining to the soul and yet not to the body of the church makes nothing against this conclusion. They indeed, teach that there is a class of persons that may be saved, who cannot be said to be *actu et proprie* [actually and properly] in the church. Bellarmine and Billuart instance catechumens and excommunicated persons, in case they have faith, hope, and charity; Perrone, so far as we have seen, instances catechumens only; and it is evident from the whole scope of their reasoning that all they say on this point must be restricted to catechumens, and such as are substantially in the same category with them; for they instance no others, and we are bound to construe every exception to the rule strictly, so as to make it as little of an exception as possible. If, then, our conclusion holds true, not withstanding the apparent exception in the case of catechumens and those substantially in the same category, nothing these authors say can prevent it from holding true universally.

Catechumens are persons who have not yet received the visible sacrament of baptism *in re,* and therefore are not *actu et proprie* in the church, since it is only by baptism that we are made members of Christ and incorporated into his body. With regard to these "there is a difficulty," says Bellarmine, "because they are of the faithful, and if they die in that state may be saved; and yet no one can be saved out of the ark, according to the decision of the fourth council of Lateran, C. 1: – *Una est fidelium universalis ecclesia, extra quam nullus omnino salvatur.* [There is but one universal Church of the faithful outside of which no

---

* F.F. Walenburch, *ubi supra,* cap. 2.

one at all is saved.] Still it is no less certain that catechumens are in the church, not actually and properly, but only potentially, as a man conceived, but not yet formed and born, is called a man only potentially. For we read, Acts ii, 41, – 'They therefore that received his word were baptized; and there were *added* to them that day about three thousand souls.' Thus the Council of Florence, in its Instructions for the Armenians, teaches that men are made members of Christ and the body of the church when they are baptized; and so all the fathers teach...Catechumens are not actually and properly in the church. How can you say they are saved, if they are out of the church?"

It is clear that this difficulty, which Bellarmine states, arises from understanding that to be in the church means to be in the visible church, and that when faith declares, out of the church no one can be saved, it means out of the visible communion. Otherwise it might be answered, since they are assumed to have faith, hope, and charity, they belong to the soul of the church, and that is all faith requires. But Bellarmine does not so answer, and since he does not, but proceeds to show that they do in a certain sense belong to the body, it is certain that he understands the article of faith as we do, and holds that men are not in the church unless they in some sense belong to its body.

But Bellarmine continues, – "The author of the book *De Ecclesiasticis Dogmatibus* replies that they are not saved. But this appears too severe. Certain it is that St. Ambrose, in his oration on the death of Valentinian, expressly affirms that catechumens can be saved, of which number was Valentinian when he departed this life. Another solution is therefore to be sought. Melchior Cano says that catechumens may be saved, because if not in the church properly called Christian, they are yet in the church which comprehends all the faithful from Abel to the consummation of the world. But this is not satisfactory; for, since the coming of Christ, there is no true church but that which is properly called Christian, and therefore if catechumens are not members of this, they are members of none. I reply, therefore, that the assertion, out of the church no one can be saved, is to be understood of those who are out of the church neither actually nor in desire, as theologians generally say when treating of baptism."*

"I have said," says Billuart, "that catechumens are not *actually and*

* *Ubi supra,* cap. 3.

properly in the church, because, when they request admission into the church, and when they already have faith and charity, they may be said to be in the church proximately and in desire, as one may be said to be in the house because he is in the vesitbule for the purpose of immediately entering. And in this sense must be taken what I have elsewhere said of their pertaining to the church, that is, that they pertain to her inchoately, as aspirants who voluntarily subject themselves to her laws; and they may be saved, not withstanding there is no salvation out of the church; for this is is to be understood of one who is in the church neither actually nor virtually, – *nec re, nec in voto*. In the same sense St. Augustine, *Tract. 4 in Joan.* n. 13, is to be understood, when he says, – *"Futuri erant aliqui in Ecclesia excelsioris gratiae catechumeni,"* [There were about to be some in the Church,catechumens of a more exalted grace] – that is, in will and proximate disposition, – *"in voto et proxima dispositione."* *

It is evident, both from Bellarimine and Billuart, that no one can be saved unless he belongs to the visible communion of the church, either actually or virtually, and also that the salvation of catechumens can be asserted only because they do so belong; that is, because they are in the vestibule, for the purpose of entering, – have already entered in their will and proximate dispostion. St. Thomas teaches with regard to these, in case they have faith working by love, that all they lack is the reception of the visible sacrament *in re;* but if they are prevented by death from receiving it *in re* before the church is ready to administer it, that God supplies the defect, accepts the will for the deed, and reputes them to be baptized. If the defect is supplied, and God reputes them to be baptized, they are so in effect, have in effect received the visible sacrament, are truly members of the external communion of the church, and therefore are saved in it, not out of it.†

Bellarmine, Billuart, Perrone, etc., in speaking of persons as belonging to the soul and not to the body, mean, it is evident, not persons who in no sense belong to the body, but simply those who, though they in effect belong to it, do not belong to it in the full and strict sense of the word, because they have not received the visible sacrament *in re*. All they teach is simply that persons may be saved who have not received the visible sacrament *in re;* but they by no means teach that persons can be saved without having received the visible sacrament at all. There is no

* *Theologia, de Reg. Fid. Dissert,* . 3, Art. 2, Sect. 3.
† *Summa,* 3, Q. 68, a.2. Corp. ad 2. et ad 3.

difference between their view and ours, for we have never contended for any thing more than this; only we think, that, in these times especially, when the tendency is to depreciate the external, it is more proper to speak of them simply as belonging to the soul, for the fact the most important to be insisted on is, not that it is impossible to be saved without receiving the visible sacrament *in re,* but that it is impossible to be saved without receiving the visible sacrament at least *in voto et proxima dispositiones.*

The case of catachumens disposes of all who are substantially in the same category. The only persons, not catechumens, who can be in the same category, are persons who have been validly baptized, and who stand in the same relation to the sacrament of reconciliation that catachumens do to the sacrament of faith. Infants, validly baptized, by whomsoever baptized, are made members of the body of our Lord, and, if dying before coming to the age of reason, go immediately to heaven. But persons having come to the age of reason, baptized in an heretical society, or persons baptized in such society in infancy, and adhering to it after having come to years of understanding, – for there can be no difference between the two classes, – whether through ignorance or not, are, as we have seen out of unity, and therefore out of charity, without which they are nothing. Their faith, if they have any, does not avail them; their sacraments are sacrilegious. The wound of sacrilege is mortal, and the only possible way of being healed is through the sacrament of reconciliation or penance. But for these to stand in the same relation to this sacrament that catachumens do to the sacrament of faith, they must cease to adhere to their heretical societies, must come out from among them, seek and find the church, recognize her as the church, believe what she teaches, voluntarily subject themselves to her laws, knock at the door, will to enter, stand waiting to enter as soon as she opens and says, come in. If they do all this, they are substantially in the same category with catechumens; and if prevented by death from receiving the visible sacrament *in re,* they may be saved, yet not as simply joined to the soul of the church, but as in effect joined or restored to her external communion. By their voluntary renunciation of their heretical or schismatic society, by their explicit recognition of the church, by their actual return to her door, by their dispostion and will to enter, they are effectually, if not in form, members of the body as well as of the soul. Persons excommunicated stand on the same footing as these. they are excluded from the church, unless they repent. If they repent and receive the visible sacrament of reconciliation *vel re, vel voto,* they may be saved, because the church in excommunicating them has willed their amendment, not their exclusion from the people of God; but we have no authority to affirm their salvation on any other conditions.

The apparent exception alleged turns out, therefore, to be no real exception at all; for the persons excepted are still members of the body of the church in effect, as the authorities referred to labor to prove. They are persons who have renounced their infidel and heretical societies, and have found and explicitly recognized the church. Their approach to the church is explicit, not constructive, to be inferred only from a certain vague and indefinite longing for the truth and unity in general, predicable in fact, we should suppose, of nearly all men; for no man ever clings to falsehood and division, believing them to be such. Their desire for truth and unity is explicit. Their faith is the Catholic faith; the unity they will is Catholic unity; the church at whose door they knock is the Catholic Church; the sacraments they solicit, they solicit from the hands of her legitimate priest. They are in effect Catholics, and though not *re et proprie* in the church, nobody ever dreams of so understanding the article, out of the church no one can be saved, as to exclude them from salvation. These being in effect members of the external communion, the distinction between the soul and the body of the church does not at all affect the assumption of the Brothers Walenburch, "out of external communion with the true church of Jesus Christ there is no salvation." [3]

[3] Although Brownson followed St. Robert Bellarmine on the possibility of catechumens being saved by an explicit desire for the sacrament of Baptism, provided they had supernatural faith and perfect charity, should they be overtaken by death before the actual reception of the sacrament, this is by no means the unanimous teaching of the Fathers and Doctors. Abbot Jerome Theisen, OSB. says that none of the Cappadocian Fathers nor St. John Chrysostom thought that salvation was possible in such circumstances.[1] Brownson mentions that his friend Archbishop Kenrick was "even more rigid and exclusive"[2] than he had ever been, probably a reference to the Archbishop's opinion on this particular point. The Archbishop writes:

> "If persons apparently sincere and well disposed, distinguished by pious sentiments and works of charity, live and die out of the Church, it is not for us to pronounce judgment; but we should refer it to the secret counsels of God, who has mercy on whom he will, and leaves whom he will in the obduracy of his heart. Pride oftentimes taints those actions which men highly prize, and many other secret obstacles may exist to the free dispensations of divine grace. Our solicitude to vindicate the Divine justice is altogether misplaced, since his judgments are righteousness, needing no support from man.

The church is always and everywhere, at once and indissolubly, as the living church, interior and exterior, consisting, like man himself, of soul and body. She is not a disembodied spirit, nor a corpse. The separation of the soul and body of the church is as much her death, as the separation of the soul and body of man is his. She is the church, the living church, only by the mutual commerce of soul and body. There may be grave sinners in her body who have no communion with her soul; these are indeed members, but not living members, – and are *in* the body rather than *of* it, as vicious humors may be in the blood without being of it, for they must have communion with the soul in order to be living members; and some theologians maintain that they who are in the body of the church without pertaining to the soul, at least by faith, though a dead faith, are not, strictly speaking, members at all. On the other hand, if as all our theologians teach, and Moehler and Perrone especially, the life of the church is in the mutual commerce of the exterior and the interior, the body and the soul, no individual not joined to her body can live her life. Indeed, to suppose that communion with the body alone will suffice, is to fall into mere formalism, to mistake the corpse for the living man; and, on the other hand, to suppose that communion with the soul and independent of it is practicable is to fall into pure spiritualism, simple Quakerism, which tapers off into transcendentalism or mere sentimentalism, a doctrine which Father Perrone expressly controverts. Either extreme is the death of the church, which is, as we have

> When it happened in the days of Augustine that a candidate for baptism, whose conduct was edifying, was snatched out of life before receiving the sacrament, this great doctor did not venture to give any assurance of his eternal happiness, although there was certainly ground for hope; much less did he undertake to plead the cause of God, who deprived him of the opportunity of regeneration; and when, on the contrary, a play-actor, or a licentious man fell sick, sought baptism, and slept in Christ, he regarded his salvation as certain. In either case, he adored the Divine counsels; and exclained devoutly, "O the depth of the riches of the wisdom of God! How incomprehensible are his judgments and unsearchable his ways!"[3]

[1] Cf. Theisen, Abbot Jerome, OSB., *The Ultimate Church and the Promise of Salvation,* St. John's University Press, Collegeville, Minnesota, 1976, p.12, n.35.
[2] "Answers to Objections," *Brownson's Quarterly Review* (October, 1874), p.394.
[3] "Life of Mrs. Eliz. A. Seton," *Brownson's Quarterly Review,* (April, 1853), pp.179,180.

said, to be regarded as always, at once and indissolubly, soul and body.* To assume that real or virtual communion with the body is not necessary, or that we may be joined to the spirit without being joined to the body is to make the body only occasionally or accidentally necessary to salvation; and, in fact, some modern speculations imply, perhaps expressly teach, that it is necessary, as if its necessity depended on the state of the human intellect, and not on the appointment of God, as if a man's disbelief could excuse or make up for his want of faith, – a doctrine taught by no father or medieval doctor, and from which we should suppose every Catholic would instinctively turn with loathing and disgust. The church is the living Temple of God, into which believers must be builded as so many living stones. It is his body, and its body is no more to be dispensed with than its soul; otherwise we could not call her always visible, for to some she would be visible, to others only invisible, and then there would be no visible *Catholic* church.

There is no name given under heaven among men but the name of Jesus Christ by which we can be saved. There is salvation in none other; and what Catholic needs to be told that Christ, as the Saviour, is in the church, which is his body, and that it is in the church, and nowhere else, that he does or will save? True, though in the church, he is also out of her, by his grace operating on the hearts of those not yet within; but he operates *ad ecclesiam,* [to the Church], to bring them within, that he may save them there, not that he may save them without. He loves his church; she is his chosen, his beloved, his spouse, and he gives his life for her. In her, so to speak, center all his affections, his graces, and his providences; and all creatures and events are ordered in reference to her. Without her all history is inexplicable, a fable, and the universe itself meaningless and without a purpose. The salvation of souls itself is in order to her, and God will have no children who are not also hers. As there is but one Father, so can there be but one Mother, and none are of the Father who are not of the Mother. Clear and explicit are all the fathers and saints as to this, and they plainly teach that it would dishonor her, and make God an adulterer, to suppose the salvation of a single soul of which she is not the spiritual mother.

God, in establishing the church from the foundation of the world, in giving his life on the cross for her, in abiding always with her, in her tabernacles, unto the consummation of the world, in adorning her as a bride with all the graces of the Holy Spirit, in denominating her his

* *Vide*, Perrone, de *Loc. Theol. p.1, cap. 2, art. 3, et cap. 4, art 1, ad 1.,*

beloved, his spouse, has taught us how he regards her, how deep and tender, how infinite and inexhaustible, his love for her, and with what love and honor we should behold her. He loves us with an infinite love, and has died to redeem us; but he loves us and wills our salvation, only in and through his church. He would bring us to himself, and he never ceases as a lover to woo our love; but he wills us to love, and reverence, and adore him only as children of his beloved. Our love and reverence must redound to his glory as her Spouse, and gladden her maternal heart, and swell her maternal joy, or he wills them not, knows them not. O, it is frightful to forget the place the church holds in the love and providence of God, and to regard the relation in which we stand to her as a matter of no moment! She is the one grand object on which are fixed all heaven, all earth, ay, and all hell. Behold her impersonation in the Blessed Virgin, the Holy Mother of God, the glorious Queen of heaven. Humble and obscure she lived, poor and silent, yet all heaven turned their eyes towards her; all hell trembled before her; all earth needed her. Dear was she to all the hosts of heaven; for in her they beheld the Queen, the Mother of grace, the Mother of mercies, the channel through which all love, and mercies, and good things were to flow to man, and return to the glory and honor of their Father. Humblest of mortal maidens, lowliest on earth, under God, she was highest in heaven. So is the church, our sweet mother. O, she is no creation of the imagination! O, she is no mere accident in human history, in divine providence, divine grace, in the conversion of souls! She is a glorious, a living reality, living the divine, the eternal life of God. Her Maker is her Husband, and he places her, after him, over all in heaven, on the earth, and under the earth. All that he can give he gives; for he gives himself, and unites her in indissoluble union with himself. Infinite love, infinite wisdom, infinite power, can do no more. All hail to thee, dear and ever-blessed Mother, thou chosen one, thou well-beloved, thou Bride adorned, thou chaste, immaculate Spouse, thou universal Queen! All hail to thee! We honor thee, for God honors thee; we love thee, for God loves thee; we obey thee, for thou ever commandest the will of thy Lord. The passersby may jeer thee; the servants of the prince of this world may call thee black; the daughters of the uncircumcised may beat thee, earth and hell rise up in wrath against thee, and seek to despoil thee of thy rich ornaments and to sully thy fair name; but all the more dear art thou to our hearts; all the more deep and sincere the homage we pay thee; and all the more earnestly do we pray thee to receive our humble offerings, and to own us for thy children, and watch over us that we never forfeit the right to call thee our Mother.

Did we reflect on what the church is, did we consider her rank in the universe, her relation to God, the place she holds so to speak, in his affections, the bare thought of the salvation of a single soul not spiritually begotten of her should make us thrill with horror. It would give the lie to all God's providences, and subvert the whole economy of his grace. We need not start at this. All may have the church for their mother, if they choose. Christ is in the church, but he is also out of the church. In the church he is operating by his grace to save those who enter; out of her he operates also by his grace, or is ready to operate, in the hearts of all men, to supply the will and ability to come in. Do not imagine that God has only half done his work, that he has merely prepared his church, fitted her up as a palace, filled her with good things, all things necessary for our salvation, when once we have entered, but that he has left us without the ability to find her out, or, having found her out, without ability to enter. He leaves nothing undone. No man has the natural ability to come into the church, any more than he has the natural ability to save himself after he has come in. All before and all after is the work of God. We can do nothing of ourselves alone, – make not even the first motion without his grace inciting and assisting us. Of no use would have been his church, – it would have been a mere mockery, or a splendid failure – if he had not provided for our entrance as well as for our salvation afterwards.

But he *has* provided for our entrance. He gives sufficient grace to all men. The grace of prayer, *gratia orationis,* is given freely, gratuitously, unto every one. All receive the ability to ask; all, then, can ask, and if they do ask, as sure as God cannot lie they shall receive the grace to seek; and if they seek, the same divine veracity is pledged that they shall find; and if they find, they may knock; and if they knock, it shall be opened to them. God has said it. Christ is in the church; and he is out of it. In it and out of it he is one and the same, and operates ever *ad unitatem.* He is out of the church to draw all men into the church; all have, then, if they will, the assistance of the infinite God to come in, and if they do not come in, it is their own fault. God withholds nothing necessary. He gives to all, by his grace, every thing requisite, and in superabundance. If we come not at his call, on our own heads lies the blame. We have no excuse, not even the least shadow of an excuse. The reason why we come not can be only that we do not choose to come, that we resist his grace, and scorn his invitations, and will not yield to his inspirations. No nice theological distinctions, no scholastic subtlety, no latitudinarian ingenuity, can relieve us of the blame, or make it not true that we could have come, had we been so disposed. If, then, we stay away, and are lost, it is we who have destroyed ourselves.

Here are the great mass of our countrymen aliens from the church of God. Why do they not come and ask to be received as children and heirs? Is it lack of opportunity? It is false. There is no lack of opportunity. God does not deny them, not one of them, the needed grace. The church is here; through her noble and faithful pastors, her voice sounds out from Maine to Florida, from the Atlantic to the Pacific. How can they hear without a preacher? But they have heard. Verily the voice of the preacher is gone out into all the earth. They have no need to say, Who shall ascend into heaven to bring Christ down? or, Who shall descend into hell to bring Christ up from the dead? The word is nigh them. It sounds in every ear; it speaks in every heart. We all know they might come, if they would. From all sections, and from all ranks and conditions, some have come, and by coming proved that it is possible for all to come; and in so proving rendered invalid the plea of ignorance or inability. Those who have not come can as well come as those who have come; and their guilt in not coming is aggravated by their knowledge of the fact that some of their own number have come; for they are no longer in ignorance.* The fault is their own. They stay away because they do not will to come. "Ye will not come to me that ye may have life, because your deeds are evil." They disregard divine grace, they disdain the church, they contemn her pastors, they scorn her sacraments. For what Catholic can doubt, if they were to seek the truth, *cauta solicitudine,* as St. Augustine says they must, even to excuse them from formal heresy or infidelity, that they would find, and, finding and knocking, that they would be admitted?

No; let us love our countrymen too much to be ingenious in inventing excuses for them, to strain the faith in their behalf till it is nearly ready to snap. Let us from a deep and tender charity, which, when need is, has the nerve to be terribly severe, thunder, or, if we are no Boanerges, breathe in soft but thrilling accents, in their ears, in their souls, in their consciences, those awful truths which they will know too late at the day of judgment. We must labor to convict them of sin, to show them their folly and madness, to convince them that they are dead in trespasses and sins, and condemned already, and that they can be restored to life, and freed from condemnation, only by the grace of our Lord Jesus

---

* S. Aug. Liv. 1, *De Bapt. contr. Donat,* . cap.5 – St. John Chrysos. *In Epist. ad Rom,* . xxvi.

Christ, whom we, and we only, preach, which is dispensed through the church, and the church only.

It has been said that our countrymen are not to be driven into the church, and that a soft answer turneth away wrath. All very true, – who doubts it? Use as soft words and speak in as honeyed tones as you please, but do not forget to set forth sound doctrine, or use hard arguments. Tell the truth in your own way, and by all means in a manner as little offensive as possible; but TELL IT. Nobody has any wish or intention to drive people into the church. There are some things so obvious, that men of ordinary sense may be presumed not to overlook them. The only driving we wish is the driving by the force of truth distinctly enunciated, by solid arguments clearly stated, and solemn appeals well put. So far as this may be called driving, which is only presenting motives to reason and free-will, we are for driving, and will do all we can to drive, till every one is driven within the fold. The lord of the nuptial feast did not command his servants to go out into the highways and hedges and *coax* people to come in, but to *compel* them to come in, that his house might be full. No man can honestly mistake the drift of our remarks, or imagine that they proceed from harshness of temper, or want of respect for the rights or the characters of those without, as well as of those within. What we urge and insist upon is, that we feel, and freely, earnestly, solemnly, without fear or palliation, set forth to our unbelieving and heretical countrymen, the danger, the sinfulness, of their present condition; that, in so far as we wish or seek their conversion, we must follow the example of the apostles and fathers, and reason of sin, justice, and judgment to come; that we must present the question of the church, not as an intellectual or aesthetical question, but as a question of life and death, of heaven and hell. Infidelity and heresy have not improved by age, and they are as hateful to God, as odious to the saints, as destructive to the souls of men, here and now, as they were in the days of St. Athanasius, St. Hilary, St. Jerome, or St. Augustine, and are to be met and conquered only in the spirit and by the weapons with which these holy fathers and great saints met and conquered them.

If any Catholics imagine, that, in some things we have said, their favorite policy has been arraigned, they will take care not to misinterpret us. We have spoken strongly, earnestly, as we have the right to speak, as it was our duty to speak; but we hope we have not spoken arrogantly, harshly, uncharitably, or without authority. We have impeached no one's motives, faith, zeal, or piety. We trust we are not so utterly destitute of Christian humility as to imagine that we have any special monopoly of true Catholic faith and zeal, or as not to feel that they who prefer a policy we may disapprove may be at least as true believers, as deeply in earnest, as solicitous for the salvation of souls, as ourselves. God forbid that we should think of drawing a parallel, or presume in the remotest degree conceivable to breathe a censure against them! We are not insensible to the pious worth, nor destitute of admiration of the labors, of those who have worn out their lives in laboring to plant the church in this moral wilderness. We are not untouched by the recital of their labors, their privations, their sufferings, their sacrifices, and we would we could aspire to their virtues. We offer our prayer at the tombs of those who have been called to their reward; we love and reverence those still living. Who are we, to judge them? We speak not of the policy they may have adopted in its relation to their times, and the frightful circumstances under which they unfurled here the banner of the cross. We speak only in relation to the country as it now is. Times have changed. Protestantism is not, as to its forms, what it was even twenty years ago. We have bitter enemies as ever, but not in the same shape. The bigot gives place to the latitudinarian. We have not now to prove that the church may be as good as the sects, or even better than the sects; for these two points are now virtually conceded to us. We have now to prove that she alone is Christianity, and that without Christianity, without Christ, there is no true life here or hereafter. It is this great fact, so solemn and so terrible, that we have wished to place prominently before our readers, – not to censure the past, but to guide our future efforts, and for the purpose of rendering such service as may be in our power to the great and glorious cause equally dear to all Catholics.[4]

[4] Almost thirty years later in 1874 Brownson was still trying to make this same point in his colorful Yankee style:

> "There can be no more fatal mistake than to soften, liberalize, or latitudinize this terrible dogma, "Out of the Church there is no salvation"... If we wish to convert Protestants and infidels we must preach in all its rigor the naked dogma. Give them the smallest peg, or what appears so, not to you, but to them; – the smallest peg, on which to hang a hope of salvation without being in or actually reconciled to the Church by the sacrament of penance, and all the arguments you can address to them to prove the necessity of being in the Church in order to be saved will have no more effect on them than rain on a duck's back."

"Answer to Objections," *Brownson's Quarterly Review,* (July 1874), pp.413,414: *Works,* Vol XX, pp.413,414.

CIVIL AND RELIGIOUS TOLERATION

(Brownson's Quarterly Review, July, 1849)

INTRODUCTION

The Know-Nothings claimed that Catholics could not be good Americans, the reverse of the famous line in the "letter to Jackie" of Commander Shea during World War II: "Be a good Catholic and you can't help being a good American." Brownson wrote many articles to answer this charge but the best of them, I think, is "Civil and Religious Toleration" written in 1849 again under the direction of Bishop Fitzpatrick. It is due in no small measure to Brownson's vigorous defence of Catholic principles that the Know-Nothing party was finally defeated. Father Ryan writes:

> *...It really seems a part of Divine Providence that to the strong Brownson was to fall the special mission of putting down hostility to the Church in America through a vigorous, crystal-clear demonstration of the reasonableness of the Catholic faith and an acceptance of Catholic teaching – that is, to all who were willing to listen to reason. His highest gifts were adapted to that end rather than to the direct winning of converts – though they operated effectively in both directions. The arguments advanced by this "Hercules of American controversy" remain unanswered to this day. Those arguments, when rightly put, are in very truth unanswerable, but if any man was needed to put them in their most forcible form, that man was Orestes A. Brownson...Msgr. Matthew Smith, founder and editor of the* Denver Register, *has said that "it is to Brownson that we owe the peace of the Church in America." [1]*

But Brownson's ideas as set forth in "Civil and Religious Toleration" are not only of historic interest, but, according to Father Ryan, were admirably prophetic of the "Declaration on Religious Freedom" (Dignitatis Humanae) of Vatican II:

> *Francis E. McMahon, author of* A Catholic Looks at the World (*at this writing [1976], lecturer in philosophy at Roosevelt University, Chicago, Illinois*),

---

[1] Ryan, *Op. cit.*, p.318.

recently drew attention to the pioneer work Brownson did already in his day preparatory to the formulation of the doctrine on religious freedom by Vatican Council II. A statement of Mr. McMahon, to the New York Times *on the matter was published on November 22, 1965:*

To the Editor:

In his dispatch from Rome (October 26) John Cogley accurately describes the Vatican Council's draft on religious liberty under consideration as the "American Schema," and rightly gives credit to Rev. John Courtney Murray, SJ., for zealously defending the thesis.

For the record it should be noted that the first prominent American thinker to advance the proposal that the individual conscience in religious matters was inviolable by the temporal power was Orestes A. Brownson (1803-1876).

My article, "Orestes A. Brownson on Church and State," which appeared in the June issue of Theological Studies, *1954 demonstrated the remarkable parallel existing between the views of Father Murray and those of Dr. Brownson...*

The forthcoming Vatican Council decree on religious liberty should be known as the Brownson-Murray formulation. Both men deserve enormous credit.

Francis E. McMahon[2]

[2] *Idem*, p.639.

Toleration, or to be more exact, religious liberty, is in every one's mouth, and the constant theme of declamation with all who would depreciate their ancestors, glorify themselves, or win the applause of the multitude; but unless we are greatly deceived, it is a theme on which there is much loose writing, and still more loose speaking and thinking. Comparatively few appear to us to understand it, or to have any passable appreciation of its reach and conditions. All men, in words at least, are staunch friends of religious liberty, ready to live and die in its defence; but the great majority seem to us to mistake it for the liberty to deny and to enslave religion. The early Protestant sects, who, wherever they were able, subjected to the secular authority, fined, imprisoned, exiled, or martyred Catholics, claimed to be the friends of religious freedom, and the liberators of religion from spiritual despotism; the old French Jacobins plundered churches, suppressed the freedom of worship, abolished the Sabbath, overturned altars as well as thrones, massacred the clergy, decreed that death is an eternal sleep, and installed the goddess of reason, under the pretence of religious liberty, and amid deafening proclamations of universal toleration; the present socialists, radicals, or red-republicans of France, Spain, Italy, Germany, Switzerland, profess to be fighting under the flag of religious no less than civil liberty, and yet their successes are everywhere marked by insults to religion, the expulsion of the religious, the spoliation of churches and convents, and the persecution of the clergy. The most superficial observer can hardly fail to perceive that the age understands, by religious liberty, not the freedom to worship God in the way and manner he prescribes, but the freedom not to worship him at all, – the freedom to enslave or suppress his worship, to plunder his temples, to desecrate his altars, to deny his existence, to blaspheme his majesty, to trample on his laws, and to live like beasts that perish.

But although we are anxious to avoid unnecessary quarrel with our age, we must tell it, that this is no religious liberty at all, that is the enslavement of religion, where not its total extinction, and the freedom of irreligion, infidelity, heresy and schism. Religious liberty, as we understand it, is *the absolute freedom of religion, in its doctrines, discipline, and worship, from all human authority,* and therefore implies the *absolute incompetency, in spirituals, of all human authority, whether public or private.* We say the absolute freedom of *religion;* by which we, of course, mean the true, that is, the Catholic religion. Consequently, we recognize no religious liberty where our church is not free in her doctrine, discipline, and worship, and where all men have not full and entire freedom to profess the Catholic religion without restraint from, or responsibility to, any human power whatever, whether vested in the king, the aristocracy, or the people. Where this freedom is wanting, there is no religious liberty. This freedom we demand, not as a favor, not as a gracious concession from the prince or the republic, but as our right, as the indefeasible right of our church, for the reason that she is the church of God, the representative of the divine sovereignty on the earth; and this freedom we are bound in conscience to assert, and to vindicate, if need be, as did the early Christian martyrs under the persecuting emperors of pagan Rome, not indeed by slaying, but by submitting to be slain.[1]

---

[1] The "Declaration on Religious Freedom" *(Dignitatis Humanae)* of Vatican II also begins as does Brownson with a statement concerning the absolute freedom of the Church.

> First, this sacred Synod professes its belief that God himself has made known to mankind the way in which men are to serve Him, and thus be saved in Christ and come to Blessedness. We believe that this one true religion subsists in the catholic and apostolic Church, to which the Lord Jesus committed the duty of spreading it abroad among all men. Thus He spoke to the apostles: "Go, therefore, and make disciples of all nations, baptizing them in the name of the Father, and of the Son, and of the Holy Spirit, teaching them to observe all that I have commanded you" (Mt. 28:19-20). On their part, all men are bound to seek the truth, especially in what concerns God and His Church, and to embrace the truth they come to know, and to hold fast to it.
>
> This sacred Synod likewise professes its belief that it is upon human conscience that these obligations fall and exert their binding force. The truth cannot impose itself except by virtue of its own truth, as it makes its entrance into the mind at once quietly and with power. Religious freedom, in turn, which men demand as necessary to fulfill their duty to worship God, has to do with immunity from coercion in civil society. Therefore, it leaves untouched traditional Catholic doctrine on the moral duty of men and societies toward the true religion and toward the one Church of Christ.

Fr. Walter Abbot, S.J., the General Editor of *The Documents of Vatican II*, makes this comment on this passage in a footnote:

> ...No man may say of the religious truth which subsists in the

From this view of religious liberty, it is evident, that, when we speak of *toleration,* we have and can have no reference to our church; for she holds immediately from God, and we recognize no power on earth that has the right to restrain her worship, and therefore none that has the right to *tolerate* it. The question of toleration lies below the question of religious liberty, and relates solely to false religions, – to infidel, heretical, and schismatical sects. Are these to be tolerated, or are they to be prohibited? Shall we assert, the natural right of every man to choose his own religion, or shall we assert, and as far as able enforce, the moral obligation of all men to profess the true religion? Shall we be intolerant and exclusive, or assert and maintain universal toleration? This is the question.

To answer this question, we must distinguish between two sorts of toleration, – political or civil toleration, and religious or theological toleration; that is, toleration of false religions in the temporal order, and toleration of the same in the spiritual order. These two tolerations are often confounded, and supposed to be inseperably connected. Hence many assert religious or theological toleration as the condition of justifying the assertion of political or civil toleration, and many also deny political toleration, in order, as they suppose, not to be obliged to assert religious toleration. But the two are in reality distinct, and one has no necessary connection with, or dependence on, the other. Political

Church: "It is no concern of mine." Once given by Christ to his true Church, the true religion remains the one way in which all men are bound to serve God and save themselves. Consequently, religious freedom is not a title to exemption from the obligation to "observe all things whatsoever I have enjoined upon you." In fine, a harmony exists between man's duty of free obedience to the truth and his right to the free exercise of religion in society. The duty does not diminish the right, nor does the right diminish the duty.

This frank profession of Catholic faith at the outset of the Declaration on Religious Freedom, is in no sense at variance with the ecumenical spirit, any more than it is at variance with the loyalty to the principle of religious freedom. Neither the spirit of ecumenism nor the principle of religious freedom requires that the Church refrain from stating publicly what she believes herself to be. The demands of truth are no more opposed to the demands of freedom than they are to the demands of love.

The Documents of Vatican II, edited by Fr. Walter M. Abbot, SJ. and Msgr. Joseph Gallagher, America Press, New York, 1966, pp.676,677; n.3 pp.676,677.

toleration of religion is the permission conceded by princes or republics to their subjects to profess the religion they choose; religious toleration is the permission granted by Almighty God to all men to profess any religion they please, or none at all, and implies the equal right, or the indifference, of all religions before God, or in reference to eternal life. Universal political toleration presupposes that all religions are compatible with the peace and safety of civil society; universal religious toleration presupposes that all religions are acceptable to God, and available for salvation. The state regards religion solely under its relation to social interests, and the theologian regards it primarily in its relation to the future life or the salvation of the soul. It is easy, therefore, if we understand the distinction of the two orders, to see that it is possible to be politically tolerant and yet religiously intolerant, if not politically intolerant and religiously tolerant.

The question of the political toleration of religion we shall consider at some length before we close; but, for the moment we must confine ourselves to religious or theological toleration. Religious or theological toleration is what is commonly called *indifferentism,* – that is, the doctrine that men may be saved in all religions, in one as well as in another, or that every one may be saved in his own religion, the religion of his country, or of his sect. To concede this doctrine is religious or theological toleration, as distinguished from political or civil toleration; to deny it is religious or theological intolerance and exclusiveness, expressed in the Catholic dogma, "Out of the church there is no salvation." Whatever conclusion we may or may not come to on the subject of political toleration, or the indifference of religions before society and the civil authority, we must, unless bereft of reason, be religiously or theologically intolerant and exclusive; for toleration in the spiritual order is, at bottom, neither more nor less than the denial of the religious principle itself.

Certain it is, from natural reason, that no man can be saved unless he renders to God an acceptable worship, and that no worship is or can be acceptable to God, except the religion which he himself prescribes. Moreover, it is equally certain, that no man can be saved who does not, at least, fulfill the law of nature. By the very law of nature, all men are bound to worship God, and to worship him in the way and manner he himself prescribes. If he leaves them to the natural law, and prescribes his worship only through natural reason, undoubtedly such worship as they can render by a prudent, diligent, honest use of reason, and the means bestowed for such a purpose, will be the acceptable worship, and all that can in justice be demanded of them; but if he prescribes a supernatural religion, and promulgates it with sufficient motives of credibility, as he must needs do if he promulgates it at all, then they are bound to worship him according to that supernatural religion, – bound by the very law of nature itself to receive and practise it; and they want even natural morality if they do not. Such a religion, with sufficient motives of credibility, he has prescribed in Christianity. How, then, can we assert the indifference of religions, and contend for religious toleration? Since God prescribes the Christian religion, the law of nature, as well as of revelation, binds us to believe and obey it. If we do not, we fail to fulfill the law of nature, as well as to render the acceptable worship, and are convicted of sin under both the natural law and the revealed. How, then, can we hope to be saved?

Christianity and Catholicity, at least in the faith of Catholics, are identical, – one and the same thing. We do and can recognize no Christianity, properly so called, out of the Catholic Church. We recognize indeed, in those who are out of her communion, many human excellences, many noble and generous sentiments, many amiable and philanthropic qualities, many just and profound thoughts, many estimable private, domestic, and civil virtues, which we delight to honor, and which we have their reward in their own order, as St. Augustine teaches us in regard to the ancient Romans; but we recognize in them no supernatural faith or sanctity, nothing distinctively Christian, nothing meritorious of eternal life. Out of the church there is no Christian religion, and therefore, if no salvation out of the Christian religion, none out of the church, as the church herself expressly teaches, and has solemnly defined in her general councils. "He cannot," says St. Cyprian, "have God for his father who will not have the church for his mother." To concede religious toleration, or the indifference of religions is neither more nor less than to deny the Christian religion itself, and to give up our faith as Catholics. If you require us to do this, you deny our right to be Christians, and are yourselves, even in defending toleration, intolerant; if you concede our right to be Christians, you concede the right of religious intolerance, and then have no right to assert or to demand religious tolerance.

Every man is obliged by the constitution of the human mind itself, and the very nature of things, to assert the principle of religious intolerance and exclusiveness. We know by natural reason, without revelation, that there is and can be but one true religion; for truth is one, individual, and most simple. This one true religion is necessarily the one which God himself institutes or prescribes; all other religions are false religions, and to suppose that one can be saved in a false religion is absurd and impious; for it is to place truth and falsehood on the same footing, and to suppose that God, who is truth itself, makes no difference between them, that is, counts falsehood as if it were truth! A man cannot believe this, unless he gives up reason; nor even then, for without reason he can believe nothing at all. Indeed, all truth, all good, all opinions even, are and must be intolerant and exclusive. Truth cannot tolerate error, or even the semblance of error; good excludes evil; right excludes wrong; holiness excludes unholiness. Nothing in the universe tolerates its opposite. In regard to all things we are obliged to assert a right and a wrong, a true and a false, and whoever asserts the one necessarily denies the other. Even he who asserts the indifference of all religions denies their difference, and is, in a manner, himself intolerant and exclusive. Hence we see, in our own days, sects formed against sectarianism; and Dr. Bushnell, just now one of our New-England "lions", is busy, consciously or unconsciously, rallying a party around his pretended Christian dogma, that there are no Christian dogmas, and should be none. Every man, who believes in any religion at all, believes his own religion is the true religion, the only true religion, and therefore that all other religions are false religions. He must, then, either believe that salvation is attainable in no other religion, or else that it is attainable in a false religion; which, as we have seen, is absurd. If he believes his religion is the true religion, he believes it is the religion that all men are bound to believe, – for truth, like right, is obligatory, – and therefore believes that all men are prohibited from believing any other. Every man must, then, do or say what he will, be religiously intolerant and exclusive.

As Catholics, it is well known that we are obliged, by our very religion, as well as by natural reason itself, to deny religious indifference, and to maintain the impossibility, *in hac providentia* [in this dispensation], of salvation out of our church. This may offend fashionable latitudinarianism, but it is nothing that we should hesitate, or in the least degree be afraid, to avow; for no severer sentence can be pronounced upon any pretended faith or church, than that it fears to assert its own indispensableness to salvation. What is it, in fact, we want a faith or church for, but to save us? and what reason have we, or can we have, for embracing any particular faith or church, but that we cannot be saved without it? A faith or church that concedes the possibility of salvation in another or outside of itself, confesses that it is not the one true faith or church of God, – therefore, virtually, that it is a false faith or church, unacceptable to God, pernicious to the souls of men, and to be eschewed by all, as they fear hell or hope for heaven. Hence all Protestant sects, of past and present times, are condemned out of their own mouths; for not one of them has, or ever has had, the courage or the audacity to assert that there is no salvation out of its communion, – that is if we understand the matter, the courage or the audacity, without contradicting itself and conceding the contrary, to assert its own truth. This, perhaps, is a fact not insignificant. Falsehood is, by its own nature, compelled to lie unto itself as well as unto others.

The age, we grant, demands religious toleration, and religious indifference is the order of the day. Many are shocked, or affect to be shocked, when they hear us say that there is no salvation out of the Catholic Church; they allege that it is harsh, illiberal, uncharitable to say so; and even some of our own Catholic friends, now and then, try to persuade themselves and their dissenting brethren that this is going a little beyond the mark, and savors somewhat of bigotry and indiscreet zeal. But he has little claim either to moral or to logical consistency, who refuses to say the true religion is the true religion; and certainly, there cannot be much bigotry or indiscreet zeal, if we use the terms in their ordinary sense, in asserting the Catholic religion is the true religion. But he who so asserts necessarily asserts that all other religions are false, and therefore, either that it is possible to be saved in a false religion or that there is no salvation out of the Catholic Church. More liberal or tolerant than this we cannot be, in the very nature of things, if we would, unless we could be foolish enough to contradict ourselves, and maintain, that, of contraries both may be true.

However this may be, as Catholics we have nothing to do with liberality or illiberality in the matter. We have not instituted the laws of mind, and they remain unchanged, whether we conform to them or not. We do not make, and cannot unmake, the truth; and it is eternally and immutably the same, whether we assert it or deny it. It is not *our* truth; it in no sense whatever depends on our intellects, or wills, or our affections; and whether it pleases or displeases us or our friends, appears to us or to them liberal or illiberal, we have just as little power as right to alter it. Should we seek to conceal it, to soften it, or to explain it away, we could only sully the chastity or destroy the integrity of our own faith, and confirm the unbelieving and misbelieving in their dangerous delusions. Still would it be as true as ever, that our religion is the only true religion, and that there is salvation in no other. The solemn truth, that out of the church no one can ever be saved, would remain in all its force unaffected by our concessions. Knowing this – knowing that it is the truth which liberates, – we dare not conceal it, and are bound in

Christian charity to proclaim it. We must not mistake natural sympathy and good feeling, or the natural kindness or softness of our tempers, for Christian charity. Christian charity, certainly, never gratuitously offends, – is never harsh, bitter, or censorious, – is always meek, gentle, affectionate, kind; but it seeks, always and everywhere, the substantial good of its objects, even at the risk of giving them momentary displeasure or pain; and, unhappily, in this perverse world, men generally have the most repugnance to that which is the most essential to their everlasting welfare.

We are not ignorant that many persons object to the intolerance and exclusiveness we assert, – that is, to the Catholic dogma, out of the church no one can ever be saved, – not only that it is harsh and illiberal, but that it is contrary even to the justice of God; for it implies, they say, that he will consign them to eternal tortures for not doing what they never had the power to do. To punish them for not doing what has never been in their power to do, is we grant, unjust, and we may be well assured that our God will never do it. But the objection has no validity, unless it be true that there are persons who live and die without ever having it in their power to become joined to the Catholic communion; consequently, they who urge this objection must prove that there are such persons, before they can have any right to insist on it, or we be under any obligation even to entertain it. An objection which rests for its validity on an uncertain principle, or an unproved assumption, proves nothing, and may always be dismissed without an answer. But is the assumption the objection makes provable? We know that our religion has been promulgated in all the earth for eighteen hundred years, and, as far as we know any thing of the matter, that, if there is any nation to which it has not been preached, it has been that nations's own fault, because it would not receive, but repelled with insult and persecution, her divinely-commissioned preachers. We know, also, that sufficient grace is given unto every man, that he who seeks shall find, and that if he knocks it shall be opened to him. Who, then, is prepared to prove that a single adult person, since St. Paul declared the Gospel has been preached in all the earth, has ever died out of the church, who could never, if he had made a proper use of the means placed within his reach, have found his way into her communion. Can they who urge the objection in any possible way whatever prove this? How can they say that even the ordinary missionary has ever failed the ready mind and the willing heart? Known unto God are all hearts from eternity; all things are at his disposal, and it can cost him nothing so to order it, that, wherever there is one ready and willing to receive the truth, there the missionary shall be ready to teach him, and to introduce him into the communion of the church. How know you that he does not so order it, and that, if any have died without actually having heard the church, it has been their own fault, – that is, because they would have rejected her in case she had been presented to them? Till you can assert the contrary with infallible certainty, your objection has no validity; for the difficulty it suggests is confessedly restricted to those who are ready and willing to receive the truth as soon as proposed to them.

But let this pass. The dogma in question certainly can in no sense impeach the justice of God, if it asserts the condemnation of none who have fulfilled the law of nature. Men are not entitled to salvation even for fulfilling that law; but they may certainly be justly condemned, if they do not fulfill it. Suppose, then, as the objection itself supposes, that in the gentile world there are persons, or may be persons, who concurring with the graces they receive, fulfill the natural law; what obliges us to suppose that they must die out of the communion of the church, even if it be conceded that they have no *ordinary* means of entering it? God may, if he chooses, use *extraordinary* means to bring them into the church; and it is far more reasonable to suppose that he will work fifty miracles to bring men into the *medium ordinarium,* if necessary, than it is to suppose, that, contrary to the whole economy of grace, he will save a single soul without it. We know that he has made use of extraordinary means to bring men into the church, as in the case of Cornelius, and that of the eunuch, recorded in the Acts of the Apostles; and, indeed, he has always used them in the conversion of nations; for in no instance has a nation been converted, in which the ordinary means employed for its conversion were adequate to the ends. Why may he not use extraordinary means in the case of individuals, as well as of nations?

Again: in asserting that no one can be saved out of the church, we do not assert that all those who die out of her communion will be condemned precisely for the guilt of not being in her communion. Invincible ignorance, unquestionably, excuses from sin in that whereof one is invincibly ignorant. If there are persons out of the church who are invincibly ignorant of her, – that is, persons who never have had the power of becoming acquainted with her, and of being joined to her communion, – they certainly are not guilty of the sin of infidelity, and cannot be condemned for that sin. But invincible ignorance, though it excuses from sin, has no saving efficacy, no positive power to advance the soul towards the kingdom of heaven. Certainly, mere negative infidels, as they are called, are excused from the sin of infidelity; yet without conversion, they cannot be saved, for, "without faith it is impossible to please God." Hence St. Thomas says, – "Infidels of this sort are damned, not, indeed, for the sin of infidelity, but for other sins, not remissable without faith." Infidelity is not the only sin for which men are damned; if it were, we should be obliged to assert, that all bad as well as good Catholics will be saved; nor is it necessarily, by any means, the only sin of those not in the Catholic communion. The condemnation of these will not be for the sin of infidelity, if they are not guilty of it, but for other sins. They will be condemned, not by reason of the guilt, but by reason of the fact, of being out of the church, for their sins against the natural law, which are remissable only through the church.

Finally, we are told that there are persons out of the church who are not only free from the sin of infidelity, but from all actual sin. But this is a gratuitous assumption; for, without a special revelation from God, we cannot know that there are such persons, and nothing, so far as we are aware, either in reason or sound theology, authorizes us to assume that there are or can be. But suppose there can be, and that there are, such persons, nothing obliges us to assert, or permits you to assume that we assert, their condemnation to the *tortures* of hell. The Catholic dogma objected to simply teaches, that no one can ever be saved out of the Catholic Church, that is, enter into eternal life, – see God in the beatific vision by the light of glory. What the dogma obliges us to assert is, that salvation, in this sense, which is supernatural both in its principle and its terminus, is unattainable out of the church. But this salvation does not necessarily stand opposed simply to the torments of hell. Hell is two-fold, and consists in the punishment of loss and the punishment of sense. None are saved who do not escape both; but not therefore does it necessarily follow, that all who are not saved are doomed to suffer both. All are guilty of original sin, and original sin itself forfeits heaven, and incurs the punishment of loss; but the church does not teach that it incurs also the punishment of sense. Hence unbaptized infants, who die before committing actual sin, – though they lose heaven can never see God by the light of glory, – do not, as our theologians teach, suffer the punishment of sense, do not, as we are permitted to hope, suffer positive pain, but will be gainers for having existed. Not of them, but of actual sinners who die in their sins, is it to be said, "Good for them if they had never been born."

Suppose now, – and if the supposition is inadmissable the objection vanishes, – that among the gentiles there are persons who die out of the church, free from all actual sin; they, certainly, will never see God, will never enter heaven, will not be saved; yet nothing obliges us to believe that they will be doomed to the punishment of sense, or to the postitive sufferings of hell. What will be their fate, beyond the fact that they will not be saved, we do not know, and do not attempt to determine. We remit them, if such there are, to the bounty of God, who, for aught we know, may place them in the category of unbaptized infants who die in their infancy. But no injustice is done them in not admitting them to the beatific vision; for to see God by the light of glory is a *gratuitous* reward, promised only to supernatural faith and sanctity, never due and never promised to mere natural innocence or to mere natural virtue. The defect of natural innocence or of natural virtue excludes from it, but the possession of either or of both does not and cannot entitle to it; and natural innocence and virtue are all that can be pretended that these have. Hence, supposing such persons, supposing them to die free from all but original sin, no injustice is done in excluding them from salvation, and therefore the dogma which denies the possibility of salvation out of the church asserts nothing contrary to the justice or even to the fidelity of God.

But granting all this as far as regards Jews, Mohammedans, and pagans, that is, unbaptized persons, it cannot apply, we are told, to persons in heretical communions, who are invincibly ignorant; for these are baptized and in their baptism have received the infused grace of faith and sanctification. But the reasoning we have used to show that it is not proved, and is not to be assumed without proof, that there are any who die without ever having had the power, if they had made the proper use of the means within their reach, of being joined to the Catholic communion, applies here in its greatest force, and renders an answer really unnecessary. The possibility of invincible ignorance, in an heretical communion, of the Catholic Church, – since the Catholic Church is always included in the formal reason of faith in those very articles which all admit are necessary, *necessitate medii ad salutem* [by a necessity of means for salvation], – may well be questioned, – and it is not to be presumed, especially since those of whom you would predicate it have received in their baptism the habit of faith which is a predisposition to believe, and a supernatural facility in believing, the truth. But let this pass. Suppose invincible ignorance in the case to be possible, and that there are persons baptized in heretical communions, who die invincibly ignorant of the Catholic Church, we grant that they are excused from the sin of heresy. If they have been sinners, they will be damned for their sins; if they have retained their baptismal innocence, – an improbable supposition, – or if they make an act of perfect contrition and die free from mortal sin, – another improbable supposition, – they will undoubtedly be saved; but not as members of heretical communions, but as members of the Catholic Church, to whose communion they were joined by baptism. Consequently, the admission of their salvation forms no exception to the dogma, that out of the church no one can ever be saved. These, therefore, present no difficulty. But we may remark, by the way, that none, whether among the schismatical, the heretical, or the unbaptized, who are aware of the dogma of the church and the explanations which Catholic theologians give of it, can be invincibly ignorant. They, whatever must be said of others, have had the opportunity of hearing the church, and their ignorance is vincible, culpable in its cause, and can no longer excuse from sin. Whatever their characters in other respects, they may, therefore, be justly condemned for the single sin of infidelity, heresy, or schism, as the case may be.

We may say, in brief, that we are obliged, by the Catholic dogma of exclusive salvation, to divide mankind, in the first instance into two classes, – namely, Catholic and non-Catholic. Salvation is predicable only of Catholics, because they only are where there is the means of salvation; it is to be denied of all non-Catholics, or who die in the second division, for they are out of the church, and at least under the penalty of original sin, and there is no remission of sin out of the church. This is all that the dogma of exclusive salvation imports.

In the second instance in regard to those who will be condemned to hell, including both the punishment of loss and the punishment of sense, we recognize four classes. 1. All who die bad Catholics. These will be damned for their sins and their abuses of the graces and privileges which have been extended to them. 2. All who have impugned the known truth, that is, persons who have actually known the Catholic Church and faith, but have rejected or refused to believe her, and died in their sin. These are formal heretics, schismatics, or infidels, and will be damned, if for no other sin, for their infidelity, heresy, or schism. 3. All who might have known the truth, if they had sought it, but did not seek it, – that is, persons who, though they have never actually known the church, yet have the opportunity of knowing her, and of becoming joined to her communion, and have neglected to avail themselves of it. These are, by implication, infidels, or heretics, and will be damned for the sin of having neglected to become Catholics when they might. 4. All who, though they may never actually have had an opportunity of becoming Catholics, have nevertheless sinned against the law of nature. These will be damned not for the guilt of not being in the Catholic Church, but for their failure to keep the natural law. On the supposition of the truth of the Catholic Church, there is nothing contrary to the justice of God in the damnation of these four classes.

In the third instance, you tell us that there is yet another class, not included in the first general division, not yet in any one of these four special divisions, – namely, a class invincibly ignorant of the church, yet innocent of all sin against the natural law, the only law by which they can be judged. But you do not and cannot prove the existence of such a class; you have no authority for alleging that there is or can be such a class, and we are unable to reconcile its existence with the publicity of the Catholic Church, the ease with which she may be distinguished, the well-known fact that sufficient grace is given unto every man, and that Christ is always, along with the church, operating by his grace to bring all men to her communion, as well as to save them in her communion after they have entered it. But, if there be such a class, they cannot be saved; for they are out of the church, – have by original sin incurred the forfeiture of heaven; and there is no remission of sin but through the church. But, as God was not obliged in justice to bring them into the church, he does them no injustice in not admitting them to the beatific vision, – the only punishment to which we are obliged by faith to hold that they are doomed.

Thus much we have thought it not improper to remark on the first branch of our subject, that no false inferences may be drawn from the fact that Catholic writers, as well as others, contend for the political toleration of the various sects. We assert rigid intolerance of all false religions, in the spiritual order; but it must not, therefore, be supposed that we deny, or do not assert, the legitimacy of their toleration in the political order. It is true, as we have said, that, in speaking of toleration, we exclude our church; for there can never be rightfully any question at all, whether she shall be free or not. She is God's church, and is free by divine right, not by the concession of the prince or the commonwealth. As much, we concede, we do not and cannot say for the sects. They are contrary to the will of God, forbidden by his law, and have no divine right to be at all. But not therefore does it follow that the civil authority is bound to suppress them, or is not bound even to tolerate them. The state

– and we beg that the fact be borne in mind – is not commissioned to execute the *whole* law of God; and, though it can never rightfully do anything contrary to that law, it has authority to enforce it only in externals, and even in externals only so far as necessary to the maintenance of the peace and welfare of society. There are mortal sins against the law of God, of daily and hourly occurrence, that transcend the reach of the civil magistrate, and which he has no right to punish. We may transgress against God in thought as well as in deed; but the state must leave our punishment to him who has said, "Vengeance is mine, and I will repay," – save when our sinful thoughts break out in deeds contrary to the rights of our neighbor or the real interests of civil society. Till then, our offenses pertain to the spiritual order, and do not fall under the cognizance of the civil magistrate, who has no competency in spirituals. There are also virtues, – such as faith, hope, charity, meekness, gentleness, humility, benevolence, – all strictly obligatory upon all men, which the civil authority cannot enforce, and has no right to enforce; for, though of the last importance to the peace and safety of society, they lie, as to their principle and motive, wholly within the spiritual order. Everybody knows this, and nobody to our knowledge, directly contradicts it. It does not, then, follow, from the exclusiveness of religion in her own order, that the political order must always enforce the same exclusiveness, and suppress whatever is opposed to it.

All must agree that the state has no right to establish a false religion, or to prohibit the true religion; because every man has from Almighty God himself full and entire freedom to profess the true religion, and no one can, under any circumstances whatever, be bound to profess or adhere, even externally to a false religion. To profess the true religion is the duty of all men, and no government has or can have the right to hinder its subjects from performing their duty. Hence Protestant, schismatics and infidel governments are justly accused of transcending their powers, exceeding their commission, and violating the first principles of religion; for, with the exception of our own, which acknowledges its own incompetency in spirituals, there is not one of them that has not prohibited, or that even now more than barely tolerates, the Catholic religion. Every state in Europe, not professedly Catholic, establishes by law even now a false religion, and in several of them the true religion is strictly prohibited, or not tolerated at all. Sweden and Denmark establish Lutheranism, deny all civil rights to Catholics, and forbid their subjects, under severe penalties, to unite themselves with the Catholic Church. In Russia, no man is allowed to leave the national church for ours; in Prussia, conversions from Protestantism to Catholicity, and efforts on the part of Catholics to effect them, are, or recently were, forbidden by law; and it is only two or three years since the Norwegian Storthing first granted partial toleration to the Catholic religion in Norway. It is still, we believe, proscribed by law in Holland, and has owed a precarious freedom, for some years past, chiefly to the connivance of the prince. In Switzerland, it is now suffering a cruel persecution from the government, and her noble prelate, the Bishop of Lausanne and Geneva, has recently been imprisoned, and is now in exile, simply for discharging his episcopal functions. We need not mention the well-known penal laws of England and Ireland, partially repealed in 1829, but still leaving the profession of the Catholic religion subject to many restrictions and vexations. By these laws, it was death for a priest to say mass in England, or to receive a member of the establishment into his church. Indeed, it is well known that Protestantism and infidelity, wherever able, have never failed to copy the example of pagan Rome, to place an interdict on the Catholic religion, and to enjoin, and to seek by pains and penalties to enforce, a false religion, or the profession of no religion. But all governmental acts of this sort are violences rather than laws, and have and can have no binding force. We are always bound to resist them, at least passively; for we must obey God rather than men; and there are times when charity to our neighbor may require us to resist them even actively.

But, though the state has no right to enjoin the profession of a false religion, or to prohibit the profession of the true religion, yet, is it not bound, we may be asked, to enjoin the profession of the true religion, and to prohibit that of the false? It certainly would be, if it were commissioned to promulgate and execute the *whole* law of God, and if there were nothing in religion left to the conscience and free will. But the latter, we know, is not true; for even the canon law strikes only external actions, and the church judges matters of conscience only in her tribunals of penance, approach to which is and must be an act of free will, and before which the culprit is his only and his voluntary accuser; and the former cannot be assumed, for that would make the state the church, and render all distinction between the secular society and the spiritual inconceivable. It would be the absorption of the church in the state, than which nothing is more to be dreaded as the history of Russia since Ivan IV, and of England since Henry VIII, abundantly testifies. The state has civil, but no spiritual functions; it is not in holy orders; it has not received the mission of evangelizing the world; and it has no vocation to preach the Gospel, or to assume the direction of consciences. It is certainly bound to recognize and protect the full and entire freedom of the true religion, and to suppress by force, if necessary, all external violence against it; for it is included in the civil rights of those who profess it; but it can legitimately use coercion, either in favor of the true or against a false religion, only for purely social reasons, and only so far as necessary to the maintenance of the order and interests of society; for, as we never cease to repeat, its functions are purely civil, and it has no spiritual competency.

Certainly the obligation or right of civil governments, not Catholic, – where there is no publicly recognized infallible spiritual authority to determine which is the true religion, – to enjoin the profession of the true worship, and to prohibit others, cannot be asserted; because the government, having only civil functions, cannot judge in spirituals, or discriminate between one religion and another. It cannot, then, enjoin one worship or prohibit another, for fear, if for no other reason, that it may enjoin a false religion and proscribe the true; and therefore it must, even in common prudence, tolerate all religions not obviously immoral, like the obscene and cruel rites of many pagan nations, or directly incompatible with the safety and welfare of society. This binds all governments not Catholic to universal toleration, because all religions but the Catholic are confessedly fallible, and can, on their own showing, offer the government no infallible judgment by which it may form, or to which it is bound to submit, its own.

With regard to Catholic governments of Catholic countries, where there is an infallible spiritual authority recognized by the nation, we distinguish between those governments which have only the ordinary obligations of civil government and those governments which hold from the church, or under the express condition of professing and defending the Catholic religion. Governments of the first-mentioned class are bound to acknowledge the true religion, and to throw their *moral* influence into its scale; for the state, as well as the individual, is bound to have a conscience, and even a good conscience; but nothing in the constitution of the state binds these governments to enforce the profession of the Catholic religion, or to prohibit that of other religions; and as these religions, if not palpably immoral, are not, in themselves, social offences, the government has no right to declare them so, or to suppress them. These governments, having by their constitution only the ordinary functions of civil governments, can do no more for the true religion or against false religions than the interests of society demand; and as such governments themselves presuppose a state of society in which false religions, as such, are not incompatible with these interests, they are bound to tolerate them, and leave their suppression to the operation of moral causes.

As to the second class of Catholic governments distinguished, that they are bound to recognize the Catholic religion as the law of the land, and are not free to tolerate all religions, we grant. But there are few, if any, such governments now in existence; and the reasons which formerly demanded and justified them have, in the social changes which have taken place in recent times, lost their force, and cannot now be urged for the establishment or the maintenance of similar governments. In the middle ages, nearly all the European governments not pagan were professedly Catholic, and did and had the right to punish open infidelity, heresy, and schism, – always sins against God, – because then they were directly crimes against society, forbidden by the public law; and crimes against society the civil government has always the right to punish. But now, when that political order has passed away, and, in the altered cirumstances of our times, these sins against God are no longer to be treated as direct crimes against society, the government is not bound, and has no right, to punish them; because civil government has never the right, we repeat, to punish any sin, except for the reason that it is a social offence, which society cannot, with a just regard to its own safety, suffer to go unpunished.

We do not assume that infidelity, heresy, and schism were social offences, merely because they were declared such by the laws, or made such by the fundamental constitution of the state. The laws, as in pagan Rome, or in England before Catholic emancipation, may establish a false religion and prohibit the true; but that does not make the profession of the true religion a social crime, or incompatible with the legitimate interests of society. If religion and the laws come in conflict, it is the laws that are to be reformed, not the religion that is to be suppressed. To say otherwise, – to say that false religions are justly punishable by civil society, simply because contrary to the civil law, – would be to concede that the profession of the true religion may be justly punished in those states in which the civil law prohibits it. The laws must themselves be just, or they do not bind; and the fundamental constitution of a state must be legitimate, or a measure is not justifiable simply because authorized by it or necessary to preserve it. What we assert is, that the political order, which, in former times, declared infidelity, heresy, and schism, when breaking out into overt acts, social offences, was itself just; because then they were such offences in fact as well as in law, and the laws only declared a truth which existed independently of them. The intolerance of the government was justifiable, because demanded by its fundamental and essential constitution, and that constitution was itself justifiable by its absolute necessity, under the circumstances, to the existence of society and the interest of civilization.

In the barbaric ages which followed the destruction of the western Roman empire – ages against which we hear so many noisy and senseless declamations, and in which we ourselves find little, except Catholicity and what proceeded from it, which does not revolt us, – the church of God had a double mission to perform, and was obliged to add to her spiritual functions the greater part of the functions of civil society itself. She was the sole repository of what had been saved from the wrecks of the old Roman civilization, and the openly civilizing force that remained after the barbarian irruption and devastations. The lay society was dissolved by the ruin of the empire and of the civilized populations, and was no longer adequate to the management of secular affairs in accordance with civilized order. The church was obliged to add to her mission of evangelizer, which is her mission of all times and places, the temporary and accidental mission of civilizer, of the nations. She must tame the wild savage, humanize the ruthless barbarian, re-establish social order, revive science and the arts, and re-store and advance civilization. All had been demolished, and she had all to reconstruct. She has to be statesman, lawyer, physician, pedagogue, architect, painter, sculptor, musician, agriculturalist, horticulturalist, bookbinder, and common mechanic or artisan, – in fine, everything but money-changer and soldier. Having thus the chief part of the work of civil society to perform, it became absolutely necessary that she should have a civil and political existence and authority, – that she should be incorporated into the state, as an integral element of the civil constitution, and have her worship, without which she could have as little social as religious influence, recognized as the law of the land as well as the law of God. There was no other condition of rescuing society from the chaos and barbarism in which it was plunged, and of reviving civilization and securing its progress. Infidelity, heresy, and schism, which were as directly in opposition to her mission of civilizing the nations as to her mission of evangelizing them, were then directly and proximately crimes against society, and as such were justly punishable by the public authorities. In attacking the church, they attacked civil society itself, struck at the very conditions of social order, and jeopardized every social interest.

But, from the nature of the case, this mission of civilizer of nations is restricted to barbarous ages and countries, for the very good reason that the church cannot be called upon to civilize nations when they are already civilized. This mission she has now, in great measure, accomplished in what is called Christendom; and the necessity of that particular political order which specially protected her in its performance, or which was requisite to enable her to perform it, does not now exist. The lay society she has rescued from barbarism, and civilized. It has now the arts of civilized life in its own possession, and does not need, as it once did, in barbarous ages, the church to teach it how to make shoes, bind books, or brew hop-beer. It is now competent, under the *spiritual* direction of the spiritual society, to the management of secular affairs. It has, in these affairs, which properly belong to it, attained to majority, and no longer needs in regard to them, so far as purely secular and as they involve no moral principle, to be under ecclesiastical tutelage. The church is now free to resign her temporary civil functions, and to devote herself exclusively to the mission of evangelizing the world. It is not necessary that she should be now incorporated into the state, in the sense she was in the barbaric ages; and consequently infidelity, heresy, and schism, though as great sins against God as ever, are not now crimes against society in the sense they then were, or to be punished as such; and therefore, as long as their adherents demean themselves peaceably, offer no external violence to the true religion, and discharge their ordinary social obligations, they are to be politically tolerated, and left to answer for their sinfulness, great as it unquestionably is, to God himself.

This reasoning cannot well be disputed. When infidelity, heresy, and schism, as well as any other sins against God, are clearly and directly crimes against society, they are justly punishable by the civil authorities; but when they only remotely offend against social interests, and are chiefly censurable only as they injure the soul, they are not so punishable, and the prince or commonwealth is bound to tolerate them. This is the principle we lay down. In former times, they were obviously and directly crimes against society, and as such were justly punishable by the civil magistrate; but, owing to the civilization effected by the social labors of the church, they are not now such crimes, and therefore not now punishable as such, but are to be politically tolerated, for they now can be, without directly or immediately endangering the existence of social order, or sacrificing the general interests of civilization. Here are the facts we assert.

All this is virtually conceded by all the respectable publicists of our times. No intelligent Protestant or infidel really denies – though we know not how long it will be so – the immense services rendered to civilization by the Catholic Church, and with one voice all those who give us philosophies of history, from Guizot to our Kentucky friend, J.D. Nourse, agree that she could not have rendered those services without the civil constitution which made hostility to her faith, discipline, or worship social offences. The present popular theory of those who are not Catholics is, that the church was the true church, and faithfully and successfully performed her mission, down to the epoch of the Protestant reformation, and that she is a false church now, because she leaves the interests of civilization to the lay society, and does not exert herself directly to promote them, which, according to them, she is bound to do, since, say they, her mission is merely that of civilizing mankind. We are aware of no intelligent voice, in even the uncatholic church, that does not defend the mutual relations of the civil and ecclesiastical societies which obtained in the barbarous ages as wise and necessary for those times, or that pretends to condemn them, except when insisted upon as equally necessary or proper in the altered state of modern civilization. Here is all we ask. Restricted to the temporary and accidental mission of the church as civilizer, we recognize a truth in what our popular authors advance. They say the political order in question was just and necessary during the barbarous ages; so say we. They say it is not just now; so say we; and therefore we, as well as they, reject it for our times. Because the church approved it in one set of circumstances, we are not obliged to maintain that she must approve it under every set of circumstances. Principles are immutable and eternal, but their application must vary according to the circumstances of time and place. This the popular authors themselves contend, and this is all we allege; and we have no quarrel with them, except when they assert that the mission of the church is primarily and exclusively that of civilizer, and contend that she is false or dead now, because she does not labor directly for the advancement of civilization, which, we need hardly say, is as silly as it is untrue.

It is evident from what we have said, that, though we assert the most rigid theological intolerance, and the wisdom and justice of the political intolerance which nobody denies was during many centuries asserted, and sometimes practiced, by Catholic states, we are bound by Catholic principles to assert for our times the toleration of all religions compatible with the existence and interests of society.

We do not, our readers will observe, justify the political intolerance in question, on the ground that it was sanctioned by the public opinion of former times, nor do we defend the political toleration of false religions now, because public opinion now demands it. Public opinion may often be pleaded in excuse or extenuation of the conduct of individuals, but it is never to be appealed to as the standard of right and wrong; especially when the question turns on principles and institutions either sanctioned or not disavowed by an infallible church. Not the public opinion, but the public necessities, the interests of society, of civilization justified the political intolerance; and these would, if they existed, justify it now as well as then, – and not only justify it, but even demand it. Let the modern political social order be broken up, the civilization which Christian nations have, by painful toil and sacrifice for so many ages, slowly worked out, be swept away, the whole of Christendom overrun with hordes of ruthless and lawless barbarians, and the world be plunged once more into the darkness and chaos of barbarism, – and let the church remain the sole repository of what has been retained of the former civilization, the only living social organism, the only living organic force, able to reduce chaos to order, to restore society to its normal condition, to reproduce and provide for the advance of civilization, – and we would say at once, revive the former political and social constitution; incorporate the church again into the state; let her resume anew her functions as civilizer, as well as evangelizer, of the nations; let her faith, discipline, and worship, without which she can have no social influence even, be made the law of the land, and whatever is repugnant to them be declared a crime against society, and, when manifesting itself in overt acts, punishable as such by the civil magistrate; – and we should have little respect for the head, little reverence for the heart, that could not or would not say as much. But now, we repeat, when such is not the state of things, and, until some terrible calamity not now foreseen, and in all human probability, not likely to occur, shall throw society out of its normal order, and bring it back, we say, let the church, be the church, and the state be the state, the two orders be distinct, and the lay society, under the *spiritual* direction of the spiritual society, manage the temporal affairs of the world, as now, thanks to the church, which did not fail in time of need, it is able to do; let the public law, where it is proper, recognize the true religion, but let it punish no sins against God any further than they are directly and immediately crimes against society. False religions are, no doubt, always offenses against society, as are all sins against God; but, as we have said more than once, when and where they are only remotely and indirectly so, when and where they are not directly and immediately so, the civil law has no right by coercive means to repress them, and could not do so if it should make the attempt. Their adherents, in all other respects discharging their social duties and demeaning themselves as good citizens, must be protected in their civil rights, and their punishment be remitted to the discipline of the spiritual society and the justice of God.

The church cannot tolerate the punishment, by the civil authority, of offences purely spiritual, because the civil authority cannot do it without trenching upon her province. She allows no one to be molested merely for his want of faith, because, for his want of faith, the unbeliever is answerable to God alone. Faith is voluntary, and cannot be forced. Whoever chooses to run the risk of the penalty of eternal damnation annexed to infidelity is free to be an infidel, and almighty God neither does violence, nor suffers any power to do violence, to his free will. He proffers eternal life to all men, tells them the conditions on which they may receive it, gives them the necessary graces to accept and secure it, urges them by the most powerful motives which can be addressed to reason, conscience, free will; but he forces no one to accept it. He demands the heart, its free, voluntary obedience, and will accept and reward only the free-will offering. Hence the church strictly and solemnly forbids any one to be forced or compelled to receive the faith. Hence her missionaries are never armed soldiers, but humble preachers, bearing only the crucifix and pastoral staff. Never has she allowed the unbaptized – Jews, pagans, Mohammadens, infidels – to be forced to profess the Catholic faith, or force to be employed against them, except to compel them to tolerate the preaching of the Gospel. If in Catholic states they have ever been disturbed or molested on account of their unbelief, it has been against her authority, or because they practised violence against the profession of the true religion; or because they were dangerous subjects to the state, and could not, under the circumstances, to be safely tolerated, – as for instance, in Spain under Charles V, when the Jews and Moors conspired in secret and with the enemies of the church, not simply to secure the peaceable enjoyment of their own religions, but to overthrow both altar and throne, both of which the state had the right, and was bound, to protect and defend, to the full extent of its power, against any and every class of enemies.

The church certainly claims authority over all baptized persons, by whomsoever they may have been baptized; for they are, in the sacrament of baptism, born her subjects, and she has a right to their obedience. Heretics and schismatics are her rebellious subjects, and she has the same right to reduce them to obedience and to compel them to conform their life to their baptismal vows, that a temporal sovereign has to reduce a rebellious province to submission to his legitimate authority. But she can reduce them only by such means as she possesses, and can inflict on them for their rebellion only such punishments as she has at her command, which are all spiritual. If they make war on her, and attempt to seize her churches, to rob her of her possessions, to desecrate her altars, and to suppress her worship or restrain its freedom, as was the case with the early Protestants in every country where they had power enough, and which caused the terrible religious wars of the sixteenth century, and the persecution of Protestants by Catholic princes, she has the right to call in the secular power to her aid, and it is bound to repel them by force; because they themselves then transfer the controversy from the spiritual order to the temporal, and attack the social and civil rights of the church no less than her spiritual rights. But when they themselves restrain their heresy and schism within the limits of the spiritual order, make no attempt to propagate their pestilential errors or iniquity by violence, and attack none of the rights of the church or of the faithful, she, as we have seen, recognizes no right in the secular authority to molest them, unless guilty of other crimes against society, and then only on principles which apply equally to all classes of social offenders. As simple heresy and schism, she cannot call in the secular authority to aid her in suppressing them. She is therefore reduced to her own spiritual resources, to addresses to their reason and their conscience, and can inflict on them only spiritual punishments, ecclesiastical censures, of which the greatest is excommunication. This, to a believer, is a terrible punishment, we grant; but to those who do not believe, who excommunicate themselves, and glory in being severed from her communion, it is not a punishment too severe to be borne.

But even in inflicting her spiritual censures, and in all of her dealings with her rebellious subjects, the church always has their reformation at heart, and never forgets that her mission is to save men's souls, and not to destroy them. She pleads with them, and leaves no measure untried that is likely to be successful; and she keeps the door always open for the return of the penitent. When she is under the painful necessity of delivering over to Satan those who set at naught her discipline, it is for "the destruction of the flesh," that "they may learn not to blaspheme." To the very last, she pleads with all a mother's sweetness, affection, and grief; and if they are finally melted, and willing to return to their duty, she opens wide her arms, and wide her heart, to receive them, and generously forgets their past disobedience. Even the much decried and calumniated Inquisition, which it is possible politicians in some instances have abused, owed its origin to her maternal solicitude, and was instituted no less for the protection than for the detection of the misbelieving. She would interpose the shield of her maternal love between her rebellious subject and the secular arm to the last, till all hope was gone, till all her resources to reclaim him were exhausted. They know little of the church of God who call her cruel, proud, haughty, revengeful, thirsting for the blood of heretics, and rejoicing in their punishment by the civil authority. Long, long does she forbear with them, – long, long does she suffer them to rend her own bosom, – before she can endure to withdraw her affectionate embrace, and abandon them to their self-chosen doom.

And here we are admonished of what should be the spirit of our intercourse with our unbelieving and heretical neighbours and fellow citizens. Rousseau asserts that the dogma, Out of the church there is no salvation, is antisocial, and that whoever professes it should be banished from the commonwealth. But he might as well have said, that the dogma, No one who dies guilty of mortal sin can be saved, is antisocial, and he who holds it should be banished from society. We certainly regard infidels and heretics as guilty of mortal sin before God, and therefore, if dying in their infidelity and heresy, as condemned to hell. But they are not the only persons whom we regard as mortal sinners; and all who die mortal sinners, even though they should die nominally in our own communion, must, according to our faith, receive the same doom. There are persons in the church who will talk, write, fight for their religion, do any thing for it but live it, whose doom will be far more severe than that of many heretics and unbelievers; nay, we know not but we ourselves may be of the number, for no man knoweth whether he deserves love or hatred, unless he has received a special revelation from God. We live in a world of sinners, and there may be in our own families, in our bosom companions, sinners for whose salvation we have as little reason to hope as we have for that of the unbeliever or heretic. These things are so, and must be so, and our rule of conduct is and should be the same towards sinners of all classes, that is, to conduct ourselves so as, if possible, to win them all to the love and practice of true religion.

It is very true that all who are not joined to the Catholic communion, if they die as they are, will come short of salvation. This we know by infallible faith; but we do not know that all who are not now joined to that communion will die as they are, and have no right to presume that they will. Nothing assures us that their hearts will not be softened, their pride subdued, their eyes opened, – that they will not one day behold, love, and conform to the truth, and enter into the kingdom of heaven, while, perhaps, we ourselves shall be thrust out into exterior darkness, where there shall be weeping and gnashing of teeth. It is no less error to hold that all out of the church will be damned, than it is to hold that they can be saved without being in the church. If we so held, there would be some foundation for Rousseau's charge; our doctrine would be antisocial, and we should be unable to discharge our social duties toward those out of our church. But we hold no such doctrine. There is a place of repentance for them as well as for us, and nothing forbids us to hope and labor for their salvation. The Lord alone knoweth who are his, and we have no right to presume, as long as there is life, that the doom of any one is sealed. We must, then, treat all men, those without as well as those within, as persons for whom Christ died, as persons who may be saved, and whose salvation is to be desired by us with an unbounded charity, and for which we are to rejoice to make any sacrifice in our power. Here is the reason why the dogma objected to is not antisocial, and why to profess it is no breach of charity to our neighbor, but if done in the proper spirit, is the very reverse, – is, in fact, the highest evidence we can give of the truth and fervor of our charity.[2]

The object of the church, in all her dealings with those without, as well as with those within, is the salvation of souls. This must be ours,

---

[2] At this point the Precious Blood Father Thomas R. Ryan comments:

> The difficulty seems to be that at least to some the dogma appears to be asserted in a partisan spirit. Not so at all. All that is asserted is that no one can be saved except through Christ, and simply that the Catholic Church is Christ in society. The American bishops put the matter succinctly in their *Collective Pastoral Letter* (January 11, 1968, p.33): "Outside of Christ, there is no salvation...Outside the Church, no salvation."

Ryan, *Op. cit.*, p.798, n.31.

also, as her faithful children. This object we shall be able to further only as we live in accordance with the spirit of our religion. It requires no deep or extensive knowledge of mankind to know that the road to their convictions lies through their affections. If we would be instrumental, under God, in converting them, we must begin by loving them, and by our love winning their love. Nothing is gained by convincing a man against his will; often the very logic that convinces, where the affections are not won, serves only to repel from obedience to the truth. We succeed in influencing others for their good only in proportion as we set before them an example fit for them to follow, – are meek, gentle, humble, charitable, kind, and affectionate in our intercourse with them. And why shall we not love these neighbors and countrymen of ours, who have not the inconceivable happiness of being in the church of God? Who are we, that we should set up ourselves above them, – that we should boast over them? What merit is it in us, that we are not even as they? or how know we that ours will not be the greater condemnation? Are they not

Brownson practiced what he preached in his own family. Neither his mother, his two sisters, or one of his brothers, ever became Catholics, yet he always remained on the best of terms with them and assisted them financially whenever he was able. Only his brother Oran followed him into the Church.

> On the other hand Brownson's effect upon his brothers and sisters was almost nil, though he remained on affectionate terms with them. We hear of his eldest brother, Daniel, obtaining some local celebrity as a public speaker, and of his sisters as Methodists even in old age. His other brother, Oran, came to visit him in 1851. He had become a Mormon, for the same reason – so he wrote on April 5, 1846 – that Orestes had become a Catholic, a belief that it was the Latter Day Saints that possessed proper spiritual authority.[90] Now he and Orestes had long arguments about religion. George Parsons Lathrop describes the scene, though of course not at first hand, and mispelling Oran's name. "Orrin," he wrote, "would put a question, which Orestes would answer with uncompromising force. Then Orrin, without saying a word would dart out of the house and walk a long time in the hot sunshine; after which he would return and put another question. The same process was repeated, Orrin still making no rejoinder. When this odd dialogue ended, there was no summing up; Orrin went away in silence. After nine years, during which the brothers had not met again, Orrin wrote to Orestes that he had become a Catholic. From Dublin, Ohio, he had gone to Dublin, Ireland, where he was received into the Church."[91]

Maynard, Theodore, *Orestes Brownson: Yankee, Radical, Catholic*, The Macmillan Co., New York, 1943, pp.147,148; n.90, Schlesinger, *Op. cit.*, p.187, n.; n.91 *Atlantic Monthly*, Vol. LXXVII (1896).

our kinsmen according to the flesh? Has not our God loved them with an infinite tenderness? Does he not proffer them his love with infinite sweetness? And has he not so longed for their love that he has died to win it? How, then, shall we not love them and labor for their salvation with a charity that burns with an intensity proportioned to their danger? Is it not here where we come short? Repelled by the bigotry, fanaticism, and hard- heartedness of some, attracted by the sweetness, affection, and kind offices of others, are we not prone to look upon these countrymen of ours who are out of the church, either as persons who need no conversion; – excusing ourselves from zealous labors to bring them to God by persuading ourselves that their conversion either is not possible or not necessary, – forgetful that in either case we sin against faith and charity, and in both show ourselves wanting in true love of our neighbor, and therefore of God? Is not here, in this double error, the reason why so few, comparatively, of our countrymen are brought into the one fold, under the one Shepherd?

There is nothing in modern heresies that should discourage us. The world, before this, has been afflicted with as deep, as wide-spread, and as obstinate heresies as it is now. We must not suppose that we have fallen upon peculiarly evil times. Evils, indeed, there are, but our lot is cast in comparatively good times. What is the situation of Catholics now in comparison with what it was under the Arian succession of Constantine? or when the wild and destructive hordes of northern barbarians overwhelmed the western empire? or when the yet more destructive Saracenic hosts, with the Koran in one hand and the scimitar in the other, shouting "There is one God and Mohammed is his prophet," overran the East, and, over more than half the known world, over the fairest provinces of even Europe herself, supplanted the Cross by the Crescent? But Arianism has been subdued, and is remembered only in the immortal records of its victors; the barbarians have been civilized; the Saracenic hosts have been checked, their power has been broken, and their once formidable empire retains a fitful existence only by the iniquitous policy of nominally Christian princes, who forget their God and the interests of civilization in a vain endeavor to maintain an ever-varying balance of power, and to arrest the march of destiny. Better the Russian than the Turk at Constantinople. Protestantism itself, which swept away a third part of Europe, as the tail of the Apocalyptic dragon swept away a third part of the stars of heaven, has spent its force, has been driven back far within its original confines, and, for two hundred and fifty years, has made no progress in the Old World, but towards destruction. True, unbelief, indifferency, socialism, communism, revolutionism, are, or just now were, rife; – true, they held during the last year their carnival, convulsed the greater part of Europe, exiled the sovereign pontiff, took possession of the Eternal City, and for a moment seemed on the point of rising to empire. But defeat follows on the heels of victory, their chiefs have fallen, are in exile or in prison, and they must soon be objects of ridicule and contempt, rather than of fear and dread. They are in the nature of things short-lived. The human race loves order, and must be a believer. It must worship, – must have a religion; and the Catholic religion alone has life, has energy, has power. Even to a superficial observer, all other religions or pretended religions are struck with death, and are in their agony. Appearances indicate that a glorious day is dawning for the church, and that there awaits her a more splendid triumph than she has ever yet enjoyed. The Lord God omnipotent reigneth. Let us not feel that these unbelieving countrymen of ours – who now, alas! have no hope but in this hollow and transitory life, who are laboring for that which is not bread, and spending their strength for that which satisfieth not – are all doomed to be lost, and that they of all the world are to have no part in the new triumphs reserved for Catholicity. Let us not feel that the time is never to come, when, for their many civic virtues and their generous contributions to an oppressed and famishing nation, they can receive no higher reward than the discovery of the gold mines of California. Let us not look upon their conversion even as difficult. They, too, are famishing, and for the bread of life. We have only to remember that this land is under the protection of the Immaculate Virgin, and to live as true children of Mary, in order to behold this noble country – whose destiny, if we are faithful, promises to surpass what the boldest imagination can conceive – won to the Cross, and standing foremost among the Catholic nations of the earth.

But to return from this apparent digression, we will simply add, in conclusion, that, while we have asserted, as we were bound by reason and faith, the most rigid intolerance and exclusiveness in the religious order, and have justified the constitution and laws of Catholic states, during the middle ages, in declaring infidel, heretical, and schismatical sects social crimes, and punishing them as such, we have shown that, in a normal or civilized state of society, Catholicity is perfectly compatible with political toleration, and concedes at least extensive toleration as is professed, and for the most part honorably maintained, by our American government. Our religion contains nothing, in case we should become the majority, and the political power should pass in this country into our hands, which would require any external changes in our existing political institutions, in our domestic and social economies, or in the present mutual relations of the civil and the ecclesiastical powers. In taking possession of a barbarous country, Catholicity must labor to change the institutions, the laws, the manners and customs, as well as the religion and interior sentiments, of the people. It has to do the same in taking possession even of a falsely civilized country, like India, China, or Japan. Catholicity can never tolerate the social institutions which are cherished by these oriental nations, as the decisions of Rome, in the controversies between the Jesuits and Dominicans, fully prove. It can tolerate any form of government; but it can, wherever it becomes resident, tolerate no despotism, no government that is not a government of law. The prince, whether monarch, aristocracy, or democracy, must govern according to law, and, as far as possible, according to just law; for she recognizes no security for the worship of God where there is no protection for the rights of our neighbour, any more than she recognizes love to God where there is none to our brother. She can never tolerate the oriental doctrine of castes, for she teaches that all men are of one blood, are brethern, equals before God, and should be equals before the law. The great reason why Christianity penetrates so slowly into these oriental nations is, no doubt, the fact, that not their religion only, but their whole order of society, their whole political, social, and domestic life, is unchristian, and must be changed in order to make them Christian nations. A Chinese or Hindu might object, with truth, to the introduction of Christianity, that it would change his political and social institutions, as well as his religious beliefs and usages.

But when Catholicity took possession of the Roman empire, it changed nothing except the spiritual order, and what held from it. It stepped into the Roman civilization as if it had been expressly prepared for it, – as it no doubt, in a great measure, had been, – abolished the false gods, purged the temples of their idolatry, cleansed them with holy water, converted them into churches, and consecrated them to the true God, – changed the manners and customs of the people as far as they depended on the false religions which had been professed, but retained the social institutions, the schools, the academies, the laws, the whole exterior domestic and social economy as she found it, only infusing her own spirit into it, and animating it with a purer, a higher, and a more vigorous life. The same will be the case here. Our civilization is founded on a right basis, – is Roman and Christian in its groundwork; and there never has been a state constituted throughout more in harmony with Catholic principles than the American. Its founders were not Catholics; far from it; but they would have been startled to have seen how much they were indebted to Catholicity for every important improvement they adopted. Their innovations were, for the most part, borrowed from Catholic teachers. Our American fathers had, unhappily for them, turned their backs upon the church; but they had been nursed in the bosom of her civilization. That civilization they brought with them to this New World, purged of the barbaric leaven which was still, in some measure, retained in the mother country, and against which the popes and the whole spiritual society had protested for ten centuries. Whoever will examine the respective civil institutions of England and this country will hardly fail to perceive, that what of England we have rejected is what she owes to her barbarous ancestors, and what we have added which she has not has been borrowed from Roman and Catholic civilization. Indeed, just in proportion, under a civil and political point of view, as we have receded from England, we have approached Rome and Catholicity. They betray no little simplicity, and ignorance of modern civilzation, who suppose that the truimph of Catholicity here would be the subversion of our political and civil constitutions. Our institutions throughout are based upon the great principles of reason and common sense, which our church presupposes and sanctions, inspired by Catholic tradition, and sustained by that portion of Catholic life which the Protestant populations were able to carry with them when they broke from its source, and which we would fain hope, is not yet wholly extinct. Indeed, the body for Catholicity seems to us to be here already prepared. It is moulded from fine, rich, red earth, in a form of majestic proportions, and of surpassing beauty, wanting nothing but the divine breath to be breathed into its nostrils in order to become a living soul. The conversion of the country would destroy, would change, nothing in this admirable body, but it would quicken it with the breath of the Almighty, and secure its continuance, and its beneficent and successful operation.[3]

[3] Like Brownson, Vatican Council II passes from the absolute religious freedom of the Church which it has received from God, to the religious freedom of man which is based on the dignity of every human person.

> 2. This Vatican Synod declares that the human person has a right to religious freedom. This freedom means that all men are to be immune from coercion on the part of individuals or of social groups and of any human power, in such wise that in matters religious no one is to be forced to act in a manner contrary to his own beliefs. Nor is anyone to be restrained from

acting in accordance with his own beliefs, whether privately or publicly, whether alone or in association with others, within due limits.

The Synod further declares that the right to religious freedom has its foundation in the very dignity of the human person, as this dignity is known through the revealed Word of God and by reasom itself. This right of the human person to religious freedom is to be recognized in the constitutional law whereby society is governed. Thus it is to become a civil right.

It is in accordance with their dignity as persons – that is, beings endowed with reason and free will and therefore priviledged to bear personal responsibility – that all men should be at once impelled by nature and also bound by a moral obligation to seek the truth, especially religious truth. They are also bound to adhere to the truth, once it is known, and to order their whole lives in accord with the demands of truth.

However, men cannot discharge these obligations in a manner in keeping with their own nature unless they enjoy immunity from external coercion as well as psychological freedom. Therefore, the right to religious freedom has its foundation, not in the subjective disposition of the person, but in his very nature. In consequence, the right to this immunity continues to exist even in those who do not live up to their obligation of seeking the truth and adhering to it. Nor is the exercise of this right to be impeded, provided that the just requirements of public order are observed.

Fr. Abbot again adds a note explaining the harmony which exists between this Declaration of Vatican II and the Constitution of the United States. He also adds a few cautions on the often loosely used word "conscience."

It is to be noted that the word "conscience," found in the Latin text, is used in its generic sense, sanctioned by usage, of "beliefs," "convictions," "persuasions." Hence the unbeliever or atheist makes with equal right this claim to immunity from coercion in religious matters. It is further to be noted that, in assigning a negative content to the right to religious freedom (that is, in making it formally a "freedom from" and not a "freedom for"), the Declaration is in harmony with the sense of the First Amendment to the American Constitution. In guaranteeing the free exercise of religion, the First Amendment guarantees to the American citizen immunity from all coercion in matters religious. Neither the Declaration nor the American Constitution affirms that a man has a right to believe what is false or to do what is wrong. This would be moral nonsense. Neither error nor evil can be the object of a right, only what is true and good. It is, however, true and good that man should enjoy freedom from coercion in matters religious.

This brings up the second question, concerning the foundation of the right. The reason why every man may claim

We have not, we grant, defended the political toleration of different religions on infidel or even Protestant principles. It would have been idle to have done so; for everybody knows that those principles are not ours, and cannot be, unless we give up our religion. We cannot place the sects on a footing of perfect equality with the church, and defend their freedom on the same ground that we do hers; because error can never exist by the same right that truth exists. The popular ground of defending the toleration of all religions by the state is the assumption of their equal right before God. This ground cannot be held by a Catholic; and if we had assumed it, on the strength of it asserted that Catholic states are bound to maintain universal toleration, who would have had any confidence in our sincerity, or not have supposed that our assertion was made merely for the purpose of escaping the odium of appearing to oppose the toleration by Catholic states of heretical or schismatical religions now, when toleration is popular, and we stand in need of it for ourselves? Every intelligent Protestant or unbeliever, with the history of the middle ages before his eyes, would have said, "Yes, these Catholics here in this country, where they are weak, are exceedingly liberal, and preach universal toleration; but let them become strong, let them once get the political power, and we shall quickly see that they are as

immunity from coercion in matters religious is precisely his inalienable dignity as a human person. Surely, in matters religious, if any where, the free human person is required and entitled to act on his own judgemnt and to assume personal responsibility for his action or omission. A man's religious decisions, or his decision against religion, are inescapably his own. No one else can make them for him, or compel him to make this decision or that, or restrain him from putting his decisions into practice, privately or publicly, alone or in company with others. In all these cases, the dignity of man would be diminished because of the denial to him of that inalienable responsibility of his own decisions and actions which is the essential counterpart of his freedom.

It is worth noting that the Declaration does not base the right to the free exercise of religion on "freedom of conscience." Nowhere does this phrase occur. And the Declaration nowhere lends its authority to the theory for which the phrase frequently stands, namely, that I have the right to do what my conscience tells me to do, simply because my conscience tells me to do it. This is a perilous theory. Its particular peril is subjectivism – the notion that, in the end, it is my conscience, and not the objective truth, which determines what is right or wrong, true or false.

The Documents of Vatican II, pp.678-690; n.5 pp.678,679.

intolerant in the political order as they are confessedly in the spiritual order. We Catholics must never forget that Protestants and unbelievers have a theory, to which they are wedded, that we are all ready to lie and swear to any thing for the sake of Catholicity, and that we can go so far as to profess indifferentism, infidelity, or even Puritanism, if we think we can thereby promote the interests of our church. Our assertions count for nothing with them. We are, in their estimation, fools when honest, and knaves when intelligent. Externally considered, it is evidently for our interest, here in this country, and indeed, in many other countries at the present time, to preach toleration; and they suppose interest governs us, as it does them, and therefore they place no confidence in our preaching, unless we show clearly and undeniably that it is in harmony with the principles of our church, where she is strong as well as where she is apparently weak.[4]

We have therefore defended the political toleration of the sects as a Catholic statesman, on strictly Catholic principles, without the least compromise, – without descending for a moment from the high ground of the infallibility and immutability of our church, – without blinking, or hesitating to justify in its fullest extent, the political intolerance manifested by Catholic states to infidelity, heresy and schism in past times. We have shown that not mere policy, but the very principles of our holy religion, require us now – on the supposition that modern unbelievers, heretics, and schismatics are civilized, and no longer barbarians, or addicted to barbarous practices – to assert and maintain as broad a toleration as our American constitution guarantees; that they forbid the punishment by the civil authority of sins against God, however great, when not incompatible with the peace and welfare of society; and that the church can of herself inflict only spiritual punishments, and no greater spiritual punishment than excommunication. If this does not satisfy, it is not our fault, nor that of our church.

[4] The Council declares that religious freedom is not only the prerogative of each individual, but also of individuals when they act in a group in the various non-Catholic churches and communities.

> 4. The freedom or immunity from coercion in matters religious which is the endowment of persons as individuals is also to be recognized as their right when they act in community. Religious bodies are a requirement of the social nature both of man and of religion itself.

Father Abbot carefully distinguishes between the religious freedom claimed by the

Catholic Church as of divine right, and the religious freedom of non-Catholic churches or communities based on the dignity of the human person.

> The freedoms listed here are those which the Catholic Church claims for herself. The declaration likewise claims them for all Churches and religious Communities. Lest there be misunderstanding, however, it is necessary to recall here the distinction between the content or object of the right and its foundation. The content or object always remains freedom from coercion in what concerns religious belief, worship, practice or observance, and public testimony. Hence the content of the right is the same both for the Catholic Church and for other religious bodies. In this sense, the Church claims nothing for herself which she does not also claim for them. The matter is different, however, with regard to the foundation of the right. The Catholic Church claims freedom from coercive interference in her ministry and life on grounds of the divine mandate laid upon her by Christ Himself (cf. below, note 13). It is Catholic faith that no other Church or Community may claim to possess this mandate in all its fullness. In this sense, the freedom of the Church is unique, proper to herself alone, by reason of its foundation. In the case of other religious communities, the foundation of the right is the dignity of the human person, which requires that men be kept free from coercion, when they act in community, gathered into Churches, as well as when they act alone.

The Documents of Vatican II, pp.681,682; n.9 p.682.

WORKS CITED

Abbot, Fr. Walter, SJ, Editor, *The Documents of Vatican II,* America Press, New York, 1966.

Brownson, Orestes A., *Brownson's Quarterly Review,* 23 Volumes, Boston, New York, 1844-1875.

Brownson, Orestes A., *The Convert, or Leaves from My Experiences, Works,* Volume V.
The Spirit Rapper, An Autobiography, Works, Volume IX.

Brownson, Henry F., *Brownson's Early Life, Brownson's Middle Life, Brownson's Latter Life,* H.F. Brownson, Detroit, 1898-1900.

Brownson, Henry F., Editor, *Brownson's Works,* Volumes I-XX, Thorndike Nourse, Detroit, 1882-1887.

Holden, Fr. Vincent, CSP., *The Yankee Paul: Isaac Thomas Hecker,* Bruce Publishing Company, Milwaukee, 1958.

Lapati, Americo D., *Orestes A. Brownson,* Twayne Publishers, New York, 1965.

Maynard, Theodore, *Orestes Brownson, Yankee, Radical, Catholic,* The Macmillian Co., New York, 1943.

Mendelsohn, Jack, *Channing: The Reluctant Radical,* Little, Brown and Co., Boston, 1971.

Ryan, Fr. Thomas R., CSSP., *Orestes A. Brownson: A Definitive Biography,* Our Sunday Visitor, Inc., Huntington, Indiana, 1976.

Scanlan, Fr. Michael J., *An Historical Sketch of the Parish of St. Rose, Chelsea, Massachusetts.*

Schlesinger, Arthur A., Jr., *Orestes A. Brownson: A Pilgrim's Progress,* Little, Brown and Co., Boston, 1939.

Swift, Lindsay, *Brook Farm,* The Macmillian Co., New York, 1900.

Theisen, Abbot Jerome, OSB., *The Ultimate Church and the Promise of Salvation,* St. John's University Press, Collegeville, Minnesota, 1976.

Whalen, Doran (Sr. Rose Gertrude Whalen, CSC.), *Granite for God's House,* Sheed and Ward, New York, 1941.

THE LOVE OF MARY

(*Brownson's Quarterly Review,* April, 1853)

Mary is the channel through which her Divine Son dispenses all his graces and blessings to us, and he loves and delights to load with his favors all who love and honor her. Thus to love and serve her is the way to secure his favor, and to obtain those graces which we need to resist the workings of concupicence, and to maintain the purity of our souls, and of our bodies, which are the temple of God. She says, "I love them that love me," and we cannot doubt that she will favor with her always successful intercession those whom she loves. She will obtain grace for us to keep ourselves chaste, and will in requital of our love to her obtain graces even for those without, that they may be brought in and healed of their wounds and putrefying sores. So that under either point of view the love and worship of Mary, the Mother of God, a mother yet a virgin, always a virgin, virgin most pure, most holy, most humble, most amiable, most loving, most merciful, most faithful, most powerful, cannot fail to enable us to overcome the terrible impurity of our age, and to attain to the virtues now most needed for our own individual salvation, and for the safety of society.

FATHER FEENEY (1950)

CONTENTS

INTRODUCTION

Orestes Brownson was received into the Catholic Church in Boston in 1844. Under the direction of Bishop Fitzpatrick he immediately began a vigorous campaign against the Native American persecution, stressing the necessity of the Catholic Church for salvation and at the same time demonstrating the complete compatibility of this claim with the duties of American citizenship. In 1949, just a little over a hundred years later, in the same city of Boston, four teachers were fired for accusing Boston College of teaching heresy, namely that it was possible to be saved outside the Catholic Church. When Father Feeney came to their defense, he was first silenced by the Archbishop of Boston, later expelled from the Society of Jesus, and finally "excommunicated" by Rome. Thirty two years later in 1972 on the initiative of Cardinal Medeiros of Boston and Bishop Flanagan of Worcester and with the approval of Pope Paul VI, Father Feeney was "reconciled" to the Catholic Church still professing the necessity of the Church and of submission to the Holy Father for salvation.

I have put the stories of these two courageous Catholics together, not just to show the difference that a hundred years made in the same city in the profession of the same Catholic doctrine, but mainly because their teachings on salvation admirably complement one another. Father Feeney did not show, as he probably should have, how the doctrine of extra ecclesiam nulla salus *was compatible with the American principle of religious freedom which was developed at length in Vatican Council II. Brownson treated this subject with great skill, especially in his* "Civil and Religious Toleration," *and it is part of the reason for his success in the campaign against the Know-Nothings. Also, although Father Feeney always thought that some persons who had* apparently *died as Protestants could have been saved (most notably Mother Seton's husband and father in his earlier writings), he never set forth the necessary conditions they would have had to meet. Again Brownson under the direction of Bishop Fitzpatrick, clearly spells out these conditions in* "The Great Question."

So while Brownson's treatment of the necessity of the Church for salvation is in general more complete than that of Father Feeney, there is one point I think in which Father Feeney's treatment is more accurate and more timely. The necessity of the sacrament of baptism for salvation was not under heavy attack in Brownson's time, and following St. Thomas Aquinas, he allowed one apparent exception to this necessity –

the case of a catechumen who had made a perfect act of love of God, but had been overtaken by death before the actual reception of the sacrament. In Father Feeney's time the necessity of baptism was, and still is, under heavy fire, and while he also followed St. Thomas in his first position paper, Reply to a Liberal, he later in his Bread of Life, in what turned out to be his final statement on the doctrine, adopted the opinion of St. Augustine who taught that a catechumen could not be saved in such circumstances.

The account which follows is drawn entirely from the major documents in the Father Feeney Case, and the interpretations expressed in the various introductions and footnotes are entirely my own, and do not necessarily represent the opinions of all the members of the various St. Benedict Center communities.

Leonard Feeney: In Memoriam

by

Fr. Avery Dulles, SJ.

(*America,* February 2, 1978)

INTRODUCTION

This book is not intended to be a biography of Father Feeney or a history of St. Benedict Center. I feel I am much too close to these events to be completely objective, so I have tried only to compile a summary of the major documents involved, confining my personal comments to the introductions and footnotes. But since the Father Feeney Case is now forty years old, a brief review at the beginning would certainly be in order.

One of the best summaries of the Case was written by Fr. Avery Dulles, S.J. at the time of the death of Father Feeney. Father Dulles, who was severely criticized by Father Feeney for his liberalism, was closely associated with St. Benedict Center only in the early forties, so some of the inaccuracies in his comments after that period are easily understandable. Although Father Dulles' appreciation is more sentimental than doctrinal, I am sure that Father Feeney, who was always grateful for any kindness, would have been pleased.

With the death of Leonard Feeney, at the age of 80, on Jan. 30, 1978, the United States lost one of its most colorful, talented and devoted priests. The obituary notices, on the whole, tended to overlook the brilliance of his career and to concentrate only on the storm of doctrinal controversy associated with his name in the late 1940's and early 1950's.

I knew Father Feeney only slightly before the spring of 1946, at which time I settled in Cambridge, Mass., for several months as I was completing my naval service and preparing to enter the Jesuit novitiate in August. I came to Cambridge in order to rejoin St. Benedict Center, a lively gathering place for Catholic students, which I had been instrumental in founding, together with Catherine Goddard Clarke, some five years earlier. Mrs. Clarke, a woman of charismatic charm and contagious enthusiasm, had run the Center almost unassisted until 1943, when she obtained the services of Leonard Feeney as spiritual director. Father Feeney was then at the height of his renown. As literary editor of America, he had become a prominent poet and essayist, much in demand on the lecture circuit. He had preached on important occasions at St. Patrick's Cathedral and had broadcast a series of sermons on "The Catholic Hour." But when he came to Cambridge he soon decided to make St. Benedict Center his single, exclusive and full-time apostolate.

By the time I returned in February 1946 the Center was teeming with activity. It was not simply a place where students could drop in for a cup of tea or a friendly chat, but also a bustling center of theological study and apostolic zeal. Equipped with an excellent Catholic library (with my own collection as part of the nucleus), the Center had set up interest groups of various kinds, most of which met in the evening on a weekly basis. For example, I joined a group led by Professor Fakhri Maluf, a Boston College professor, in which we exchanged papers, week by week, first on the angelology of St. Thomas and then on St. Bernard's doctrine of the love of God. With Fakhri and several others, I was part of a smaller group that systematically worked through Joseph Gredt's Latin textbook on scholastic philosophy, beginning with the formal logic. There was also a weekly evening on Dante, directed by Professor Louis Solano of the Harvard faculty, at which distinguished Boston converts, such as Daniel Sargent and Hugh Whitney, were frequent visitors. Other groups at the Center specialized in modern literature and dramatics. Shortly before leaving I took the primary responsibility for putting out the first issue of *From the Housetops*, a quarterly journal intended to disseminate the Center's vision of an integrally Catholic culture. Soon after I left, the Center was to become officially registered as a Catholic school eligible to receive benefits under the G.I. Bill of Rights.

Thursday nights at St. Benedict Center were, in a special way, for Father Feeney. He gave a carefully planned course of lectures, beginning with the act of faith and then passing on to the sacraments. His leading idea in these lectures seemed to be the integration of nature and grace. Faith he viewed as a sacrifice in which the believer offers to God the most excellent gift of reason. For the sacrifice to be meaningful it was essential, in Father Feeney's estimation, to have a proper esteem for the value of reason. In these lectures he therefore taught us to love the senses, the imagination, the memory and all the faculties of the mind. So, too, when he came to the sacraments, he labored to instill into his hearers a deep appreciation of the elements used in the church's rituals – water, oil, bread, wine and the like. Following the same pattern, when he spoke of celibacy, Father Feeney took great pains to communicate a high regard for Christian marriage, on the ground that the renunciation of marriage could not be an acceptable sacrifice unless one regarded marriage as truly good.

Not only was the doctrine solid; the oratory was superb. Never have I known a speaker with such a sense of collective psychology. Father Feeney would not come to his main point until he had satisfied himself that every member of the audience was disposed to understand and accept his message. In the early part of his lectures he would tell anecdotes, recite poems and in various ways gain the attention and good will of all his hearers. Totally aware of the reactions of every person in the room, he would focus his attention especially on those who seemed hostile, indifferent or distracted. When at length he had the entire audience reacting as a unit, he would launch into the main body of his talk, leading them from insight to insight, from emotion to emotion, until all were carried away, as if by an invisible force permeating the atmosphere.

Week by week the audience grew. Every seat in the auditorium was filled; then every foot of standing space was taken up, and at last people gathered in groups at every open door or window to catch whatever fragments they could of these Thursday-evening talks.

To Father Feeney, however, the popular lectures were not the most important part of his work. They were intended for a relatively wide public, not for the inner group of disciples. His main interest was in those who made the Center their principal occupation in life – those for whom it was a kind of family, school and parish all rolled into one. For this group Father Feeney would make himself available every afternoon, hearing confessions and giving personal direction. Later in the afternoon he would emerge for tea and a social hour. Then at suppertime a group of us would generally pile into Catherine Clarke's decrepit sedan so that we could continue our discussions over hamburgers in a restaurant. In the company of Catherine Clarke and Leonard Feeney conversation was never known to lag.

I regret that I did not make notes on some of Leonard Feeney's conversation. His table talk was brilliant and memorable. He would teach us to look on the world with fresh eyes and to delight as he did in the variety of God's creation. He was particularly fascinated by the animals, as appeared in many of his poems. One of them, written for children, begins characteristically: "Moo is a cow/ When she makes a bow/ To a meadow full of hay./Shoo is a hen/ When she's back again/ And you want her to go away."

As a spiritual director Father Feeney carefully trained his disciples. Although he was capable of sharp admonitions and rebukes, his general practice was to lead by positive encouragement. He was generous in praising others, both in their presence and when they were absent. When he noticed faults in the members of the group, he would correct these in a good-humored way, with playful mimicry, rhymes and puns. (For his views on the value and limits of the pun it would be worthwhile to read his little article, "How Much Do I Like a Pun?" *Am.*, 9/26/36.) Father Feeney's light-hearted mockery extended not only to members of the Center but to the public figures of the day. Parodying their rhetoric and mannerisms, he would deliver with mock solemnity imaginary speeches such as Al Smith on the fallacies in Descartes's philosophy ("putting Descartes before the horse"). Fulton Sheen on the merits of Coca-Cola ("Ho, everyone that thirsteth for the pause that refreshes!")) and Franklin Roosevelt on the decline of sacramental religion ("Some of our underprivileged are having to get along on two paltry sacraments, or even none"). In other imitations he presented Katharine Hepburn reporting a championship prizefight and Eleanor Roosevelt broadcasting the events of Good Friday.[1] We listened to these imitations with our sides splitting, almost sick with laughter. Then at a crucial moment Father Feeney would be likely to remove his clerical collar, put it over his head like a wimple and begin to speak in the broken English of Mother Cabrini.

But the humor, too, was only marginal to Father Feeney's real

---

[1] Eleanor Roosevelt broadcasting the events of Good Friday was not an original with Father Feeney, but was from his friend Clare Booth Luce. Father Feeney gradually dropped this skit from his repertoire, I suspect, because he considered Good Friday too sacred a subject for comedy.

concern. Most of all he enjoyed speaking directly about the truths of the Christian faith. With unbelievable vividness he would make the Gospel episodes come alive: scenes of the rich young man, of Zacchaeus in the sycamore tree and countless others. When he quoted from the letters of Paul one had the impression that Paul himself was speaking. To this day, I imagine St. Paul with the features and voice of Leonard Feeney.

While teaching us to love the New Testament (not only in English and Latin, but in the Greek text he always had at hand), Father Feeney led us also to study the fathers and doctors of the church. We easily memorized the list of the 29 doctors, and their names were more than names to us. Father Feeney taught us the issues that made Athanasius an exile from his native Egypt. He explained why Cyril stood up against Nestorius and why Augustine wrote fiery tracts against the Pelagians and the Donatists. Under his direction we came to appreciate the equable wisdom of Aquinas and the more intuitive metaphysics of Duns Scotus, who especially appealed to the poet in Feeney, as he had to Gerard Manley Hopkins. Father Feeney familiarized us, also, with the Christian poets. His memory never seemed to falter when he quoted from Hopkins or Francis Thompson, from Belloc or Chesterton or, in English translation, from Peguy or Claudel.

In addition to the lore of historical theology and Christian poetry, we were introduced into the profundities of speculative theology. Here again the oral teaching of Leonard Feeney was our principal guide. Outside St. Benedict Center, was there any place in the world where lay people in our day were so eagerly discussing the processions in the Blessed Trinity, the union of the two natures in Christ, the presence of Christ in the Mystical Body, the marvels of transubstantiation, the divinizing effects of sanctifying grace and role of Mary in God's plan of salvation?

The systematic theology that I learned from Father Feeney has stayed with me through the decades, while I have forgotten much of what I studied more recently. In part this is because he had an imcomparable gift for putting the deepest mysteries in the simplest terms, as may be seen, for example, from his masterly essay, "The Blessed Sacrament Explained to Barbara." It must also be said that at the Center the Catholic faith was never just abstract doctrine to be memorized for an examination but was always a truth to be lived and prayed. Nearly all the Center family were daily communicants and made great sacrifices of one kind or another to live their faith to the full. We had periodic days of recollection. Every evening at the Center ended with night prayers, when we would recite in common from memory the

Prologue to the Fourth Gospel and pray to the Blessed Virgin for protection and fidelity.

Life at the Center had an indelible effect on all the associates. Before long about 100 members of the Center community had accepted vocations to the priesthood or the religious life, and an equal number, I would estimate, entered into deeply Christian marriages. All the time, new members kept pouring in. At least 200, it is reported, became converts to the Catholic faith. All the Center's projects seemed to prosper. An option for some was to affiliate themselves permanently with the Center. Already when I was there the Center was beginning to take on certain characteristics of a religious community – one open to both men and women, single and married, with Father Feeney in the role of superior and novice master. Only later did St. Benedict Center draw up a rule of life for its members as "Slaves of the Immaculate Heart of Mary."

Were there, at the time I was present, any signs of the coming cataclysm? I did notice, toward the end of my stay, that Leonard Feeney was becoming increasingly polemical. His attacks on materialism, skepticism and agnosticism became sharper and more personal. He used bitter invective against Hume and Kant, Marx and Freud. At times he denounced "liberal Catholics" who had failed to support Genralissimo Franco. Even Jacques Maritain was in his eyes infected by the poison of liberal culture. Father Feeney's attitude toward the Jews was ambivalent. He felt that they could not achieve their true vocation except in Christ, but that when they accepted this vocation they excelled all other Christians. In his lectures and conversation he made us savor the total Jewishness of Mary, of Jesus and of Paul. He used to talk of a certain Jewish taxi driver in New York whom he had instructed in the faith and who had become, in Father Feeney's judgment, a true mystic.

On the question of salvation outside the church, Father Feeney had not as yet adopted any clear position. He was convinced that Catholics must not hesitate to present the full challenge of the Gospel, which for him included the whole system of official dogma. He felt that too many tended, out of politeness and timidity, to evade the task of forthright witness. As long as any person was alive, Father Feeney used to say, we should urge the necessity of his accepting the fulness of the faith. But after death, the situation was different. We could confidently leave our loved ones to the unfathomable mercy of God, to which we could set no limits. "I would infinitely rather be judged by God," Father Feeney would say, "than by my closest friend."[2] Hence the damnation of non-Catholics was not at that stage, as I recall, any part of the Feeney gospel.

How did Leonard Feeney later become a proponent of the rigid and almost Jansenistic position attributed to St. Benedict Center? I have no personal knowledge of what happened in the late 1940's. Perhaps Father Feeney was somewhat embittered by his encounters with the non-Catholic universities about him; perhaps, also, he was led into doctrinal exaggerations by his own mercurial poetic temperament. Then again, he and others may have been somewhat intoxicated by the dramatic successes of the Center and too much isolated from opinions coming from outside their own narrow circle. It occurs to me also that the religious enthusiasm of some of Father Feeney's convert disciples may have led him further than he would have gone on his own. He was ferociously loyal to his followers, especially those who had gone out on a limb to defend what they understood as his own teaching. Thus, when several faculty members at Boston College were dismissed for their teaching on salvation, he backed them to the hilt. From that moment the developments leading to Father Feeney's excommunication and to the interdiction of the Center were all but inevitable.

For those who loved and admired Father Feeney it was painful to see illustrated newspaper articles about him on Boston Common, flanked by burly bodyguards, shouting vulgar anti-Semitisms at the crowds before him. No doubt he did become angry and embittered in the early 1950's, but happily this was only a passing phase. St. Benedict Center, after it moved to Still River, Mass., in January 1958, became a different kind of community, more in keeping with the Benedictine spirit to which Father Feeney himself had long been attracted. Thus it became possible for the major portion of the community, including Father Feeney himself, to be reconciled to the Catholic Church in 1974. Two years later two members of this community were ordained to the priesthood so that they could carry on Father Feeney's ministry to the "pious union of Benedictine Oblates" that has sprung forth from the St. Benedict Center. It would have been tragic if Leonard Feeney, the great apostle of

2 Even after Father Feeney adopted his literal interpretation of "no salvation outside the Church," he never spoke of the damnation of individual Protestants. He remembered daily at the altar the parents of his disciples who had apparently died Protestant. In a recent talk show Cardinal O'Connor of New York was asked about "no salvation outside the Church." He is reported to have answered: "Well you have to hold that it means what it says, but this does not mean that we judge anyone. We leave non-Catholics to the mercy of God." This was Father Feeney's position exactly.

salvation within the church, had died excommunicate.

There are certain texts from the Bible that I can never read without hearing, in my imagination, the voice and intonations of Leonard Feeney. Among them is the following, which he frequently quoted in Latin from the liturgy for the Doctors of the Church: "The time of my departure has come. I have fought the good fight, I have kept the faith. Henceforth there is laid up for me the crown of righteousness, which the righteous judge, will award to me on that day, and not only to me but also to all who have loved His appearing." (2 Tim. 4:6-8.)

Cursum consummavi, fidem servavi: These words could serve as Leonard Feeney's epitaph. They express his overriding concern to resist any dilution of the Christian faith and to pass it on entire, as a precious heritage, to the generations yet to come. In an age of accommodation and uncertainty, he went to extremes in order to avoid the very appearance of compromise. With unstinting generosity he placed all his talents and energies in the service of the faith as he saw it.

A CHRONOLOGICAL OUTLINE
OF THE FATHER FEENEY CASE

Part I   From 1940, the founding of St. Benedict Center, through 1949,
the dismissal of Father Feeney from the Society of Jesus.

(Part I is taken almost entirely from *The Loyolas and the Cabots: The
Story of the Boston Heresy Case* by Catherine Goddard Clarke.)

INTRODUCTION

"Father Feeney entered the Jesuit Order when he was seventeen years old, from his home in Lynn, Massachusetts. He had two younger brothers and a sister. His two younger brothers became priests, also, one a Jesuit and the other a secular priest. Father's mother and father are still living, thank God. They have both been a source of strength and joy to us during what would have been, for most parents, a time of humiliation. They were taught 'our' doctrine as children, and they have never doubted our cause was any other than that of the Blessed Mother of God, for the protection of the Church of her Divine Son.

After he had made his Jesuit studies in America, Father Feeney was sent to England and France for further study. When he returned to the United States, he taught in the Graduate School at Boston College, and from there he was sent to New York, to be Literary Editor of *America,* the national Jesuit weekly. Father spent four years in New York, writing, editing, lecturing – part of the intellectual life of a great city.

Cardinal Hayes, of New York, was his friend, and so was Monsignor Lavelle, the Vicar General of the Archdiocese. Father gave the course of sermons for Advent, in St. Patrick's Cathedral. He lectured to Catholic audiences in New York, and from there went off for lectures all over the country.

He confessed, however, to being lonely for parish work, such as he had done in Manchester, England, while he was studying there. And so he found a small apostolate for himself among the taxicab drivers, in New York City. These friends have never left him. They have remained faithful to this day.

Father found work to do also among college students. His message to both groups was exactly the same. It is Father Feeney's message to everybody: the Holy Catholic Church for salvation; the Son of God in the Holy Eucharist for adoration; and Mary, God's Mother, for our Mother." [1]

[1] Clarke, Catherine Goddard, *Gate of Heaven,* Ravengate Press, Boston, 1952, pp.31,32.

March 19, 1940 St. Benedict Center, a student center for Catholics at Harvard and Radcliff, founded by Catherine Goddard Clarke.

> We decided on a name by which we would be known, and we dedicated the work to Mary, the Mother of God, under the patronage of St. Joseph. We chose for our name Saint Benedict Center. We had been studying the doctrine of the Mystical Body of Christ, and we felt that the spirit of St. Benedict embraced beautifully the doctrine of community living. Too, we were told that the college students, coming upon St. Benedict in their history courses, knew him and seemed to have affection for him.[1]

1942 Fr. Leonard Feeney, SJ. becomes Spiritual Director of Saint Benedict Center.

September, 1946 First issue of St. Benedict Center quarterly *From the Housetops* appears.

> The first issue of FROM THE HOUSETOPS came out in September 1946. It was well received. Monsignor Hickey called upon us to tell us how much he liked it. Monsignor Wright said that His Excellency, Archbishop Cushing (to whom we had gone when we first conceived the idea of the magazine, for his approval and blessing) would be glad to contribute some articles for it. In the December 1946 issue, Archbishop Cushing had an article in the HOUSETOPS entitled, "Catholics and Communism." In the March 1947 issue, His Excellency wrote on "The Catholic Chaplains"...
>
> The circulation of our magazine resembled very much the representation of people in the Center. Subscriptions came from countries in Europe, from India, the Near East, the Far East, South America,

---

[1] Clarke, Catherine Goddard, *The Loyolas and the Cabots,* Ravengate Press, Boston, 1950, pp.6,7.

Canada, most of the states of the United States, the Philippines. College libraries subscribed to it. Priests contributed to it; nuns wrote for it. We came to have a group of distinguished writers, as well as a list of distinguished readers.

As our message grew clearer, and our voice stronger, the general praise of us grew more wary. We were startling the Liberals [2] who had expected that under Father's direction the HOUSETOPS would take on the charming humor, the delightful wisdom, the joyous entertainment of his own earlier books. [3]

September, 1947 First article in HOUSETOPS to mention "No salvation outside the Church," "Sentimental Theology" by Fakhri Maluf, appears.

It was not until the second year, however, that the shouting FROM THE HOUSETOPS really pierced the ears of the Liberals. One article, principally, caught their attention. It was in Volume II, No. 1, the September, 1947, issue of the HOUSETOPS. It was called "Sentimental Theology," and was written by Fakhri Maluf...

Dr. Maluf had written in his article...

...I know I am not wasting punches at a straw man. Sentimental thinking about religious matters is very much with us today. A great deal of what is being said by Catholics today sounds in very sharp contrast with the accent of the authentic voice of the Church, teaching, warning, and defining. The sharp weapons of Christ are being blunted, and the strong, virile doctrines of the Church are being put aside in a conspiracy of silence.

[2] A complete explanation of what St. Benedict Center understands by the term "liberal" will be found in the article *Reply to a Liberal* by Raymond Karam, which appears in its entirety in Appendix I.
[3] Clarke, *Op. cit.,* pp.49,50.

While talking to a Catholic group recently, I was shocked to a realization of what is happening to the faith under the rising wave of liberalism. I happened to mention casually the Catholic dogma, *"There is no salvation outside the Church."* Some acted as if I were uttering an innovation they had never heard before, and others had the doctrine so completely covered with reservations and vicious distinctions as to ruin its meaning and destroy the effect of its challenge. In a few minutes, the room was swarming with the slogans of liberalism and sentimentalism, utterances which are beginning to have the force of defined dogma. Taken in their totality and in the manner in which they were used and understood by their utterers, these slogans constituted an outlook incompatable with the Catholic faith and with the traditions of the Church. "Salvation by sincerity," "Membership in the soul of the church," "Don't judge," "Don't disturb the good faith of unbelievers," "It is not charitable to talk about hell or to suggest that anybody may go there," and "Isn't faith a gift?" and "How about baptism of desire?" and so on. I am not concerned with these phrases as they might occur in a theological treatise with sufficient explanations and with only proportionate emphasis; I am rather concerned with a practical attitude of mind which seeks and selects precisely these phrases and builds them into a closed system of thought, ready to justify every act of cowardice and disloyalty to the Church...

...The Catholic Church does not proclaim the exclusive salvation of one race or one class of people, but invites every man to the great joy of being united with Christ in the communion of saints. The Catholic truth is not a sad story for which we need apologize; it is a proclamation of the greatest good news that could ever be told. No matter how sternly its message is phrased, it is still the one and only hope in the world. Only love and security can afford to be severe. When we say that outside the Church there is no salvation, we are also and at the same time announcing that inside the Church there is salvation. The world already knows the sad part of our story, because the world finds no salvation in the world. The Church does not have to tell unbelievers that they are in sin and in despair; they know that in the depths of their hearts. What is new to the world in the Christian story is that, through Mary, the gates of heaven are opened and that we are invited to become brothers of Jesus in the Eternal Kingdom of God. This is not a story which can be told with the subdued and hesitant voice of sentimental theology."

September, 1947, FROM THE HOUSETOPS, *No Salvation Outside the Church.* For the first time, censorship for our magazine was being talked about. Why, we asked ourselves? Other Catholic magazines had no *imprimatur.* Had we said something that was not sound doctrine? No, we were told, we hadn't, but we had said something controversial. Was a defined doctrine of the Church controversial? No one answered us. [4]

October, 1947 Archbishop Cushing publicly praises Father Feeney to capacity audience at St. Benedict Center.

Archbishop Cushing, in October of 1947, came to the Center. Notice of his coming had been posted, and the crowd which awaited his arrival, both inside the Center and outside in the little square, was so large that it was necessary to telephone for police officers to take care of the jam. Students were standing in every available place, even five abreast on the long radiators by the windows. Father Feeney presented Monsignor Hickey to the audience, and he, in turn introduced His Excellency.

Friends later told us that never had they heard Archbishop Cushing endorse anyone so wholeheartedly as he endorsed Father Feeney, in his speech to

[4] *Idem,* pp.53,73-75.

the Center that evening. Five times, in various ways. His Excellency said that the Center had the official sanction and gratitude of the Archdiocese. If ever there were anything he could do for us, the Archbishop told us and our guests, he would be very happy indeed to do it. He had known about and was grateful, he went on, for the religious vocations which had gone out from the Center. The Center students, he said, had the best teachers in the world.

"As regards Father Feeney," the Archbishop declared, "we feel about him the way the little boy felt, when he knelt down one night and said his prayers, this way: 'Dear God, please bless my mother and daddy, and all my aunts and uncles; and please, dear God, *please* take care of Yourself. If anything happens to *You,* the whole show's over!'" [5]

May 2, 1948 1200 friends of St. Benedict Center carry Infant Jesus of Prague in procession on Archbishop's grounds.

In February of 1948, a great honor came to St. Benedict Center. A statue of the Infant Jesus of Prague was presented to us, blessed by the Archbishop of Prague, His Excellency Josef Beran. The statue arrived on February 22nd, the day the Communists took over Czechoslovakia.

The story of the miraculous statue of the Infant Jesus of Prague is one familiar to almost every Catholic. It is a devotion which had been precious to Catholics for centuries, and grows more beautiful with time. Through it, the Christian pays homage to Him Who, even as an infant and Mary's child, was at the same time the King of Kings. The statue is dressed royally, in rich vestments for the King who was also the Great High Priest. The small right hand is raised in a Bishop's blessing, and on the infant head is a tall crown, majestic and heavy...

[5] *Idem,* pp.71,72.

On Sunday, May 2, 1948, over 1200 people from St. Benedict Center carried His Infant Majesty in procession through the grounds of His Excellency, the Archbishop, to the altar in the garden at the back of Archbishop's house. The Archbishop received us, and listened to the promises of the St. Benedict Center students to the Infant Jesus, Who was so beautifully symbolized in our statue, and to the addresses which followed the promises. Archduke Rudolph, of the House of Hapsburg, and Count Edmund Czernin, of Prague, were significantly among the speakers, significantly because both their families figured for centuries in the history of the miraculous statue of the Infant Jesus of Prague. It was through Count Czernin, who was a member of the Center, that the precious statue came to us. He told us:

"If Prague had remained faithful to the Infant Jesus, all that has befallen it today would not have happened. Devotion to the miraculous statue spread all over the world, and yet thousands of people in Prague knew nothing of it, cared to know nothing of it. We have had Chinese come to Prague, Americans come to Prague, people from everywhere, just to visit the statue, only to be told by someone who lived a few streets from it that he did not know where it was.

"This statue of yours is *exactly* like the original. If Prague goes down before the Communists, at least the Holy Infant is here, honored and beloved." [6]

August 25, 1948   Father Feeney ordered to Holy Cross By Jesuit Provincial.

August 25, 1948

Dear Father Feeney: PC

You are to go from St. Benedict Center to Holy

---

[6] *Idem,* pp.75,76.

Cross College. You are to report there on September 8th. This will give you time to report at Holy Cross and get things cleared up at St. Benedict Center. I am sure you will be very happy in your new position and will continue to do as wonderful work as you have in the past. I have already informed the Vicar General of this change.

(signed) *J.J. McEleney, S.J.*
Provincial

...Doctrine or Discipline! St. Benedict Center knew, as far back as the fateful September 8, 1948, the day on which Father Leonard Feeney was to leave the Center and report for duty as a teacher of English at Holy Cross College in Worcester, Massachusetts (outside the diocese of Boston), that failure by Father to go to Holy Cross would constitute for our liberal superiors an opportunity to obscure the doctrinal challenge by making the whole thing appear to be disciplinary...

Father's two shabby black bags were packed and waiting beside the door, not to take him on a lecture tour this time, but for the trip to Worcester, and away from us, for good...Father Feeney was asked to leave the diocese because the truth he was teaching was embarrassing to too many people. The feeling of College officials about the resignations of students from Harvard, and social Catholics with Harvard connections – on the one hand – and, on the other, the hierarchical policy of expediency, had conspired to bring about Father's removal from St. Benedict Center. The Church in Boston was saying, not so much in words so much as in action, "Hush, hush! Father Feeney. This isn't the time to preach the doctrine of No Salvation Outside the Church. There is a time for that, but this is not the time."

Not even with Christ saying through His Apostle, "Behold *now* is the acceptable time. Behold, *now* is the day of salvation?"

No, not even then.

Our choice finally lay between two courses of action: (1) Father Feeney's remaining at St. Benedict Center – in which case the doctrine would be upheld and championed, even though Father would appear as merely a disobedient priest, and St. Benedict's a center of recalcitrants. Or (2) Father would leave St. Benedict Center and go to Holy Cross – in which case the doctrine would be completely discredited and Liberal Catholicism more deeply entrenched than ever, with no challenge to it worth mentioning in the United States. With the first course there was, too, the hope of a hearing eventually, when Archbishop Cushing returned from Europe. With the second course Father Feeney's distinguished reputation as a Jesuit writer would be saved, and St. Benedict Center would enjoy its former esteem.

We chose the first course. We would so choose again. Despite the avalanche of prestige, power and politics which has been hurled upon us for over a year, despite the cry of "Discipline!" which has been made against our protest of "Doctrine!" people everywhere know that there is a group of Catholics who hold for the safeguarding of the Deposit of Faith in the way the Church has always protected the Faith for its children – by the unequivocal rendering of the defined doctrines of the Church. It were better that we should lose all we have than that the Truth should die...

We turned, finally to St. Thomas Aquinas for confirmation of what our consciences told us to be true. We found it in the *Summa Theologica*, Secunda Secundae, Question 104, Article 5, wherein St. Thomas distinguishes three kinds of obedience:

"Accordingly we may distinguish a threefold obedience; one, sufficient for salvation, and consisting in obeying when one is bound to obey; secondly, perfect obedience, which obeys in all things lawful; thirdly, indiscreet obedience, which obeys even in matters unlawful...(Moreover), it is written (Acts V 29): 'We ought to obey God rather than men.' NOW SOME-TIMES THE THINGS COMMANDED BY A SUPE-RIOR ARE AGAINST GOD. THEREFORE SUPERIORS ARE NOT TO BE OBEYED IN ALL THINGS,"...

It is true we were tempted to belittle our stand by asking ourselves the question: Are *you* the only orthodox Catholics? Are you the only group in the United States who are holding the doctrine of No Salvation Outside the Catholic Church or without personal submission to the Holy Father?

Father Feeney answered for us: "We hope not. However, we take great courage from the fact that the great Catholic saint and Doctor of the Church, St. Athanasius, was exiled five times and excommunicated by every Bishop in the East for holding out alone for Catholic doctrine. The creed which bears his name, the Athanasian Creed, states, 'Whosoever wishes to be saved, before all things it is necessary that he hold the Catholic Faith, which unless one preserves whole and inviolate without doubt he will perish eternally.'

"The great jurist and Chancellor of England, St. Thomas More, on trial for his life, was asked by the prosecutor, 'What More? You wish to be considered wiser and of better conscience than all the bishops and nobles of the realm?' St. Thomas More replied: 'My lord, for one bishop of your opinion I have a hundred saints of mine; and for one parliament of yours, and God knows of what kind, I have all the general councils for a thousand years.'" [7]

December, 1948 Article entitled "Liberal Theology and Salvation" by Raymond Karam appears in *Housetops*.

---

[7] *Idem,* pp.100,111-113,117,118.

January, 1949 Paper entitled "Some Observations on the Question of Salvation Outside the Church" by Philip Donnelly, SJ., head of Department of Theology at Weston College, circulated at Boston College and Harvard.

January 17, 1949 Father Feeney and Catherine Clarke found religious commuinity, The Slaves of the Immaculate Heart of Mary.

We took our vows and became Slaves of Our Lady's Immaculate Heart on the 17th of January, 1949...

We live a community life, as Slaves of the Immaculate Heart of Mary, with hours of prayer, hours of study, and hours of work. Father Feeney and the young men who some day hope to be ordained priests live in one of our houses known to us as Sacred Heart Hall. Our girls who have dedicated their lives in singleness to Our Lord and Our Lady, live in a house which we call, among ourselves, Immaculate Heart Hall. Our families live in houses just below Sacred Heart Hall.[8]

January 24, 1949 Three professors at Boston College, members of St. Benedict Center, protest liberal teachings at college to Rector, Fr. William Keleher, SJ.

---

[8] Clarke, Catherine Goddard, *Gate of Heaven,* Ravengate Press, Boston, 1952, pp.138-140. The title "Slaves of the Immaculate Heart of Mary" was from Sister Catherine and was inspired by St. Louis Marie de Montfort's *True Devotion to the Blessed Virgin* and William Thomas Walsh's *Our Lady of Fatima* which we were all reading at the time. This editor was among the 20 or so members of St. Benedict Center who took simple, private vows on the night of January 17, 1949: "I promise to make the first interest of my life the doctrinal crusade of St. Benedict Center, and I promise obedience to Father, and to whomever he may delegate." Thus the "doctrinal crusade" plus the Slavery to the Immaculate Heart of Mary were the original charisms of our religious community.

Cambridge, Mass.
January 24, 1949.

Very Rev. William L. Keleher, S.J.,
President, Boston College,
University Heights,
Chestnut Hill 67, Mass.

Dear Father Keleher:

It is a matter of conscience with us to inform you, as the Rector of Boston College, that we are scandalized and grievously concerned about some of the doctrines being taught in this college, and we are especially concerned about the salvation of souls entrusted to the care of the faculty of Boston College. We have intimated to you before, in personal discussions, our worry, and it is clear you have done absolutely nothing about it.

We are placing before your conscience the duty of thoroughly investigating whether, among other things, implicitly or explicitly, the following heresies are being taught at Boston College: (1) that there is salvation outside the Church; (2) that any man can be saved without submission to the authority of our Holy Father the Pope.

Respectfully yours,

Charles Ewaskio
Fakhri Maluf
James R. Walsh. [9]

February 11, 1949 Members of St. Benedict appeal to Pope Pius XII.

St. Benedict Center decided to write His Excellency, Archbishop Cushing, a candid statement of its feelings. The letter was delivered at Archbishop's

---

[9] Clarke, Catherine Goodard, *The Loyolas and the Cabots,* Ravengate Press, Boston, 1950, pp.145,155.

House that evening. No answer to it, however, was ever received, and St. Benedict Center was then at a loss to know where next to turn. The words and actions of the Archbishop and Bishop grew every day more Liberal, and both they and the Jesuit Order were bringing to bear upon us more and more pressure. We knew that every Catholic had the right, in a matter of doctrine, to appeal directly to the Holy Father, and so, out of our completest need, we brought our problem to the Chair of Peter.

St. Benedict Center
23 Arrow Street
Cambridge, Massachusetts.

Feast of Our Lady of Lourdes,
February 11, 1949.

To His Holiness, Pope Pius XII,
Vatican City.

Your Holiness:

We, your faithful children, watchful for the preservation of our Holy Faith and deeply concerned about the rising and most imminent danger of false doctrines being fostered and spread even by Catholic colleges and seminaries, wish to place this anguish of soul before Your Holiness, and on our part and on the part of hundreds of our colleagues and students who share our concern and who, after constant prayer, feel we must come to you personally, the Vicar of Our Lord and Saviour on earth, to say to you what the Apostles said to the Master, "Save us, for we perish!"

We are convinced that in this our country there is at this moment a very real and grievous threat to the integrity of our Holy Faith. The wave of error is not beyond control yet, but it will be very soon if not checked, for the poison of false doctrine is spreading by means of educational institutions, magazines, newspapers, books, even receiving official Catholic approval, and the people to whom the Faith is still the pearl of great price can only appeal to you, the successor of St. Peter, for protection.

The insidious heresy that there may be salvation outside the Catholic Church and that submission to the Supreme Pontiff is not necessary for salvation has been taught by implication in many ways but is now getting to be more and more of an explicit teaching.

In more than one way people are made to believe that a man may be saved in any religion provided he is sincere, that a man may have baptism of desire even while explicitly refusing baptism of water, that a man may belong to the soul of the Church while persisting in his enmity to the true Catholic Church, indeed even while actively persecuting the Church.

These dangerous doctrines are beginning to manifest themselves even in the practical order in such popular demonstrations as interfaith meetings where a common denominator is sought, giving people to believe that something less than the entirety and integrity of the Catholic Faith may be sufficient for salvation, to the detriment of every dogma that is peculiar to the Catholic Church. Such slogans as "one religion is as good as another"; "we are saved by personal sincerity"; the "things on which we agree are vastly more important than the things on which we differ" – such slogans are being accepted even by Catholics as substitutes for the Creed.

We assure Your Holiness, as your most loyal children, that if this avalanche is allowed to continue, it will lead to a veritable catastrophe to the Kingdom of Christ and for the scandal and perdition of souls. We will be always ready, at the command of Your Holiness, to present documentary evidence in support of our concern.

We have the honor to be
Your Holiness, humble servants in Jesus and Mary,

Fakhri Maluf
Asst. Professor of Philosophy, Boston College
Catherine Clarke,
President, St. Benedict Center...
James R. Walsh,
Instructor in Philosophy, Boston College
Charles Ewaskio,
Asst. Professor of Physics, Boston College...
David Supple,
Instuctor in German, Boston College High School.[10]

February 24, 1949 Teachers at Boston College and Boston College High
School, members of St. Benedict Center, appeal to
General of Jesuits, Fr. Jean Baptiste Janssens, SJ.

90 Putnam Ave.,
Cambridge, Massachusetts.
Feast of St. Matthias,
February 24, 1949.

The Very Rev. Jean Baptiste Janssens, S.J.,
General of the Society of Jesus,
Borgo Santo Spirito 5,
Rome, Italy.

Dear Father General:

We are appealing to you on a matter of great
gravity, involving the protection of our Holy Faith
and the salvation of many souls.

We are professors at Boston College, which is
under the direction of the Society of Jesus. We are
convinced that at Boston College many doctrines are
being taught by members of the Society of Jesus
which are contrary to defined dogmas of the Faith.
They are teaching implicitly and explicitly that there

---

[10] Clarke, *Op. cit.,* pp.159,160. This is the first of two appeals made by members of
St. Benedict Center to the Holy Father: this one written in simple, child-like
language, the second in more legal form.

218 THEY FOUGHT THE GOOD FIGHT

may be salvation outside the Catholic Church, that a man may be saved without admitting that the Roman Church is supreme among all the churches, and that a man may be saved without submission to the Pope. We assure you that we would not have appealed to your high office unless we had exhausted every legitimate means of alerting all the proximate authorities of the Society without avail. We further assure you that we have very ample evidence to support our charges, which evidence will be produced at your demand.

We are Your Reverence's humble servants in Christ,

Fakhri Maluf
Asst. Prof. of Philosophy at Boston College
James R. Walsh
Instructor in Philosophy at Boston College
Charles Ewaskio
Asst. Professor of Physics, Boston College...
David Supple
Instructor of German, Boston College High School.[11]

April 5, 1949 Acknowledgment of appeal to Holy Father received from Monsignor Giovanni Battista Montini, Pro-Secretary of State, later Pope Paul VI.

Vatican City, March 25, 1949.

SEGRETERIA DI STATO
DI
SUA SANTITA

N. 196925/SA

The Secretariat of State, at the gracious bidding of the Holy Father acknowledges receipt of the document submitted to Him by Mr. Fakhri Maluf, and

[11] *Idem,* pp.171,172.

bearing the signatures of various Professors of Boston College High School and of St. Benedict Center, and while communicating that it has been forwarded to the Supreme Congregation of the Holy Office for consideration and attention, has pleasure in assuring the signatories that His Holiness, appreciating the Catholic sentiments which prompted their gesture, cordially imparts to them His paternal Apostolic Blessing.

(stamped with the seal of the secretariat of State)[12]

April 13, 1949 Fakhri Maluf, James Walsh, Charles Ewaskio, and David Supple, four teachers whose names appeared on appeal to General of Jesuits, fired from Boston College and Boston College High School.

Boston College
University Heights
Chestnut Hill 67
Massachusetts.

Office of the President   April 11, 1949

Dr. Fakhri Maluf,
90 Putnam Avenue,
Cambridge, Massachusetts.

Dear Doctor Maluf:

I have just received from Father Janssens word of your letter to him under date of February 24th. In connection with this matter, I would like to see you in my office on Wednesday, April 13th, at 2:30 p.m.
In the event that any teaching assignment here at Boston College may conflict with this hour, I have notified the various deans that I shall expect you here

---

[12] *Idem*, p.172.

and they will take care of the classes.

> Very sincerely yours,
> (signed) William L. Keleher, S.J.
> President.

Mr. Charles Ewaskio and Mr. James Walsh received letters identical to Dr. Maluf's...

Fr. Keleher:[13]

> "I have written to you in connection with the letter you sent to the General of the Jesuit Order. I have received instructions to the effect that the signatories of that letter be presented singly before a Board of one priest and two laymen and be asked certain questions by me."

Dr. Maluf:

> "Your letter invited us to meet with you personally, Father, and if we are to be presented before a Board we should have been given the right to know that ahead of time."

Fr. Keleher:

> "This arrangement was indicated to me by the General and I was asked to send you only the information that was given you in the letter. And besides, the members of the Board are not going to ask any questions, because I am going to do all the talking."

Dr. Maluf:

> "What directions you might have received from the General do not concern us. We are shocked at the way the General handled our appeal, because we made it clear to him that

[13] All important converstions were recorded from memory in "The Center Log" as soon as possible after they had occurred.

we had no confidence in you to be the judge
in this matter. And whatever directions you
have received from him, we still feel that it
is our right to know what we were invited
for and whom we were invited to meet. In
your letter you explicitly invited us to meet
you, personally."

Fr. Keleher:

"You will merely be asked to retract your
statements and, in case you refuse to do
that, your connection with Boston College
will be severed as of this moment.".…

The three teachers walked out of the President's
Office dismissed, for doctrine, from Boston College.
This dismissal affected also one other teacher, since
the General had included all signers of his letter.
David Supple, instructor in German at Boston College High School, had signed the letter. He could not
in conscience retract, and so he, too, lost his job…

The report of one morning newspaper, the *Boston
Post,* for Thursday, April 14th, is similar to that
carried in the other Boston papers. The *Post* account
read:

FOUR B.C. TEACHERS
FIRED AFTER PROBE

College President Discharged Them, They Claim,
When They Refused to Retract Statements Made to
General of Jesuit Order – Charged Father Keleher
with "Heresy" – One of Men is Teacher in B.C. High
School – Other Three on College Faculty – Had Been
Told Theories They Held Not Approved – Final
Action Immediate.

Four columns of the story followed with a clear
statement of the propositions which the teachers had
accused Boston College of teaching, in their letter to

the General of the Jesuits. The *Boston Post* said:

> The propositions which were accused to the General are – at Boston College are taught both explicitly and implicitly that (1) there may be salvation outside of the Catholic Church; (2) that a man may be saved without admitting that the Catholic Church is supreme among the churches; (3) that a man may be saved without submission to the Pope...

...The *Boston Evening Globe,* April 14th, 1949, carried it in headlines on the front page:

B. C. REPLIES TO
OUSTED TEACHERS

...Father Keleher's statement today was as follows:

"These gentlemen in question were under contract at Boston College to teach philosophy and physics. They had been cautioned by me and others to stay within their own fields and leave theology to those who were adequately and competently prepared.

"They continued to speak in class and out of class on matters contrary to the traditional teaching of the Catholic Church, ideas leading to bigotry and intolerance.

"Their doctrine is erroneous and as such could not be tolerated at Boston College. They were informed that they must cease such teaching or leave the faculty." [14]

April 18, 1949 Father Feeney supports "Four Professors."

Father Feeney then decided that this was the time for him to come to the defense of the four teachers... And so he released a statement to the press...

It read as follows:

[14] *Idem,* pp.185,186,190,195,196.

"I was very much surprised to learn from newspaper reports that Father Keleher had said that a profession – and where needed, an explanation – of the truths of our Holy Faith, which Father Keleher seems to have relegated to a specialist under the title 'theology,' is forbidden any Catholic teacher speaking to Catholic students at a Catholic college. Inasmuch as very few – I might almost say a bare minimum – of the classes are directly concerned with religion and in the hands of what the President calls 'competent theologians,' this procedure would leave the principles of our Holy Faith almost totally unmentioned for the greater part of the four-year course of a college boy's life."

I know many erroneous things that have been uttered by irresponsible teachers in Catholic colleges, but why the three basic premises of Catholic life, – the very direction signs by which one finds it, – should be forbidden Professor Maluf, Professor Walsh, and Professor Ewaskio is beyond my competence to understand."...[15]

April 19, 1949   Father Feeney silenced and St. Benedict Center placed under interdict by Archbishop Cushing.

Each newspaper gave the entire text of the Archbishop's ruling against us, with the decree, which was as follows (*Boston Globe,* April 19, 1949)

Text of Decree
on Fr. Feeney

"Rev. Leonard Feeney, S.J., because of grave offense against the laws of the Catholic Church has lost the right to perform any priestly function, including preaching and teaching of religion."

Any Catholics who frequent St. Benedict's Center, or who in any way take part in or assist its activities

15 *Idem,* p.209.

forfeit the right to receive the Sacrament of Penance and Holy Eucharist.

"Given at Boston on the 18th day of April, 1949.

"Richard J. Cushing,
Archbishop of Boston." [16]

May 28, 1949 Father Feeney appeals to Holy Father.

May 28, 1949

To Pope Pius XII

Your Holiness:

It is with the deepest anguish that I write to you, the Vicar of Christ on earth, to ask you to protect me in the crusade which God has given me to wage in Your defense and in the defense of our Holy Faith in the United States of America...

Your Holiness must believe me when I tell You that the condition of the Church in the United States of America in the matter of doctrine is utterly deplorable. There is no doubt about it that we are slowly becoming a National Church, controlled not in the least by Your Holiness, but by the National Catholic Welfare Council of Washington, D.C. Americans are not being taught the Catholic Faith as it is contained in the writings of the Fathers and the Doctors and in the definitions of the Councils of the Church. They are being taught what a committee of extremely deficient American theologians think will interest the American mind without ever embarrassing or challenging it.

I am writing this letter to Your Holiness simply, and as a child. Your Holiness may see already that it is not a legally organized document. It is a cry of

16 *Idem,* pp.219,220.

anguish from my priestly heart. In order not to tire you with too many details, may I tell you in brief statement what is the fundamental heresy universally taught by Catholics, priests and teachers, in the United States of America. This is the doctrine which American Catholics are being taught.

"The way to be saved is by being sincere to your convictions and living a good life. If one of your convictions happens to be that the Roman Catholic Church is the true Church of Christ then you are obliged to join it. If you do not sincerely think it is the one way to salvation, then you are invincibly ignorant and God will save you, apart from the Church. You are then said to belong to the soul of the Church, and whatever you desire for yourself in the way of salvation, Catholic theologians are prepared to call 'Baptism of Desire.' Were you to sincerely think that the Roman Catholic Church is not the true Church of Christ, it would be a sin for you to join it."

Your Holiness, I assure You in all my honour, in the sanctity of my Sacrament and whatever voice I have to be heard in profession of Faith, that the above statement is the substance of what is being taught all Americans as the means of eternal salvation. I am bold enough to say that You know what I am telling You is the truth. There is no Pope in history who has been as close to the American mind as you have been. I personally heard you speak in New York City when I was one of the editors of *America*, and I know that this is true. Every day you defer calling a halt to the wild Liberalism of the American hierarchy, a Liberalism which pays not the slightest attention to Your messages against Interfaith movements and against exposing our Catholics to the dangers of heretical perversion, the more will grow the spirit of indifference and apostasy in our land, and ten years from now will be too late to save it. I know along with this challenge which I offer to Your Holiness, while prostrate at Your feet in reverence and love, there go thousands of graces to enable You as Christ's Vicar to save this world for our Holy Faith. Unless You are the thundering leader of the world, other thunderers will take Your place, be they the Hitlers, the Mussolinis, the Stalins or the Roosevelts, who have already so confused the world that is waiting for our Pontiff to speak.

...Every one of my thousands of readers in America knows that I will never give up my Faith, and many are scandalized that I received so little protection in my profession of it. I beseech the protection of the Vicar of Christ on earth.

With profoundest respect, I am...

(signed) Father Leonard Feeney, SJ. [17]

---

[17] This letter to the Holy Father which was sent in 1949 did not appear in *The Loyolas and the Cabots* which came out in 1950, presumably because Father Feeney was still hoping for an answer at that time. The letter was first made public in 1953 in *Saints to Know and Love* by the Slaves of the Immaculate Heart of Mary published by St. Benedict Center.

Father Feeney was completely crushed by the failure of the Holy Father to support him in his doctrinal stand. He thought that his condemnation must somehow have been brought about without the Holy Father's knowledge or consent. Yet Cardinal Wright, the auxiliary Bishop of Boston at the time of the condemnation, later wrote:

"...It was suggested that I should make a trip to Rome to answer certain questions about the movement in the mind of the astonished Supreme Pontiff. The 'Boston Heresy' was inevitably condemned by the then Holy Office over the signature of Cardinal Marchetti-Selvaggiani, but the Pope personally wished to supervise and, indeed, *make* the official English translation which would be sent to the Archbishop of Boston for promulgation in the battle zone. As a result I spent three hours one sunny morning in the Holy Father's study at Castelgandolfo while he personally, with infinite care, reviewed and revised a document which would mean so much to the peace of mind of thousands.

I shall never forget how painstaking, precise and scholarly was the Chief Shepherd of Christendom as he labored on a document designed to restore peace to a relatively small corner of the Christian world...When the work of translation

September 3, 1949 Portions of letter dated August 8, 1949 from Holy Office to Archbishop Cushing published in *The Pilot,* official organ of the Archdiocese of Boston.

HOLY OFFICE CONDEMNS
TEACHINGS AND ACTIONS
OF ST. BENEDICT'S CENTER

An official letter has been received by Archbishop Cushing from the Supreme Sacred Congregation of the Holy Office, through the Apostolic Delegate in Washington, the Most Rev. Amleto G. Cicognani, answering what are called "the opinions and contentions" of the followers of Saint Benedict's Center in Cambridge. Included in this group are four young professors who accused the faculty of Boston College of teaching heresy, and two students of Emmanuel College who resigned from that institution on the eve of Commencement last Spring. The letter from Rome bears the signature of His Eminence Cardinal Marchetti-Selvaggiani.

The Holy office, over which the Pope himself presides, is the Congregation which safeguards the teaching of faith and morals. The Roman pronouncement reveals that this Sacred Congregation met in plenary session on Wednesday, July 27, 1949, and that the decisions set forth in this letter were approved by His Holiness, Pope Pius XII, in an audience on the following day.

The Holy Office declares: "This Sacred Congregation is convinced that the unfortunate dispute is due to an insufficient study and understanding of the well known dictum 'Extra Ecclesiam nulla salus,' and

was done to his satisfaction he read it through with great silence and, again, great solicitude. I remember that he closed his eyes as if in prayer when he had finished the reading of the English version and then with a gesture of finality, he put it to one side."
Wright, Cardinal John, "Pope Pius XII: A Personal Recollection," *The Pilot,* March 26, 1976, Boston.

that the dispute has been rendered more acrimonious because of the serious disturbance of discipline occasioned by the refusal of some members of the aforementioned group to revere and obey duly constituted authority." The Sacred Congregation refers to the axiom as "an incontestable principle," but continues: "However, this doctrine must be understood in the sense in which the Church herself understands it. Surely it in not to private judgment that Our Savior committed for exposition the deposit of faith, but to the teaching of the Church."

The Roman letter points out that the teachings of Saint Benedict's Center are inconsistent with pronouncements of His Holiness Pope Pius XII concerning the relationship to the Church of those who are not of the Fold. The Holy Office condemns the teaching of the Cambridge group in these terms: *"From all the foregiong it is clear that the doctrine presented by the periodical* FROM THE HOUSETOPS *(Vol.3) as genuine Catholic teaching, is far from being such, and can do nothing but grave harm both to those who are in the Church and to those outside it."*

With regard to recent actions of the Center leaders, the Holy Office employed severe terms of censure, declaring it beyond understanding how St. Benedict's Center can consistently claim to be a Catholic school, and desire to be called such, while actually refusing to conform to the prescriptions of Canon Law, and while functioning as a source of discord and revolt against Church authority, and as a cause of great upset to many consciences."

The letter singled out by name the sole priest associated with the Center and declared: "Similarly it is beyond understanding how a member of a religious society, namely Father Feeney, can present himself as a 'defender of the faith,' and at the same time not hesitate to attack the catechetical teaching proposed by legitimate authorities, and not even fear to bring upon himself the weighty sanctions of Canon Law leveled against his grave violations of duty as a religious, as a priest, and as an ordinary member of the Church."

The Sacred Congregation reproved the publishing activities of Saint Benedict Center, saying: "...it is nowise to be borne that Catholics should arrogate to themselves the right to publish a magazine for spreading theological doctrines without that permission of competent Church authority which is called an 'imprimatur,' and which is exacted by Canon Law."

Center spokesmen have repeatedly declared that they would be content only with a pronouncement from the Holy See itself. The letter from the Holy Office points out that now "Rome has spoken," and ends with a solemn warning to the dissident group "at the peril of their souls" immediately to return to Church unity in belief and practice....

The next day many of the newspapers pilloried us in the headlines and in the news. The *Boston Daily Record* ran two-inch headlines which screamed from every news stand: POPE ASSAILS FEENEY GROUP – Censures St. Benedict's Center As Source of Discord and Revolt. The *Boston Daily Globe* wrote:

VATICAN CONDEMNS
CAMBRIDGE CENTER

The Vatican has condemned the teachings of the St. Benedict Center, Cambridge, and has warned Rev. Leonard Feeney, S.J., four discharged Boston College professors and their followers at the Center that they remain outside the authority of the Catholic Church "at the peril of their souls," it was revealed last night.

Announcement that Rome had acted in the matter of the doctrinal dispute was made by Archbishop Cushing, who disclosed that the Vatican ruling was contained in an official letter from the Supreme Sacred Congregation of the Holy Office...

The story went on for columns.

The next serious consequence, from the standpoint of doctrine, was headlined in the *Worcester Telegram,* for Friday morning, September 2, 1949. We sent this first page of the *Worcester Telegram* to the Holy Office. The headlines ran:

VATICAN RULES
AGAINST HUB
DISSIDENTS
holds no salvation
outside church
Doctrine *to be false* (the italics are ours)

There it was, plain as day. The Vatican holds No salvation Outside the Church to be a *false* doctrine. No one could deny that this was one wolf the shepherds had let into the sheepfold. That the *Worcester Telegram* should draw this conclusion is not surprising. It would have been surprising if someone had not drawn it.[18]

October 10, 1949 Father Feeney dismissed from the Society of Jesus.

In the name of the Lord:

10, October, 1949

...Fr. Leonard Feeney, solemnly professed and a member of the New England Province of the Society of Jesus, received an order under Holy Obedience on

---

[18] Clarke, Catherine Goddard. *The Loyolas and the Cabots,* Ravengate Press, Boston, 1950, pp.289-294.

This letter of the Holy Office to the Archbishop of Boston has never been put in the *Acta Apostolicae Sedis* ("The Acts of the Apostolic See.") It appeared in Denzinger (the *Enchiridion Symbolorum*) for the first time in the 1963 edition. Fr. Karl Rahner, SJ., who had been the editor up to that time, gives as his source for this document, not the usual *Acta,* but *The American Ecclesiastical Review,* which is highly unusual, to say the least.

the 21st day of April 1949 from the Superior of his Province which was given in the city of Cambridge, Massachusetts (U.S.A.) where he was residing, that he proceed within twenty four hours to the College of the Holy Cross in Worcester...

...Considering the obstinacy involved the following questions officially proposed must be answered by this final sentence:

1. Whether it is certain that there is a crime of serious and permanent disobedience, after virtually three warnings in this case.

2. Whether the failure of amendment is certain.

3. Whether Fr. Leonard Feeney should be dismissed from the Society of Jesus...

To the first AFFIRMATIVE...
To the second AFFIRMATIVE...
To the third AFFIRMATIVE...

Wherefore by the authority which the Sacred Cannons give us, we declare Fr. Leonard Feeney dismissed from the Society of Jesus.

John Baptist Janssens
Superior General of the Society of Jesus
President of this Tribunal[19]

[19] St. Benedict Center Archives. Translation from the Latin by John Post.

It should be noted that Father Feeney was expelled from the Society of Jesus, not for doctrinal, but for disciplinary reasons, namely his refusal to go to Holy Cross. The Jesuits steadfastly refused to give Father Feeney a doctrinal hearing. Frank Sheed who was Father Feeney's friend, but no friend of his doctrine, wrote in his autobiography:

"...He [Father Feeney] was condemed but not answered. When Boniface VIII said in the bull *Unam Sanctam* that it was 'altogether necessary for salvation for every human creature to be subject to the Roman Pontiff,' he seemed to be saying not only what Father Feeney was condemned for saying, but what a vast number of yesterday's Catholics had grown up believing. Everybody would have been helped by a full-length discussion." Sheed, Frank, *The Church and I,* Doubleday and Co., Garden City, New York, 1974, p.166.

PART II

From 1950, the encyclical *Humani Generis,*
through 1952, the excommunication of Father Feeney.

(Part II is taken almost entirely from the *The Loyolas and the Cabots,
Part II: A Documentary Survey* compiled by the archivist of St.
Benedict Center.)

1950   *The Loyolas and the Cabots*, a history of St. Benedict Center
        from 1940 to 1950, By Catherine Goddard Clarke, appears.

August 21, 1950 Encyclical *Humani Generis* of Pope Pius XII appears.

> ...The *New York Times* telephoned and asked for
> Father Feeney.
> "We have the translation of the Pope's encyclical,
> *Humani Generis*," the *Times* man said, "and we have
> checked his pronouncement on no salvation outside
> the Church with the release you gave us when you
> were silenced. In that release you said theologians
> today are making the doctrines of the Church abso-
> lutely meaningless. Did you know the Pope says the
> same thing in his new encyclical? He says, 'Some
> reduce to a meaningless formula the necessity of
> belonging to the True Church in order to gain salva-
> tion.' Will you give us a statement?"
> The editions of the *New York Times* for the next day
> carried Father Feeney's statement, and newspapers
> all over the United States printed the United Press
> release of Father's story of his joy and relief - for the
> salvation of souls - at the Holy Father's confirmation
> of the Church's solemn doctrine.[1]

1952 *Gate of Heaven* by Catherine Goddard Clarke appears, a popular
     defense of the doctrinal postion of St. Benedict Center substan-
     tially the same as that of *Reply to a Liberal* which appears in its
     entirety in Appendix I.

1952 *Bread of Life*, a collection of lectures by Father Feeney given at St.
     Benedict Center, appears.

---

[1] Clarke, Catherine Goodard, *Gate of Heaven,* Ravengate Press, Boston, 1952,
p.23.
   This editor was present when the call from the *New York Times* came in. It was
Sister Catherine's birthday and when Father Feeney announced the news, there
was wild cheering for several minutes. Father then made a little speech which
began, "Now that we've won, we don't want to lose our high ideals..." We all
thought at the time that it was all over – little did we know.

September 4, 1952 Father Feeney receives letter from Archbishop Cushing threatening to reduce him to the lay state.

ARCHDIOCESE OF BOSTON
One Lake Street
Brighton 35, Massachusetts
(SEAL)

Office of the Archbishop   September 4, 1952

Rev. Leonard Feeney
c/o St. Benedict Center
23 Arrow Street
Cambridge 38, Massachusetts

Dear Father Feeney:

By direction of the Supreme Sacred Congregation of the Holy Office, with the complete approval of His Holiness, Pope Pius XII, I am ordered to invite you to come to me and to make explicit profession of your submission both to the local Ordinary and to the Apostolic See. This profession is to be made on or before the fourth day of the month of October, 1952. I pray and hope that you will humbly comply with this order of the Sacred Congregation and of the Holy Father. If, unfortunately, you should refuse to do so, the same Congregation, with the full approval of the Holy Father, has ordered me to tell you at this time that you will be reduced to the lay state. With paternal interest, I shall await your priestly response to this invitation. It will be a pleasure to arrange an appointment for you. You may ask for it either by writing to me or by telephoning me at the Chancery office or at my own home.

By direction of the same Sacred Congregation, again with the full approval of the Holy Father, you are also warned to desist immediately from your activities as leader of the St. Benedict Center movement, under threat of still graver punishments to be determined by the Sacred Congregation.

The Holy Office, with the full approval of the Holy Father, has placed St. Benedict Center under local interdict and yourself under personal interdict. The local interdict applies to all properties owned and controlled by St. Benedict or its members. As you know, it forbids "divine office, or sacred rite," for example, the celebration of Mass, administration of the Sacraments, preaching, etc. These interdicts are in force immediately, but their existence will not be published at the present time. I am praying and hoping that you will submit voluntarily to the wishes of the Sacred Congregation and of the Holy Father. If you do not do so, however, it will be necessary to publish these interdicts, after October 4th, 1952.

For your further knowledge and guidance, the Holy Office, with the full approval of the Holy Father, has ordered the publication of the entire text and translation of the letter sent to me by the same Sacred Congregation under date of August 8, 1949. You have already received from me copies of this letter; for your convenience, I enclose herewith copies of the original text and the officially approved translation.

The Holy Office, with the approval of His Holiness, the Pope, has also ordered the withdrawal from circulation of the book GATE OF HEAVEN. The author, Mrs. Catherine Goddard Clarke, has been notified of this order.

May the grace of God guide and keep you

Faithfully yours in Christ,

+ Richard J. Cushing
Archbishop of Boston.[2]

---

2 *The Loyolas and the Cabots, Part II: A Documentary Sequel,* 1970, pp.7,8.

September 6, 1952 Full text of Protocol No. 122/49 published in Boston *Pilot*. This letter appears in its entirety in Appendix II.

September 24, 1952 St. Benedict Center again appeals to the Holy Father, accusing Archbishop Cushing of heresy, and declaring the "Letter of the Holy Office to the Archbishop of Boston" heretical and canonically invalid.

The Slaves of the Immaculate Heart of Mary
of Saint Benedict Center in
The Archdiocese of Boston

To:

The Sovereign Pontiff, Pius XII,
Gloriously Reigning over the Universal Church

*Notification to Your Holiness in the
External Forum of the Existence of the
Disability of Excommunication for Heresy
Incurred by Richard Cushing, Archbishop of
Boston, under the provisions of Canon 2314 of
the Sacred Code of Canon Law and Petition for
Further Relief Against the Same*

Most Holy Father:

On April 18, 1949, Richard Cushing, Archbishop of Boston, without previous notice or hearing, and through the public press, issued a decree suspending Father Leonard Feeney by depriving him of his right to exercise his priestly faculties in the Archdiocese of Boston and censuring the members of Saint Benedict Center by depriving them of the Sacraments of Penance and Holy Eucharist. Later, by oral order of the Chancellor, Mgr. Walter J. Furlong, in a telephone conversation, the scope of the decree was extended to include the Sacrament of Matrimony. By its own terms, the decree stated that the censures which it imposed were for grave offenses against the Catholic Church. The issuance of this decree was the direct result of the public defense made by the Reverend Leonard Feeney of four professors who were discharged from Boston College, a Catholic institution in the Archdiocese of Boston conducted by the Society of Jesus, for holding and teaching that there can be no salvation outside the Catholic Church. For the holding and teaching of this doctrine these professors were accused by the rector of that institution, Rev. William Lane Keleher, S.J. of disseminating ideas which lead to "bigotry and intolerance."

Although all the parties affected thereby have questioned the canonical validity of this decree, they have since observed its provisions in order to avoid public scandal to the extent that they have been able to do so without compromising the doctrines of the Faith...

This action of the Archbishop in the midst of a controversy concerning the doctrine that "there is no salvation outside the Catholic Church" has had the substantial effect of denying and calling into doubt this doctrine and has been the direct occasion of propagating and disseminating heresy. On several occasions it has been stated in the public press; and consequently, the impression has been created in the public mind that the Archbishop of Boston holds that there can be salvation outside the Catholic Church. The said Richard Cushing, Archbishop of Boston has never taken any action to dispel such an impression. His failure to do so in a matter that is the subject of public controversy on a doctrine of the Faith indicated his assent to the doctrinal holdings attributed to him...

On August 8, 1949, the Supreme Congregation of the Holy Office issued a document which is Protocol No. 122/49 of that Congregation. This Protocol is substantially defective in that it contains heresy insofar as it states that one can be saved under certain conditions outside the Roman Catholic

Church and without personal submission to the Roman Pontiff. It is formally defective in that it was never published in the *Acta Apostolicae Sedis* and consequently is without any binding effect as an Act of the Holy See. This Protocol, which contained heresy, was published in part in the *Pilot,* the official organ of the Archdiocese of Boston on September 3, 1949. On September 6, 1952, the full text of the same Protocol was published in the aforementioned Boston *Pilot* at the direction of the said Richard Cushing, Archbishop of Boston, who signed his name to the published letter authorizing the publication of the Protocol...

For the aforementioned publication of the said Protocol No. 122/49 of the Supreme Congregation of the Holy Office which heretically states that under certain conditions one can be saved outside the Catholic Church and without submission to the Roman Pontiff and for the consequent dissemination of its substance throughout the secular and Catholic press of the United States of America with disastrous consequences to the integrity of the Faith and the salvation of souls, we accuse the said Richard Cushing, Archbishop of Boston, of the crime of heresy as defined by Canon 1325 of the Sacred Code of Canon Law...

The order of September 4, 1952 of the said Richard Cushing, Archbishop of Boston exacts compliance on the part of the Reverend Leonard Feeney under the threat of reducing him to the "lay state." The purpose of such threat is to create in the public mind the impression that the sublime dignity of the priesthood does not have the indelible character of a sacrament but is a simple office that can be given or taken away. Such contemplated action is explicitly forbiddden under the penalties for heresy by a decree of the Holy Council of Trent...

(Canon 4 "If anyone shall say that through this sacred order the Holy Spirit is not given, and that therefore in vain do the bishops say 'receive the Holy

Spirit'; or that through it a character is not impressed or that he, who was once a priest, can again be made a layman, let him be anathema.)

We beg your Holiness to protect us from this proposed attempt of the said Richard Cushing, Archbishop of Boston, to defend himself from the accusation of heresy by a vicious attack on the sanctity of the Sacrament of Holy Orders...

In this dark hour when the plague of heresy has paralyzed the very government of the Church, we the members of Saint Benedict Center have consecrated ourselves to the religious life as the Slaves of the Immaculate Heart of Mary for our own sanctification and for the preservation and propagation of the Faith. We place our little religious community under the personal protection of Your Holiness and we pray that the Immaculate Mother of God, the Destroyer of All Heresy, will give you the courage to grant us relief against the heretical bishop who rules the Church of Boston.

But I have prayed for thee, that thy faith fail not: and that being once converted, confirm thy brethern." (Luke 22:32.)

> Your Holiness's Most Obedient Children
> in the Immaculate Heart of Mary
>
> The Slaves of the Immaculate Heart of
> Mary
> of Saint Benedict Center...
>
> Feast of our Lady of Ransom, 1952[3]

---

[3] *Op. cit.,* pp.14-21. This document is very long and I have edited out various newspaper clippings and citations from Canon Law.

October 25, 1952 Father Feeney summoned to Rome by Cardinal Pizzardo, Secretary of Holy Office.

(Seal)

Suprema Sacra Congregation Ex Aedibus S. Officii,
   SANCTI OFFICII   die 25th October 1952

(Prot. N) 122/49
(In responsione fiat mentio
   huius numeri)

Rev. dear Father,

The Supreme Sacred Congregation of the Holy Office has been obliged repeatedly to make your teaching and conduct in the Church the object of its special care and attention, and recently, after having again carefully examined and calmly weighed all the evidence collected in your cause, it has found it necessary to bring this question to a conclusion.

However, His Holiness, Pope Pius XII, in His tender regard and paternal solicitude for the eternal welfare of souls committed to His supreme charge, has decreed that, before any other measure be carried into effect, you be summoned to Rome for a hearing. Therefore, in accordance with the express bidding and by the special authority of the Supreme Pontiff, you are hereby ordered to proceed to Rome forthwith and there to appear before the Authorities of the Supreme Sacred Congregation of the Holy Office as soon as possible.

Yours sincerely in Christ
/s/ Joseph Cardinal Pizzardo
(Secr.)

Rev. Father L. Feeney
Saint Benedict Center   /s/ A Ottaviani[4]
Cambridge 38, Mass.   ass.
U.S.A.

4 *Idem*, p.40.

October 30, 1952 Father Feeney requests statement of charges against him.

In re: (Prot. N) 122/49

October 30, 1952

His Eminence, Joseph Cardinal Pizzardo,
Secretary, Supreme Sacred Congregation
of the Holy Office,
Palazzo del S. Uffizio
Vatican City, Italy

Your Eminence:

I have just received a letter from the Holy Office, written in English and signed with Your Eminence's name. It is dated October 25, 1952. This is the first official notification I have received of the existence of a cause, judicially cognizable, in which I am an interested party. Your letter not only informs me that such a cause exists but also that there is to be a hearing for its disposition. A hearing or trial presupposes some formal complaint or accusation which serves as a legal basis for the proceedings and which also informs the accused of the charge against him so that he can prepare to defend himself. Before I can participate in a trial I would like to know with more adequate particularity what I am to be tried for.

I want to take this opportunity to call to Your Eminence's attention a document transmitted to the Sovereign Pontiff by the Slaves of the Immaculate Heart of Mary. The date of this document is the Feast of Our Lady of Ransom, 1952. It was accepted by the Postmaster at Boston, Massachusetts on September 25, 1952, and numbered 265987; the Holy Father acknowledged its receipt on September 28, 1952. A copy of this document was also transmitted to the Cardinal Archbishop of New York on the Feast of Saint Jerome, 1952.

In closing, I beg your Eminence's prayers for myself and for the nearly one hundred Catholic young men and women associated with me, who are most loyal and devoted children of our Holy Father the Pope.

I have the honor to remain your Eminence's humble servant in the Immaculate Heart of Mary.[5]

November 22, 1952 Cardinal Pizzardo again reiterates order without statement of charges and informing Father Feeney that expenses will be paid by Apostolic Delegate.

(Seal)
Suprema Sacra Congregation Ex Aedibus S. Officii,
    SANCTI OFFICII   die 22 Nov. 1952

Prot. N. 122/49
(In responsione fiat mentio
    huius numeri)

Dear Father,

Your letter of the 30th October clearly shows that you are evading the issue, instead of obeying promptly the order which was given you in the name of His Holiness, as was clearly expressed in my letter of the 25th October.

You are to come to Rome immediately where you will be informed of the charges lodged against you.

I wish to inform you that if you do not present yourself at the Congregation of the Holy Office before the 31st December this act of disobedience will be made public together with the canonical penalties.

Yours very sincerely in Christ

/s/ J. Cardinal Pizzardo
(scr.)

Rev. Fr. L. Feeney
St. Benedict's Center   /s/ A. Ottaviani
Cambridge, Mass.

[5] *Idem*, p.41.

N.B....The Apostolic Delegate has been authorised to provide for the expenses of your journey.[6]

December 2, 1952 Father Feeney replies quoting Canon Law to the effect that he is legally entitled to a statement of charges.

> Feast of Saint Bibiana of Rome,
> December 2, 1952.

His Eminence, Giuseppe Cardinal Pizzardo,
Secretary, Supreme Sacred Congregation of the Holy Office,
Palazzo del S. Uffizio,
Vatican City.

Your Eminence:

I have received Your Eminence's letter of November 22, 1952.

Your Eminence seems to have misconstrued my motives in replying to your letter of October 25, 1952. I had presumed that your first letter was to serve as a canonical citation to appear before your Sacred Tribunal. As a citation, however, it is fatally defective under the norms of Canon 1715 especially in that it did not inform me of the charges against me. This canon requires that the citation contain at least a general statement of the charges. Under the norms of Canon 1723 any proceedings based on a citation so substantially defective are subject to a complaint of nullity.

While under Canon 1555 the Supreme Sacred Congregation of the Holy Office may judge causes according to its own proper custom, I do not think that these customs dispense with the substantial requirements of justice of the "Ius Communale" of the Church. In this way the law of the Church gives effect to the Apostolic injunction that no priest shall be con-

---

[6] *Idem,* p.42.

246 THEY FOUGHT THE GOOD FIGHT

demned except by the universally accepted modes of judicial proceedings.

"Against a priest receive not an accusation, but under two or three witnesses...Them that sin reprove before all; that the rest may have fear." (1 Tim. 5:19-20.)

This text gives Scriptural authority to the establishment of the external forum for the purpose of judging causes according to the basic requirements of justice for the conduct of legal proceedings. See Bellarmine, *De Romano Pontifice*, Liber Quartus, Caput XVI; "Probatur testimoniis verbi Dei posse pontifices veras leges condere."

I am concerned at the suggestion in Your Eminence's letter of the impostion of vindictive penalties without the formalities of a trial. Canon 1959 would seem to prevent this. I can see no grounds for proceeding against me "ex informata conscienta." My offense, if any, is not occult. On the contrary, it is a notorious public fact that I am in the anomalous position of being under censure for holding and teaching the Catholic doctrine that there can be no salvation outside the Catholic Church, nor without submission to Our Holy Father, the Pope.

I am at a loss to understand why Your Eminence should threaten me with the penalties for contumely when there is no indication of it on my part. I have no intention of being contumacious of the authority of your most Sacred Tribunal. The questions, however, which I have raised in this letter, and in my previous one, are legitimate under Canons 1842 and 1843.These questions are: (1) What are the charges against me; and (2) What is the nature of the proceedings to which I have been summoned? Under Canon 1715 a description of the charges and the nature of the proceedings should be in the citation, for its validity.

I am also unfamiliar with the procedures proper to the Holy Office under Canon 1555. Since such procedures are to govern the conduct of the proceedings,

I would like to have them made available to me so that I can familiarize myself with them in order to protect my rights under them. I would also like to know whether in this instance under Canon 247, your Supreme Sacred Congregation is acting as a court of the first instance or as a court of appeal from the actions of the Archbishop of Boston. Your Eminence must admit that proceedings before your Supreme Sacred Tribunal, whether original or appellate, even by special provision of the Code are so extraordinary in their nature that neither a priest nor a canonist can be expected to have a ready familiarity with them.

There is also the question as to whether, for the sake of convenience, the jurisdiction of your Supreme Tribunal can be exercised by either a delegated tribunal or by delegated judges in this country. Furthermore, since the issue of orthodoxy is immediately involved, it is also possible that questions of recusation might be raised.

I am the only spiritual father of a religious congregation of approximately one hundred American young men and women completely consecrated to Our Lady as Slaves of the Immaculate Heart of Mary. They have suffered and are suffering untold persecution at the hands of both ecclesiastical and civil authorities in the United States. Ecclesiastically, this persecution has taken the form, in several provable instances of the circulation of unpublished documents of the Holy See for the purposes of intimidation, in violation of Canon 2333. Civilly, it has also, in several provable instances, with the cooperation of the ecclesiastical authorities, reached the point of physical violence.

Furthermore, the rumor has falsely and maliciously been circulated and countenanced by ecclesiastical authorities, that I and the members of my Congregation are excommunicated and are no longer members of the Catholic Church. My spiritual children suffer this because they hold and preach that there is no salvation outside the Catholic Church, nor without personal submission to our Holy Father, the Pope.

Because I am immediately responsible in such extraordinary circumstances for their spiritual welfare, I am reluctant to leave the country readily, if other provisions are either feasible or convenient under Canon 1555 as proper to the Holy Office. I fear for my children lest my absence from the country be seized on by my enemies as an opportunity to persecute them still further:

"I will strike the shepherd, and the sheep shall be dispersed." (Mark 14:27.)

The extraordinary situation in which I and my spiritual children find ourselves has been brought to the attention of the Sovereign Pontiff, in accordance with the provisions of Canon 218. This was done informally in a letter to His Holiness, dated May 28, 1949, and formally by a document, dated on the Feast of Our Lady of Ransom, September 24, 1952. This latter document was called to Your Eminence's attention in my letter to you of October 30, 1952.

The document of the Feast of our Lady of Ransom was a petition to His Holiness that he give us the protections in this situation which are ours as of right under Canon 2232. A copy of the document was also transmitted to the Cardinal Archbishop of New York.

The state of the Faith existing in the Archdiocese of Boston as recounted in this document is most grave. For example, it has even reached the point where, in a predominantly Catholic city, a heretical minister, on the occasion of the definition of the Assumption of the Most Blessed Virgin Mary, publicly attacked her virginity by a paid advertisement in every secular newspaper in the city, without any public protest by either the ordinary or the clergy. I am the only priest in the Archdiocese of Boston who has attempted to remedy this situation by my public utterances and by proper recourse to the Holy See.

Because of the direct and indirect responsibility I have for the care of souls in this deplorable situation, which approximates conditions under which the See is embarrassed under Canon 429, I hope that some way can be found in which the necessary preliminary questions can be settled without imposing on me, and those dependent on my pastoral care, the unnecessary burden of my absence from the country.

With renewed assurance of my profound obedience, I have the honor to remain

Your Eminence's most respectful servant,

Leonard Feeney
Slave of the Immaculate Heart of Mary.[7]

January 9, 1953 Final communication from Cardinal Pizzardo.

(Seal)

Suprema Sacra   Del Palazzo del S. Offizio
Congregazion,   9th Jan. 1953
Del Santo Offizio

Prot. N. 122/49
(Nella risposte si prega
citare quesro numero)

Rev. dear Father,
    In reply to your letter of the 2nd Dec. 1952 asking for further explanations, the Supreme Sacred Congregation of the Holy office communicates to you herewith the orders received from His Holiness, that you are to present yourself to this Congregation before the 31st January 1953, under pain of excommunication incurred automatically (ipso facto.) in case of failure to present yourself on the date indicated. This decision of His Holiness has been made after the arrival of the latest documents from St. Benedict Center.

Yours sincerely in Christ
/s/ J Cardinal Pizzardo
(Sec.)

[7] *Idem,* pp.43-48.

> Rev. Father Leonard Feeney   /s/
> 23 Arrow Street   A. Ottaviani
> Cambridge 38, Mass.   ass.[8]

January 13, 1953 Father Feeney complains that the "secret" proceedings of the Holy Office have been leaked to the public press. Again questions the validity of the "Letter of the Holy Office to the Archbishop of Boston."

January 13, 1953

His Eminence, Giuseppe Cardinal Pizzardo,
Secretary,
Supreme Sacred Congregation of the Holy Office,
Palazzo del S. Uffizio,
Vatican City.

Your Eminence:

I have received your letter of January 3, 1953, I have been in communication with your Eminence since October 25, 1952. I was under the impression that all bona fide communications from your most Sacred Tribunal, acting as the Inquisitors-General of the Holy Roman Church, were protected by the "secrecy of the Holy Office," which, if violated, is punishable by the penalty of automatic excommunication – absolution from which is reserved to the Sovereign Pontiff. It is most irregular that the substance of your communications to me was divulged both publicly and privately on several different occasions by several persons.

These instances are as follows:

(1) On Sunday, November 16, 1952, a Mrs. Weiler of Boston, Massachusetts, in collaboration with a Mr. and Mrs. Joseph Uberti of Waltham, Massachusetts, called out to me, "Why don't you go to Rome as they have asked you to? They'll give you the money now."

[8] *Idem,* p.50.

(2) On Sunday, November 23, 1952, this same person, under identical circumstances, again called to me, "Why don't you go to Rome as they have asked you to? They will give you the money now."

(3) On Wednesday, January 7, 1953, the Very Reverend William E. Fitzgerald, the Provincial of the New England Province of the Society of Jesus, asked my brother, the Reverend Thomas B. Feeney, S.J., why I didn't go to Rome as ordered by the Holy Office. He further said, "All these delays, excuses and subterfuges with which he is carrying on are a scandal."

(4) On Thursday, January 8, 1953, George Croft, a reporter for the Boston *Globe,* a secular newspaper, came to Saint Benedict Center, on instructions from his paper, to seek out information on a story that "Father Feeney was to go to Rome." Mr Croft said that he had been sent by his superior, Mr. William R. Callahan, who is the Catholic religious editor of the Boston Globe.

(5) On Friday, January 9, both Mr. Callahan and Mr. Haviland, the Managing Editor of the Boston Globe, confirmed the report that they had received information to the effect that Father Feeney was to go to Rome.

Such divulgence of my communications with the Holy Office, together with your threat to publicize my failure to be in Rome, whether or not such failure is justified, indicates that our correspondence is not subject to the "secrecy of the Holy Office." It further indicates that your purpose is not to inflict spiritual penalties for any crime of which I might be found guilty, but to intimidate me by threats of "smearing" in the public press. This is an unconscionable use of documents of the Holy See for the purposes of intimidation, for which you, under the provisions of Canon 2333, incur the same penalty with which you threaten me – automatic excommunication.

Your letter of January 3, 1953, states that if I do not appear in Rome on or before January 31, 1953, I incur *automatic excommunication* (excommunication *ipso facto*). The most diligent search of the

Sacred Canons fails to indicate any authority for this, and your letter is equally obscure on this point. Once more your letter threatens the impostion of a penalty without stating the crime for which it is imposed, in violation of Canon 2225.

I hope that you are not implying that my repeated efforts to determine this controversy were in bad faith. My correspondence with you will stand in the archives of the Church, and before the whole Catholic world, to show that I have been firm in my respect for ecclesiastical authority, as well as adamant in my refusal to compromise the Sacred Dogma of our Faith, that there is No Salvation Outside the Catholic Church, nor without personal submission to the Pope. Your threat to impose penalties without either accusations or proceedings, as required by the Sacred Canons and the *ius communale* of the Church, is outrageous and barbarous.

You know as well as I do that the action which you threaten is subject to the Complaint of Nullity under Canon 1680. The Cardinals of the Supreme Sacred Congregation of the Holy Office, as the Inquisitors-General of the Holy Roman Church, are bound by the decree which the Fourth Lateran or Twelfth Ecumenical Council applies to all proceedings before inquisitors.

"The accused shall be informed of the charges preferred against him, that an opportunity may be given him of defending himself. His accusers shall be made known to him, and he himself shall have a hearing before his judges."

The fact that the Sacred Code makes provision for the excommunication of those who would forge or tamper with documents of the Holy See (Canon 2360) indicates that it is a practice that is not beyond the realm of possibility.[9] This suspicion is further con-

---

[9] It is interesting to note that Galileo was condemned on the strength of what many historians consider a "forged" document. For example, the Jesuit historian Fr. James Brodrick says:

"What, then, is to be thought of the document dated Feb-

firmed by the fact that one of your previous letters on this controversy (Protocol 122/49) has been disseminated as a doctrinal pronouncement of the Holy See and it was never published in the *Acta Apostolicae Sedis.*

I want to again protest Protocol Letter 122/49 of August 8, 1949, to the Archbishop of Boston. *This heretical letter says that there can be salvation outside the Catholic Church.* There has been a diabolical plan to convey to the minds of the people that this protocol Letter of the Holy Office is, in effect, an infallible pronouncement of the Pope *ex certa scientia, motu proprio,* presuming to abrogate the "Solemn judgment of the Church," as expressed in the following infallible pronouncements:

(1) The Decree of the Jacobites, of the Council of Florence;

(2) The Decree against the Albigenses, of the

---

ruary 26 in the Vatican files and produced by the prosecution in 1633 in proof that Galileo *had* been given an absolute injunction by the Commissary of the Holy Office, in 1616?... The dark truth of the matter is that the document of February 26, 1616, in the Vatican files is not an original text, but somebody's concoction, probably that same year, to embroil Galileo with the Inquisition, should he at any time seek to maintain Copernicanism as a physical reality.

The bogus injunction is in the same handwriting as that of neighboring and certainly genuine documents, so the man responsible must have been some unscrupulous curial official hostile to Galileo, whom it is now impossible to identify. He succeeded beyond his wildest hopes seventeen years later, when his imaginary injunction was produced as a trump card against the unfortunate astronomer during his trial in Rome. He was taken completely by surprise, and maintained that he had never been given such an injunction. In proof, he produced Cardinal Bellarmine's certificate in 1616, and it is incomprehensible, if the Dominican Commissary, Firenzuola in 1633 was really trying to discover the truth and not predetermined on a verdict of guilty, that he should not have seen the complete incompatibility between the fake injunction and St. Robert's certificate."
Brodrick, Fr. James, SJ., *Robert Bellarmine,* The Newman Press, Westminster, Maryland, 1961, pp.376,377.

Fourth Lateran Council;

(3) The Bull, *Unam Sanctam.*

All of these pronouncements have infallibly declared that there is No Salvation Outside the Catholic Church, nor without personal submission to the Pope.

This pernicious Protocol Letter has been circulated throughout both the secular and Catholic press of the United States of America as the doctrine of the Church. What is more deplorable is that there are provable instances where Catholics have been threatened with ecclesiastical penalties for not assenting to the heretical contents of this letter.

I very seriously question both the good faith and the validity of any attempt to excommunicate me because I dared to call the substance of this decree to your attention, and because I dared to insist on my rights under it in both my letters of October 30 and December 2, 1952...

I am your Eminence's respectful servant

Leonard Feeney
Slave of the Immaculate Heart of Mary[10]

July 16, 1953 Letter from St. Benedict Center to Pro-Secretary of State, Msgr. Giovanni Battista Montini, later Pope Paul VI. This document is extremely long with many attached newspaper clippings, and reviews the material already submitted to the Holy Father and to the Holy Office. Evidently the Center's thinking was that since the Holy Office was persisting in dealing with the Father Feeney Case as a political matter, rather than doctrinally, the Center might as well be dealing with the Vatican Office for political affairs, the Secretariat of State. Also the Pro-

---

[10] *Idem,* pp.51-59. This was Father Feeney's last communication with Cardinal Pizzardo. Father Feeney himself did want to go to Rome, but was prevented by some of his more over-protective disciples. In retrospect it seems that he should at least have sent a delegate to show his genuine respect for Cardinal Pizzardo's authority, no matter what he thought of his orthodoxy.

Secretary of State, Cardinal Montini, was the only Vatican official who ever responded favorably to the Center's communications. (See *The Loyolas and the Cabots*, p.172 quoted above.)

February 13, 1953 Father Feeney excommunicated.

Translation

SUPREME SACRED CONGREGATION OF THE HOLY OFFICE

DECREE

The Priest Leonard Feeney
is Declared Excommunicated.

Since the priest Leonard Feeney, a resident of Boston (Saint Benedict Center), who for a long time has been suspended from his priestly duties on account of grave disobedience of Church Authority, being unmoved by repeated warnings and threats of incurring excommunication ipso facto, has not submitted, the Most Eminent and Reverend Fathers, charged with safeguarding matters of faith and morals, in a Plenary Session held on Wednesday 4 February 1953, declared him excommunicated with all the effects of the law.

On Thursday, 12 February 1953, Our Most Holy Lord Pius XII, by Divine Providence Pope, approved and confirmed the decree of the Most Eminent Fathers, and ordered that it be made a matter of public law.

Given at Rome, at the Headquarters of the Holy Office, 13 February 1953.

Marius Crovini, Notary

AAS (February 16, 1953) Vol. XXXXV, Page 100.[11]

[11] *Idem,* p.62. Father Feeney would always insist that he was not excommunicated, claiming that he could not be excommunicated for merely professing a dogma of the faith. It should be noted that this document does not contain the seal of the Holy Office, nor is it signed by Cardinal Pizzardo or the Holy Father. The only signature is that of a notary public. Also again the excommunication is not for doctrine, but for discipline, Father Feeney's failure to go to Rome. John Deedy who can hardly be considered partial to *extra ecclesiam nulla salus* writes:

> "...It seems a mistake...not to have given Feeney the doctrinal hearing he desired, or at least to have thrown open the salvation topic to the theological community for debate...
>
> Likewise, it seems a mistake to have formalized the excommunication of Leonard Feeney. (The Holy Office declared in its 1953 decree that Feeney 'automatically incurred excommunication' by displaying 'stubborn disobedience to an order' enjoining him to appear in Rome 'before the authorities of the Sacred Congregation.') However much patience, charity and the 'rules' had been abused, the pronouncement of excommunication seems superfluous, coming as it did on top of the silencing, the withdrawal of faculties, interdiction of St. Benedict Center, and other measures. This was over-kill. The church's disapproval of Feeney and his doctrine was more than apparent. A more sensitive reading of the situation, particularly after 1949, should have suggested referral of the Feeney case to others than to excommunicators. Under the circumstances, the excommunication was excessive.
> Deedy, John, *Seven American Catholics,* The Thomas More Press, Chicago, 1978, pp.119,120.

PART III

From 1958, St. Benedict Center moves to
Still River, to 1978, the death of Father Feeney.

(Part III is taken from newspaper clippings.)

January 30, 1958 St. Benedict Center moves to large farm in Still River, Massachusetts, diocese of Worcester. Adopts more monastic life-style.

December 15, 1958 Archbishop Cushing created Cardinal by Pope John XXIII.

April 2, 1968 Timothy J. Harrington made Auxiliary Bishop of Worchester.

August 8, 1968 Death of Catherine Goddard Clarke (Sr. Catherine), foundress of St. Benedict Center, co-foundress of Slaves of Immaculate Heart of Mary. Father Feeney's community begins to break up into several separate groups.

September 8, 1970 Umberto Medeiros becomes Archbishop of Boston.

November 2, 1970 Death of Cardinal Cushing.

November 22, 1972 Reconciliation of Father Feeney to Church.

> Still River, Mass. (NC)
> "...The...reconciliation came November 22, 1972, when Father Feeney met with Rev. Richard J. Shmaruk, a priest of the Boston Archdiocese acting as an agent of Bishop Bernard Flanagan of Worcester, in whose diocese the community lives. But behind the scenes as the agent of reconciliation was Cardinal Medeiros, who as a seminarian often attended lectures at Father Feeney's center.
> Father Shmaruk...said...that the circumstances of the reconciliation were informal and private because of Father Feeney's advanced age and state of health, and because the Church did not want to intervene in the internal difficulties of Father Feeney's community of followers.
> Father Feeney was not required to retract his literal interpretation of the doctrine 'outside the

Church there is no salvation,' Father Shmaruk said." [1]

1974 "Reconciliation" of majority of members of St. Benedict Center.

Worcester, Mass. (NC) – Father Leonard Feeney, a Jesuit who was excommunicated in 1953, and 29 of his followers have been reconciled with the Church, according to Bishop Bernard Flanagan of Worcester.

On September 26 Bishop Flanagan confirmed rumors that last spring he accepted back into the Church most of the members of Father Feeney's community, the Slaves of the Immaculate Heart of Mary, at St. Benedict Center, Still River, Mass.

He also confirmed that Pope Paul VI personally accepted Father Feeney back into the Church two years ago through the intervention of Humberto Cardinal Medeiros of Boston...

The group of 23 men and 6 women who followed Father Feeney "sought and obtained reconciliation earlier this year," Bishop Flanagan said, "after we had submitted their petition to the Sacred Congregation for the Doctrine of the Faith in the Holy See."

Eighteen members of the community have not been reconciled.

The Bishop said he personally accepted the 29 persons into full communion with the Church in the chapel of their home, St. Benedict Center.

The only condition set down in receiving the men and women into the Church, the Bishop said, was that each individual "make the usual profession of faith according to the traditional formula." Each did so, he said, in his presence.

"The men and women were then absolved," he said, "of any canonical censures which they might

---

[1] *The Advocate,* October 31, 1974, Newark. The reconciliation of Father Feeney and later of members of St. Benedict Center was approved by Pope Paul VI and expedited in Rome by Cardinal Wright, Prefect of the Sacred Congregation for the Clergy, who had been Auxiliary Bishop of Boston at the time of the excommunication.

have incurred while members of the religious community...Oblates of Still River." [2]

January 30, 1978 Death of Father Feeney.

February 20, 1978 Memorial Mass for Father Feeney celebrated in the
Cathedral of St. Paul, Worcester, by Bishop Ber-
nard Flanagan.

> ...To all who loved and revered Father Feeney in life,
> let me say, that your best memorial will be to remem-
> ber him in prayer, particularly to ask Our Blessed
> Lady to whom he had such great devotion and great
> love in life, to recommend him to her as Advocate,
> that he may quickly enter into the life of the Beatific
> Vision, and there intercede for us in bringing about
> that oneness, that unity in the true faith, which
> Christ willed for all who live and believe in Him.[3]

---

[2] On February 10, 1988 the status of an additional 14 sisters from St. Benedict
Center was "regularized" by Bishop Timothy Harrington of Worcester. Being
asked to make a profession of faith, the sisters chose to recite the Athanasian
Creed which begins: "Whoever wishes to be saved must, above all, keep the
Catholic faith: for unless a person keeps this faith he will undoubtedly be lost
forever" (Denz. 6). At the ceremony Bishop Harrington said in his homily, that if
Father Feeney were still alive "... he would speak to you in a more poetic fashion
than I have done. I know too that he is rejoicing that I your bishop, your spiritual
father and brother am here with you and that you are with me, in your love for the
Church." *(Catholic Free Press,* February 12, 1988.)
[3] From eulogy of Father Feeney by Bishop Flanagan. Tape, St. Benedict Center
Archives.

A PICTURE GALLERY
OF THE FATHER FEENEY CASE

1. Father Feeney in New York.
2. Catherine Goddard Clarke.
3. Blessing of Pope Pius XII.
4. Father Feeney and Catherine Clarke.
5. Infant Jesus of Prague.
6. Father Feeney and Infant of Prague.
7. St. Benedict Center residence in Cambridge.
8. Richard Cardinal Cushing.
9. Father Feeney at time of silencing.
10. Newspaper headlines.
11. Father Feeney at time of excommunication.
12. Pope Pius XII.
13. St. Benedict Center, Still River.
14. Humberto Cardinal Medeiros.
15. Bernard J. Flanagan, Bishop of Worcester.
16. Father Richard Shmaruk.
17. John Cardinal Wright.
18. Pope Paul VI.
19. Timothy J. Harrington, Bishop of Worcester.
20. Graves of Father Feeney and Sister Catherine.
21. Memorial Mass for Father Feeney by Bishop Flanagan.

1. Father Feeney at height of literary fame.

2. Catherine Goddard Clarke, Foundress of St. Benedict Center, and Co-Foundress of the Slaves of the Immaculate Heart of Mary.

*3. Blessing of Pope Pius XII on St. Benedict Center,
the Feast of St. Joseph, March 19, 1940.*

4. Father Feeney and Catherine Clarke in front of St. Benedict Center.

5. Infant Jesus of Prague,
blessed by Archbishop Beran of Prague.

6. *Father Feeney and Infant of Prague.*

7. One of several St. Benedict Center residences in Cambridge.

8. Richard Cardinal Cushing, Archbishop of Boston (1944-1977).
Silenced Father Feeney and interdicted St. Benedict Center in 1949.

9. Father Feeney at time of silencing.

The Boston Daily Globe

BOSTON, TUESDAY MORNING, APRIL 19, 1949

36 PAGES—FIVE CENTS

GUIDE TO FEATURES

ARCHBISHOP SILENCES PRIEST

Sternly Disciplines Jesuit in Ruling on B. C. Dispute

Catholics Are Barred From St. Benedict's, Directed by Fr. Feeney

Abp. Cushing Indorses College Action on Ousted Instructors

Leandersson and Cote Rank as Marathon Co-Favorites

Marathon Entries
Page 14

2 'Lonely Heart' Slayings Linked to Widow, Sons

Spahn and Bickford Pitch for Braves in Doubleheader Against Phils Today

AUDIE MURPHY IN ACTION

Globe Gets
Great human document; stark account by most decorated G.I. in whole Army

10. Newspaper headlines at time of silencing.

11. Father Feeney at time of excommunication.

*12. Pope Pius XII (1939-1958). Approved "Letter of
Holy Office to Archbishop of Boston" (1949) against
Father Feeney's teaching. Encyclical* Humani Generis
(1950) interpreted by press as pro Father Feeney.

13. St. Benedict Center, Still River.

14. *Humberto Cardinal Medeiros, Archbishop of Boston (1970-1983). Attended lectures at St. Benedict Center when he was a seminarian. Initiated "reconciliation" of Father Feeney.*

15. Bernard J. Flanagan, Bishop of Worcester, (1959-retired 1983). Worked for reconciliation of Father Feeney 1972. Received reconciliation of majority of members of St. Benedict Center 1974.

16. *Fr. Richard J. Shmaruk, priest of the Archdiocese of Boston. Acted as agent for Cardinal Medeiros and Bishop Flanagan. In 1972, with faculties from Rome, absolved Father Feeney of any censures "he might have incurred."*

17. *John Cardinal Wright, Auxiliary Bishop of Boston
(1947-1950), Prefect of the Sacred Congregation
for the Clergy (1969-1979). Expedited removal of
censures from Father Feeney (1972) and from
majority of members of St. Benedict Center (1974).*

*18. Pope Paul VI (1963-1978). Approved
reconciliation of Father Feeney and
members of St. Benedict Center.*

*19. Timothy J. Harrington, Bishop of Worcester,
(1983-). "Regularized" status of additional
members of St. Benedict Center 1988.*

20. *Graves of Father Feeney (1897-1978)*
and Sister Catherine (1900-1968) in Still River.

21. Memorial Mass for Father Feeney by Bishop Flanagan Worcester Cathedral 1978.

APPENDIX I

REPLY TO A LIBERAL

by

Raymond Karam

INTRODUCTION

by
Editor

Unfortunately Father Feeney never sat down and wrote a treatise on his position on salvation, but he did supervise and give his approval to this long article by Raymond Karam, *Reply to a Liberal.* The article's occasional somewhat sophomoric tone is explained by the fact that its author was only twenty-two years old when it was written. One of Father Feeney's sympathizers once wrote: "if he had only stuck to St. Thomas Aquinas, they never would have been able to touch him." Sometimes it is hard to see the forest for the trees, because that is just what this article tried to do. Let me extract then a few of the quotes in the article from St. Thomas to present a little summary of his teaching on salvation.

On submission to the Pope:

"To be subject to the Roman Pontiff is necessary for salvation." *Contra Errores Graecorum,* In Titulo, "Quod ad eum (Petrum) pertinet determinare quae sunt Fidei."

On the Catholic Faith:

[After the Incarnation, all men if they wish to be saved are] "bound to explicit faith in the mysteries of Christ chiefly as regards those which are observed throughout the Church and publicly proclaimed such as the articles that refer to the Incarnation."* [And, after the Incarnation, all men in order to be saved] "are bound to explicit faith in the mystery of the Trinity." + *Summa Theologica,* Part II-II, qu.2, a.7; + *Idem,* a.8.

On invincible ignorance:

[But what St. Robert says about children applies to

adults as well, for even though some of them could die unbaptized because they never heard of Christ, and hence without being guilty of this ignorance, yet these will perish eternally because they have original sins and because of their actual sins, as St. Thomas unmistakably teaches in the *Summa.*] "If however we find it [unbelief] in those who have heard nothing about the faith, it bears the character not of sin but of punishment, because such like ignorance of Divine things is the result of the sin of our first parents. If such like unbelievers are damned, it is on account of other sins which cannot be taken away without faith, but not on account of their sin of unbelief. Hence Our Lord (Jo. xv,22); *If I had not come, and spoken to them, they would not have sin;* which Augustine expounds (*Tract. lxxxix, in Joan.*) as *referring to the sin whereby they believed not in Christ."* Summa Theologica, Part II-II, qu.10,a.1, In Corp.

On Baptism:

"For just as a man cannot live in the flesh unless he is born in the flesh, even so a man cannot have the spiritual life of grace unless he be born again spiritually. This regeneration is effected by Baptism: 'Unless a man be born again of water and the Holy Ghost, he cannot enter the kingdom of God.'"* "It is manifest that all are bound to receive baptism, and that without it there cannot be salvation for men." + *Collation de Pater, etc.,* Exposition of the Apostles Creed, Tenth Article; + *Summa Theologica,* Part III, qu.68, a.1, In Corp.

Baptism of Desire or *in voto* (in intention) limited to martyrs and to catechumens overtaken by death:

"It is necessary, in order that a man might enter into the kingdom of God, that he approach the baptism of water *actually* (*in re*), as it is in all those who are baptized; or *in voto,* as it is in the *martyrs* and *the catechumens who were hindered by death before they could fulfill their intent (votum)." On St. John,* ch. III, Lect. I, n.4.

These are just a few of the many quotes from St. Thomas Aquinas in *Reply to a Liberal.* Let me add just two more of my own to round out his teaching on salvation.

On the necessity of the Church: (This teaching of St. Thomas was cited in part in Vatican Council II.)

"In any community existing around an altar, under the sacred ministry of the bishop, there is manifested a symbol of that charity and 'unity of the Mystical Body, without which there can be no salvation.'" The Dogmatic Constitution on the Church, Chapter 3, Article 26. The full quote from St. Thomas reads: "The content [*res*] of the sacrament [of the Eucharist] is the unity of the mystical body without which [unity] there can be no salvation. There is no access to salvation outside the church just as in the flood there was no salvation outside the ark (which signifies the church); so one reads in 1 Peter 3,20-21." *Summa Theologica,* Pars III, qu.73, a.3. (Quoted in Theisen, Abbot Jerome, OSB., *The Ultimate Church and the Promise of Salvation,* St. John's University Press, Collegeville, Minnesota, 1976, p.45, n.19.)

On the necessity of explicit faith:

"Is it necessary to believe explicitly?

Difficulties:

It seems that it is not, for
1. We should not posit any proposition from which an untenable conclusion follows. But, if we claim that explicit belief is necessary for salvation, an untenable

conclusion follows. For it is possible for someone to be brought up in the forest among wolves, and such a one cannot have explicit knowledge of any matter of faith. Thus, there will be a man who will inevitably be damned. But this is untenable. Hence, explicit belief in something does not seem necessary...

Answer to Difficulties:

1. Granted that everyone is bound to believe something explicitly, no untenable conclusion follows even if someone is brought up in the forest or among wild beasts. For it pertains to divine providence to furnish everyone with what is necessary for salvation, provided that on his part there is no hindrance. Thus, if someone so brought up followed the direction of natural reason in seeking good and avoiding evil, we must most certainly hold that God would either reveal to him through internal inspiration what had to be believed, or would send some preacher of the faith to him as he sent Peter to Cornelius. (Acts 10:20.)" *The Disputed Questions on Truth,* Question 14, Article 11.

FROM THE HOUSETOPS

Vol. III, No. 3   Spring, 1949

CONTENTS OF "REPLY TO A LIBERAL"

REPLY TO A LIBERAL

Raymond Karam

INTRODUCTION

We have been asked many times to explain what we mean by the term "liberal Catholic." Articles in each issue of FROM THE HOUSETOPS have referred to these "liberals," accusing them of religious indifferentism, or lack of concern for the Faith, of absence of loyalty to the Church, to the Pope, to the officially appointed teachers of Catholic doctrine, and, at times, of open heresy. We have been warning Catholics against the dangers of liberalism, letting them infer, from our statement of the erroneous doctrines, who these liberals are. This policy does not, however, serve to make the issue clear and definite enough, and so it becomes necessary at this point to name our opponents, or at least some of them, and to refute their heretical teachings openly.

This task has been made easier for us than we could have anticipated. In answer to one of the articles which appeared in the December 1948 issue of FROM THE HOUSETOPS, Father Philip J. Donnelly, S.J., Professor of Dogmatic Theology at the Jesuit Seminary at Weston, has, for the benefit of Boston College, issued a paper under the heading: *Some Observations on the Question of Salvation Outside the Church*. A weaker defense of a theological opinion could not be found, nor a more perfect expression of liberalism.

Those who read my article in the last issue must have noticed the long line of authorities quoted in support of the often-defined dogma that no person can attain eternal salvation unless before he dies he becomes a member of the Roman Catholic Church. The priest who attempts to refute my article never refers to the authorities I quoted. He ignores them. Although he is himself a professor of Dogmatic Theology, and therefore one who should know better, all he offers in support of his own liberalism is the theory of a French liberal called Caperan and the statement of an Italian Jesuit called Lombardi, both of whom have no more authority on dogmatic questions than Father Donnelly himself.

He gives us three allocutions composed by Pope Pius XI, one in 1927, one in 1930, and one delivered in 1938 to a group of scientists, all of which are quoted from the L'OSSERVATORE ROMANO. And, to give a final touch to this comedy, there is appended to Father Donnelly's notes an additional note by his editor, who quotes one sentence from a speech delivered by Pope Pius XII, as it was reported in the *New York Times!*

Is this the way a Catholic is expected to know the revealed and defined truths of his Faith? Since when does a teacher of Dogmatic Theology have to depend on the good pleasure and honesty of newspapers in order to know what is the Catholic Faith and what he is supposed to teach? And what about the generations of Catholics who lived before the September 6th, 1948 issue of the *New York Times?* Was it impossible for them to have known the unadulterated Catholic truth? Does Father Donnelly prepare his course in Dogmatic Theology dependently on how a newspaper quotes or misquotes some radio address of the Pope? Or is it that the techniques of our advanced and progressive century require the introduction of a course on Journalism as an indispensable part even of the theological training of our priests? We writers in the HOUSETOPS who are full of a "spirit of smug Protestant righteousness," according to Father Donnelly, may be greatly misinformed, but no news from Rome has reached us as yet announcing a papal definition of the infallibility of newspapers!

Apart from these "authorities," Father Donnelly makes use of the two main documents used by liberals: an allocution by Pope Pius IX in 1854, and an encyclical by the same Pope in 1863. And, as liberals always do, he at times misquotes the Holy Father, misrepresents his intention, and invariably makes the Pope's statements serve his own preconceptions. All this I have shown in my article on *Liberal Theology and Salvation,* which appeared in the December 1948 issue of FROM THE HOUSETOPS.

The one and only infallible pronouncement used by Father Donnelly in his paper is taken from the decree on Justification, Chapter 4, of the Council of Trent. However, this decree is erroneously explained, and, as I shall show later on in this article, is made to mean the very opposite of what was intended.

Perhaps before taking up in detail every point of Father Donnelly's paper, it would be well to quote it in full, so that no reader will be misled, and so that no point will be left confused in his mind, from not having read the original document. The article runs as follows:

Department of Theology

BOSTON COLLEGE

Chestnut Hill, 67, Massachusetts

SOME OBSERVATIONS ON THE QUESTION OF SALVATION OUTSIDE THE CHURCH

At present there is no work in English that covers adequately the question of salvation outside the Church. Perhaps the best thing to do in the present circumstances is to indicate the contents of two books on this subject:

  a) The classic work by Caperan, *Le probleme du salut des infideles: essai theologique* (1934);
  b) The more recent work by Fr. Riccardo Lombardi, S.J., the famous apostle of Italy, *La salvezza di chi no ha fede* (Rome, 1945, "Edizione: La civilta cattolica").

The first point to be made is that the formula "extra ecclesiam nulla salus" must not be understood in the sense that salvation is impossible for any one who does not believe explicitly in the Catholic Church, and does not accept all the revealed truths proposed by her for belief. The same infallible authority which proposes this formula also teaches that sanctifying grace, and consequently, a title to the Beatific Vision are conferred by baptism of desire. Therefore, the insinuation of a writer in the latest issue of a magazine called "From the Housetops" that baptism of desire is a device of "liberal" Catholics to christianize heretics, is in direct contradiction to the doctrine of the Council of Trent, which teaches that justification of the unbaptized may be described "as the transfer from that state, in which a man is born as the son of the first Adam, to the state of grace and adoptive sonship of God, through the second Adam, our Savior Jesus Christ; and after the promulgation of the Gospel this transfer cannot be accomplished without the water of regeneration *or the desire of it...*" (Denz. 796.)

Secondly, baptism of desire confers membership in the Church "in voto." For Pius IX, who taught so unmistakably that "extra ecclesiam nulla salus," also taught just as unmistakably that those who through no fault of their own do not recognize the Catholic Church as the only true Church..." and who yet keep the precepts of the law of nature graven by God in all men's hearts, who are prepared to obey God, and who lead an honorable and upright life, are able, by the powerful workings of God's light and grace, to attain eternal life. For God, who sees distinctly, who searches into and knows the mind, spirit, habits and thoughts of all men, would never of His supreme goodness and mercy permit anyone to be punished eternally unless he had incurred the guilt of voluntary sin." (*Denz.* 1677.)

He likewise teaches in the same place that only those who are "contumaciter" and "pertinaciter" divided from the Church cannot be saved outside the Catholic Church, and that those who *contumaciously* resist her authority and definitions and who *obstinately* remain separated from the unity of that Church and from Peter's successor the Roman Pontiff – to whom the custody of the vine was entrusted by our Savior – cannot obtain eternal salvation." (*Denz.* 1677.)

Pius IX likewise forbids unconditionally any manifestation by Catholics of a spirit of enmity toward those outside the Catholic Church. "But let the children of the Catholic Church *in no way whatsoever* be hostile to those who are not one with us in faith and love..." (*Denz.* 1678). As for that spirit of hostility manifested in the scarcely veiled assumption that Protestants are to be convicted of bad faith, and henceforth to be treated as formal heretics, the same

Pope said: "We have to hold as of faith that no one can be saved outside the Apostolic Roman Church, that she is the one Ark of Salvation, that whosoever does not enter her will perish in the flood. *But at the same time it is to be held equally certain* that those who labor under ignorance of the true religion will never – provided their ignorance is invincible – be held guilty in the eyes of God of this fault. *Who would dare claim to be able to assign limits to such ignorance* when he reflects on the diversity he sees among peoples, localities, characters and a host of other points? Assuredly when, released from the fetters of the body, we shall see God as He is, we shall then clearly see the intimate and exquisite way in which the mercy and justice of God are combined; but let us, so long as here on earth we are weighed down by this mortal body which dulls the soul, hold firmly to our Catholic doctrine: 'one God, one faith, one baptism'; *to try and probe deeper is criminal...*" (Denz. 1647).

These statements are the more pertinent, since they are located in the strongest statements of any Pontiff against religious indifferentism. It is quite one thing to maintain that Protestants or pagans are just as favorably situated with regard to salvation as Catholics, and quite another thing to maintain that they are in bad faith and are to be spurned because they do not submit to a distorted interpretation of Catholic doctrine (Cf. Caperan, *op. cit.,* pp. 138-142).

The spirit of these two citations of Pius IX were several times repeated and developed by Pius XI. "Sad are these conditions, it is true, but nevertheless, they provide some consolation, because the greater the ignorance – and who can ever presume to judge a person's good faith except God? – the less the responsibility. So true is that that Jesus Himself sought, as it were, His last consolation in the fact of ignorance, when He cried out from the Cross to the Father: 'Pardon them, because they know not what they do.'" (Allocution of Pius XI, January 11, 1927; *L'Osser-*

vatore Romano of this date.) More explicitly Pius XI said: "The limits of vincible and invincible error are among the most difficult to define, even for the most penetrating intellect. Only God, who is TRUTH, who is ALL TRUTH, who calls every creature to the TRUTH, who gives the means according to His measure to arrive at the TRUTH, only God can with certainty define the limit between vincible and invincible ignorance." (Allocution published in the *L'Osservatore Romano,* 31 January 1938.)

Even more remarkable and to the point, in an exhortation not to judge those outside the faith, is the following: "We are filled with sadness when We see so many countless souls so neglectful of the guarantees which God gives of His continuous presence and of His activity [in the Catholic Church]. Truly, in the light of this consideration, some have been tempted to conclude that these souls, without grace, have reached such a stage of degradation, that they are inexcusable. But such a judgment is beyond our pertinence or power: God alone knows the limits of vincible ignorance and of good faith, and we have an obligation to leave to Him all decision and judgment on this question." (Pius XI, "Discourse of March 10, 1930, at the reading of the Decree approving the Miracles for the Canonization of Blessed Catherine Thomas," *L'Osservatore Romano,* 11 March 1930.)

Father Lombardi, in concluding his survey of Papal doctrine, adds the following practical consideration: "In addition to these authoritative statements, there is a reason of the practical order, which urges a benevolent attitude towards infidels: it is the importance for the Apologist or the Missionary of starting his work with the greatest possible amount of good-will. This is only in accord with the example of Christ; true, He never countenanced the approval of *evil* to obtain good-will; but, on the other hand, He laid it down as a duty, to love and to excuse as far as possible all *persons;* He forbade us to judge temerariously, bitterly, or to interpret actions as due to evil motives or malice: 'Judge not and you will not be judged, condemn not and you will not be condemned' (Luke, 6:37)." (Lombardi, *op. cit.,* II, p. 229.)

In this question of the possibility of salvation outside the Church and the related problem of the invincible ignorance of those outside the Church, it is periously easy for some Catholics, whose zeal outruns their knowledge of Catholic truth, to fall into the state of mind that they condemn so bitterly, namely, a spirit of smug Protestant righteousness, of arrogating to oneself the prerogative of judging others with the mercilessness of a Lutheran or Calvinistic God, and of superficial private judgment in a totally unfounded interpretation of the subjective state of Protestants generally, and in a corresponding depreciation of authority, which borders on contempt. Such a spirit not only alienates Protestants of good faith but is also a positive scandal to Catholics.

Philip J. Donnelly, S.J.,
Professor of Dogmatic Theology,
Collegium Maximum Sancti Spiritus, Weston

EDITOR'S NOTE:

On September 5th, 1948 in a speech delivered in German and broadcast by the Vatican radio on the occasion of a Catholic celebration in Mainz, Pope Pius XII, referring to movements outside the Catholic Church for the unification of Christians said: "We know how insistent is the desire in many, both Catholics and non-Catholics, for unity of faith; the [Catholic] Church surrounds dissenters in the faith with sincere love and prayer for their return to her, their mother, from which God knows how many are separated without any fault of their own." (Cf. *New York Times,* Monday, 6 September 1948, p. 1, col.4.)

PART I

ANSWER TO FIVE MINOR POINTS

1. It seems to be a habit of liberal theologians to give more weight to the opinions of theologians of their own type than to the infallible definitions of the Church. Some of them never quote the Scriptures and the Councils; others do, usually by way of pious preamble. Father Donnelly, in his "observations" on the "question" of salvation outside the Catholic Church, uses only one statement from a Council of the Church. This lone statement turns out to be wholly to his disadvantage. In the same way, a famous French liberal, J. Bainvel, S.J., in his book entitled *Is There Salvation Outside the Catholic Church?* gives more than thirty quotations from Holy Scriptures, from the Fathers and Doctors and Councils – which unmistakably prove what the whole book is trying to explain away. The only texts which might be in Father Bainvel's favor are taken, with the usual mistranslations and mutilations, from Pope Pius IX's allocution and encyclical which I have mentioned in the introduction to this article, together with two or three sentences chosen out of the works of St. Augustine, again always mutilated and presented in such a way as to mean the very opposite of what they were intended to mean.

2. Liberal theologians give the impression that the dogma that "Outside the Church there is no Salvation" is still a question under debate. Father Donnelly says that "at present there is no work in English that covers adequately the question of salvation outside the Church." How can a dogma, after twenty centuries of Christianity, be still a "question" under discussion and debate? Not only is the teaching of the Church very clear on this point, but Pope after Pope has infallibly defined the same dogma.

There is no other dogma which has been so many times defined, and so many times proclaimed by Fathers and Doctors. But even if the dogma had not yet been infallibly defined, would that make it less a doctrine to be believed by all Catholics under pain of mortal sin? The Assumption of the Blessed Virgin, for example, has not yet been defined by the Church, and still it is a revealed dogma, and not a debatable question. The Divinity of Christ, likewise, was a dogma even before its definition in the Council of Nicea in 325, as was the oneness of the Person of Christ before its definition at the Council of Ephesus in 431. They were preached and defended as doctrines contained in the Deposit of Faith by St. Athanasius, St. Basil, St. Augustine, St. Jerome, St. Cyril of Alexandria, and all the orthodox teachers, before the dogmas were defined by councils. Would St. Athanasius have said, with the cold and measured utterance of a modern liberal theologian, "At present there is no work in Greek that covers adequately the question of the Divinity of Christ?" Or would Pope Leo the Great have said, "At present there is no work in Latin which covers adequately the question of the two natures in Christ?"

We may ask Father Donnelly: Why is it that there is no work in English which covers adequately this question of salvation outside the Church? Is it not a central doctrine of the Church? Has not the English language been in use for centuries? It would seem to be the office of the theologian to put the infallible pronouncements of the Popes and the teachings of the Doctors of the Church in clear and simple English, and to see that these pronouncements are kept in their purity of utterance and not confused by the comments of liberals, which destroy their meaning.

3. All liberalism is essentially skeptical. The liberals have studied Descartes, Hume, Kant, Einstein to such an extent that they have become skeptics and relativists themselves. If you were to ask liberal theologians, "Is it, or is it not, a dogma of the Church that there is no salvation outside the Church?" some would answer, "No it is not. There *is* salvation outside the Church." But most of them, knowing the danger in such a clearly heretical answer, would reply, "Yes, it is a defined dogma; BUT this does not mean that one who is not a Catholic cannot be saved."

For example, Father Donnelly admits that the Church has been teaching "extra Ecclesiam nulla salus," (Is the statement always kept in Latin in order not to offend Protestants? Is the heresy of Americanism still surviving, even after its condemnation by the Pope?) But Father Donnelly does not go so far as to call this teaching of the Church a *dogma*. He calls it a *formula*. Father Bainvel calls it an *axiom*.[1] Father Donnelly concedes the existence of this "formula" BUT says it "must not be understood in the sense that salvation is impossible for anyone who does not believe explicitly in the Catholic Church and does not accept all the revealed truths proposed by her for belief."

Father Bainvel, S.J., is guilty of the same inconsistency. He says that it is against the teaching of the Church to say that a person can be saved by good faith alone, or by belonging to the soul of the Church, or by belonging to the invisible Church. It is absolutely necessary for salvation, Father Bainvel says, that a man believe in the truths of the Church and belong to her body, and *visibly*. Moreover, he goes on, some theologians say that the Church is necessary for salvation by a necessity of precept so that a person totally ignorant of its existence could be saved without belonging to it. This, he says, is against the teaching of the Church, and we must hold that the Church is necessary for salvation by a necessity of means, so that without it salvation is *absolutely* imposs- ible. BUT, he adds, good faith and invincible ignorance can easily excuse a man so that he could attain salvation without joining the Catholic Church, without knowing about the Church, and without believing in its truths!

Now, I ask Father Bainvel, what is the use of asserting a dogma of the Faith if a BUT is going to undo it? Or why should the Church take so much care in defining a dogma if her intention is to say the very opposite of what she states in the definition? This we know is not the intention of the Church, but is, rather, the practice of the liberal theologian, which practice breeds skepticism and doubt.

4. One of the most common ways in which liberals confuse people on the teachings of the Church (and a very dishonest way, as everyone must admit) is to claim to quote a Pope or a Council, and then, by mistranslating the text and leaving out the most important words and clauses, misrepresent it completely. Let me give an example:

Pope Pius IX, in his allocution *Singulari quadam,* says: "But at the same time it is to be held equally certain that those who labor under ignorance of the true religion, if their ignorance is invincible, will not be held guilty *of this* in the eyes of the Lord. (Sed tamen pro certo pariter habendum est, qui verae religionis ignorantia laborent, si ea sit invin- cibilis, nulla ipsos obstringi *huiusce rei* culpa ante oculos Domini.)" [2]

Father Bainvel translates this statement (I am quoting from an authorized English translation of his book, *Is there Salvation Outside the Catholic Church?*): "It may be equally held as certain that ignorance of the true faith, if it be invincible, *excuses one from all fault* in the eyes of the Saviour." [3]

This is more than a mistranslation.

Now, Father Donnelly, in *his* paper, uses nine quotations. One of these is from R. Lombardi, S.J., and three from journalistic sources. Although these contain some distortions and notable omissions, I shall leave them aside for the moment as being of no importance whatsoever for deciding a dogmatic issue. In the remaining five quotations, there are two extremely serious mistranslations, and one major omission which completely changes the meaning of the passage. Here are the two mistranslated passages (I shall come to the third one later):

After saying that those who are invincibly ignorant of the Catholic

Faith will not be held guilty *of this* in the eyes of God, Pius IX says: "But now who would claim to himself to be able to designate limits to such an ignorance *according to the nature and variety of peoples,* regions, temperaments, and so many other things? (Nunc vero quis tantum sibi arroget, ut huiusmodi ignorantiae designare limites queat *juxta* populorum, regionum, ingeniorum aliarumque rerum tam multarum rationem et varietem?)" [4]

Father Donnelly renders the above passage of Pius IX in this way: "Who would dare claim to be able to assign limits to such ignorance *when he reflects on the diversity he sees among peoples,* etc..." What the Holy Father is warning us *not* to do is exactly what Father Donnelly is doing, namely, he is intimating that anyone can easily judge that there are many more people who are invincibly ignorant than we would think there are, by reflecting on the diversity that can be seen among peoples, regions, temperaments, etc. Pope Pius IX is warning us, on the contrary, not to judge of the invincible ignorance of people according to such superficial and sociological norms as diversity of peoples and customs. What do the liberals do? They make it their main concern to *reflect* on this very diversity and to judge of the invincible ignorance of people *according to this consideration.* When a Pope warns them not to take sociology and other purely rational studies as a norm to decide theological or dogmatic questions, they misconstrue his utterances and proceed to become experts on sociological and scientific problems, and they misinterpret Catholic dogmas in accordance with their secular studies!

The second mistranslated passage is the following: Father Donnelly claims that Pope Pius IX says: "For God, who sees distinctly, who searches into and knows the mind, spirit, habits and thoughts of all men, would never of His supreme goodness and mercy permit anyone *to be punished eternally* unless he had incurred the guilt of voluntary sin."

It is true that this passage is taken from an encyclical which is not infallible. But how can a professor of dogmatic theology have so little concern for the truth and so much less concern for the orthodoxy of a Pope as to claim that the Vicar of Christ could have made a statement like that? To say that God would never permit anyone *to be punished eternally* unless he had incurred the guilt of voluntary sin is nothing short of Pelagianism. It took all the strength and militancy of St. Augustine to destroy this heresy, and here it appears once more in our century, in the utterances of liberal professors of theology who try to hide behind a Pope by misquoting him.

If God cannot *punish eternally* a human being who has not incurred the guilt of voluntary sin, how then, for example, can He punish eternally babies who die unbaptized? Did these babies incur "the guilt of voluntary sin?" Or would Father Donnelly assert that they are not punished eternally, but are rewarded with the Beatific Vision? Or would he say that they are sent to Limbo, but that Limbo is not a place of eternal punishment but of reward? Is the teaching of the Church obscure on this point, too? Or is it not rather one more instance of the way liberal theologians confuse Catholics by misquoting a passage and never giving an explanation?

What Pius IX says is that "God, who sees distinctly, who searches into and knows the mind, spirit, habits and thoughts of all men, would never of His supreme goodness and mercy permit anyone to be *punished with eternal torments (aeternis puniri supplicis),* who has not incurred the guilt of voluntary sin." [5] What is due in justice to original sin is punishment and not reward, but it is the punishment of loss, the loss of the Beatific Vision (poena damni); and what is due to personal sin is the punishment of the senses, the fire of hell (poena sensus). But the punishment of loss can be and actually is inflicted on those who die free from personal sin but unbaptized, hence still under the sway of original sin..

Thus Innocent III said: "The penalty of original sin is the loss of the vision of God; the penalty of actual sin is the torment of everlasting hell." [6] And St. Bonaventure says: "...the punishment of being deprived of the sight of God and the loss of heavenly glory affects both adults and children who are unbaptized. The children are punished with the others, but by the mildest punishment because they deserve only the punishment of loss but not the punishment of the senses." [7]

The remaining two texts which Father Donnelly uses, one taken from the Council of Trent and the other from the same encyclical of Pope Pius IX, *Quanto Conficiamur,* fortunately are not mistranslated, but they are wrongly interpreted. Several words are emphasized in such a way as to give a false meaning to the whole passage, as I shall show later in this article. Thus there is not one authority used by Father Donnelly which does not disprove his ideas – when correctly quoted.

5. In the beautiful ages of the Faith, Theology was the queen of the sciences. Philosophy was her handmaid. There came the day when sophists like Hegel and Berdiaev completely subjected theology to philosophy and reason. But modern liberal theologians subordinate this fairest queen even to inferior sciences, such as sociology, astronomy and historical criticism. Every Catholic knows that, along with the Holy Scriptures and the infallible pronouncements of the Popes, the greatest authorities in theological and dogmatic questions are the earliest

teachers of Catholic truth. The authority of the Fathers is so powerful that all the Councils refer to their works in order to determine beyond question the body of truth contained in the Deposit of Faith.

Liberal theologians, however, impressed by the methods of modern scholarship, depart from the traditional way, and seek the latest work on a subject. They offer this as a solution of the matter, as witness Father Donnelly's use of Caperan and Lombardi. What has the revealed truth of Jesus Christ to do with novelty and recent research? Does the truth of our Faith change with time? Or does a modern liberal pretend to understand Our Lord's doctrine better than His immediate followers and all the centuries of Faith have understood it?

Nobody can deny that in the minds of liberal theologians what the early Christians held is not of great importance. And nobody can deny that in everything they say they imply that the dogmas of the Faith do change with time. How often have we heard liberals openly say that the Church has been teaching *since the Middle Ages* that people can be saved outside the Church, and without the knowledge of the truths of the Faith! Some of them do not hesitate to say that the reason this change in the doctrine of the Church has occurred is because we now know of the existence of peoples living in countries and continents undiscovered and unknown during and before the Middle Ages.

We know that Bainvel admits most of humanity into heaven, in his arrangement. His solution of the "problem" of salvation outside the Church consists in saying that pagans and heretics and schismatics and open enemies of the Church belong to the Catholic Church, both to her body and her soul. And yet he openly confesses that this was not the teaching of the early Church on the subject. He says, "From these various statements we may rightly conclude that, in the early stages of Christian thought, the Church was as necessary for salvation as Christ Himself." [8] Is this not clearly implying that the dogmas of the Church change with time? Is Father Bainvel carrying over into the sacred realm of theology the pseudo-scientific theories of so-called evolution? What does he mean by early *stages* of Christian thought? His presumption borders on blasphemy.

It is very noticeable that in Father Donnelly's paper the earliest authority quoted is the Council of Trent in 1547. He immediately passes on without further explanation, to the nineteenth and twentieth centuries. Furthermore, although Father Donnelly quotes (or rather misquotes) some recent Popes, the two works which are the basis of his paper, as he attests at the beginning, are (1) a "classic work by Caperan" (1934), and (2) "the more recent work by Father Riccardo Lombardi"

(1945).* It is evident, from these data, how much support Father Donnelly was able to find in the tradition of the Church as preserved in the works of the Fathers and the Doctors.

PART II

OUTSIDE THE CHURCH THERE IS NO SALVATION

1. *Explicit Faith in the Catholic Church and in Her Teachings is Necessary for Salvation*

We now come to something more positive and more doctrinal. "The first point to be made" says Fr. Donnelly, "is that the formula 'extra ecclesiam nulla salus' must not be understood in the sense that salvation is impossible for any one who does not believe explicitly in the Catholic Church, and does not accept all the revealed truths proposed by her for belief."

---

*   The story of Father Lombardi's interview with Sister Lucia, to whom Our Lady appeared at Fatima, is told in "The Secret of Fatima" by Fr. Joaquin Maria Alonso, CMF.

> "...On February 7, 1954 Father Lombardi, after much insistence, but at an inopportune time for Sister Lucia, managed to speak with her in the parlor of the Carmelite convent in Coimbra. He wrote later of the impression she made on him:
>
> Her face was simple, her voice clear and without the slightest trace of artificiality which can be so easily assumed in certain situations. She was not well; in fact she was running a temperature. I questioned her:
>
> "Tell me if the Better World Movement (which was already known to her) is the Church's response to the words Our Lady spoke to you.
>
> "Father," she replied, "there is certainly need of this great renewal. Without it, and considering the present state of humanity, only a limited part of the human race will be saved."
>
> "Do you really believe that many people go to hell? I myself hope that God will save the greater number, and I even wrote a book entitled *The Salvation of Those Who Have No Faith.*
>
> "Father, many are condemned."
>
> "It is certain that the world is an abyss of vice...Still, there is always hope of salvation."
>
> "No, Father, many, many, are lost."

Alonso, Fr. Joaquin Maria, CMF., *The Secret of Fatima, Fact and Legend,* The Ravengate Press, Cambridge, Massachusetts, 1979, p.106. (Raymond Karam's notes are numbered and appear at the end of the article. My own are indicated by an asterisk and are at the bottom of the page.)

Is this really the teaching of the Church on this point? Let us see what Holy Scripture and the tradition of the Church have to say.

Our Lord, sending His Apostles to preach His Gospel, said to them: "He that believeth and is baptized shall be saved; but he that believeth not shall be condemned." (Mk. 16,16.)

St. Paul, in his Second Epistle to the Thessalonians, (I, 7-10), says: "And to you who are troubled, rest with us when the Lord Jesus shall be revealed from heaven, with the angels of His power: in a flame of fire, *giving vengeance to them who know not God, and who obey not the Gospel of Our Lord Jesus Christ.* Who shall suffer eternal punishment in destruction, from the face of the Lord, and from the glory of His power: when He shall come to be glorified in His saints, and to be made wonderful in all them who have believed; because our testimony was upon you in that day."

Again in the same Epistle (II, 8-11) the Apostle says: "And then that wicked one shall be revealed whom the Lord Jesus shall kill with the spirit of His mouth; and shall destroy with the brightness of His coming, him, whose coming is according to the working of Satan, in all power, and signs, and lying wonders, and in all seduction of iniquity *to them that perish; because they receive not the love of the truth, that they might be saved.* Therefore God shall send them the operation of error, to believe lying; *that all may be judged who have not believed the truth,* but have consented to iniquity."

St. Thomas Aquinas, the official teacher of Catholic Doctrine, on the authority of the Apostle (Heb. XI, 6): "Without faith it is impossible to please God," says that faith in truths revealed by God is absolutely necessary for salvation.[1] Moreover implicit faith is not enough, nor is it possible to have implicit faith in some truth if one does not hold explicitly other truths.[2] "Therefore, as regards the primary points or articles of faith, man must believe them explicitly, just as he must have faith." [3]

Now, according to St. Thomas, what are the primary points or articles of Faith which must be believed explicitly by a man who wishes to be saved? They are (besides the belief that God is, that He is a rewarder and a punisher): (a) explicit faith in the mystery of the Incarnation, and all the points which are related to it which are found in the Creed; and (b) explicit faith in the Trinity, and in all the points related to it which are found in the Creed. Saint Thomas speaks as follows:

> After the Incarnation, all men if they wish to be
> saved are "bound to explicit faith in the mysteries of

Christ, chiefly as regards those which are observed throughout the Church and publicly proclaimed, such as the articles that refer to the Incarnation." [4] And, after the Incarnation, all men in order to be saved "are bound to explicit faith in the mystery of the Trinity." [5]

We see, therefore, that explicit faith in the articles of the Creed is necessary for salvation. But is this enough? Saint Thomas teaches that it is enough only if the person is unable to know more truths explicitly, and does not deny *any* articles of the Faith.[6] On the contrary, a man who professes to hold the truths of the Faith and at the same time explicitly denies even one truth, does not have the Faith at all, and therefore cannot be saved.[7] This would be true in the case of a man who denied the supremacy and infallibility of the Catholic Church and the necessity of the Church for salvation.

The above clearly refutes Father Donnelly's statement that explicit belief in the Catholic Church and acceptance of all the revealed truths proposed by her are not necessary for salvation. For further proof that explicit belief in the Catholic Church IS necessary for salvation, let us quote St. Thomas and St. Alphonsus Liguori. St. Thomas says, "Neither formed nor formless faith remains in a heretic who disbelieves one article of faith...Consequently whoever does not adhere, *as to an infallible and divine rule,* to the teaching of the Church, which proceeds from the First Truth manifested in Holy Scripture, has not the habit of faith, but holds the things which are of faith otherwise than by faith." [8]

St. Alphonsus Ligouri says that the motive for believing any truths of the Faith is "that God, the Infallible Truth, has revealed them, and that the Church proposes them to our belief. Behold, then, how we should make an act of faith: 'My God, because You, Who are the Infallible Truth, have revealed to the Church the truths of the Faith, I believe all that the Church proposes to my belief.'"[9] Hence it must follow that belief in the truths which the Church proposes is impossible without belief in the Church itself. Therefore, only those who adhere to the teaching of the Church *as to an infallible and divine rule* can have real faith and find salvation.

Proof of the necessity of explicit belief in the Catholic Church and the acceptance of all the revealed truths proposed for belief in order to be saved is found all through the writings of the Fathers, the Doctors, and in the Councils. Let us list here a few additional statements:

St. Thomas says, commenting on the Apostles' Creed: "No man can obtain the happiness of heaven – which is the true knowledge of God – unless he know Him first by faith: 'Blessed are they that have not seen, and have believed' (Jn. 20,29)." [10]

The Council of Trent, which Fr. Donnelly thinks is in his favor, teaches unmistakably: "Indeed, since the Apostle said that man is justified by *faith* and freely (Rom. 3, 22-24), these words must be understood in that sense, which the perpetual consensus of the Catholic Church held and expressed, namely that we are thus said to be justified by faith, since *'faith is the beginning of human salvation,'* the foundation and root of every justification, ' *without which it is impossible to please God* (Heb. 11,6)' and to come to the fellowship of His children." (Sess. VI, Chap. 8.) [11]

St. Robert Bellarmine, S.J., Doctor of the Universal Church, says at the very beginning of his *Doctrina Christiana:* "We begin the exposition of the *dogmas of the Faith of Christ, whose knowledge is necessary for every one who earnestly desires the salvation of his soul.*[12]

St. Alphonsus Liguori teaches that God calls us in two successive vocations, which necessarily follow a definite order: "This was the first and sovereign grace bestowed upon us, – our vocation to the Faith; which was succeeded by our vocation to grace, of which men were deprived." [13] Thus sanctifying grace cannot come to an adult in whom faith did not come first.

Pope Pius XI, whom Fr. Donnelly quotes from newspapers, says in his Encyclical *Mortalium Animos:* "Moreover, when the only Begotten Son of God commanded His legates to teach all nations, *He then bound all men with the duty to believe* what was announced to them by 'witnesses preordained by God.' He attached to His command the sanction, 'He that believeth and is baptized shall be saved; but he that believeth not shall be condemned.' Now this double commandment of Christ, which must be observed, *to teach and to believe so as to attain eternal salvation,* cannot even be understood if the Church does not propose the evangelical doctrine entire and clear and if in the teaching of it, it is not free from all danger of error." [14]

Pope Pius IX, whose utterances have been so pitilessly mutilated and mistranslated by the liberals of our day, says in his Allocution *Singulari Quadam:* "It is necessary that you inculcate this salutary teaching in the souls of those who exaggerate the power of human reason to such a point that they dare, by its power, to investigate and explain the mysteries themselves, than which nothing is more foolish, nothing more insane. Strive to call them back from such a perversity of mind, explaining indeed that nothing was granted to men by God's Providence more excellent than the authority of the divine faith, that this faith is to us like a torch in the darkness, that it is the leader that we follow to Life, that *it is absolutely necessary for salvation,* since 'without faith it is impossible to please God,' and 'he that believeth not shall be condemned' (Mk. 16,16)." [15]

Moreover, concerning explicit faith in the Incarnation and the Most Holy Trinity, Pope Innocent XI, in his condemnation of certain errors on moral questions "Errores varii de rebus moralibus," includes the following heretical proposition:

(*It is error to believe that*) 64. "A man is capable (capax) of absolution, however much he may labor in ignorance of the mysteries of the faith, and even though through negligence, be it even culpable, he does not know the Mystery of the Most Holy Trinity and of the Incarnation of Our Lord Jesus Christ." [16]

Concerning explicit faith in the Catholic Church and in her supremacy, the Council of Constance condemned the 41st proposition of John Wycliff in which this heretic said that it was not necessary for salvation to believe in the supremacy of the Roman Church. [17]

In connection with the question of the necessity of the Catholic Faith for salvation, let me point out the fact that Fr. Donnelly and the other liberals quote texts without seeing that they can be easily turned against them. Thus the Encyclical *Quanto conficiamur* by Pius IX is universally quoted by the liberals to support their doctrine that a man totally ignorant of the Catholic Faith can be saved. But what does Pius IX say?

"It is known to Us and to you that those who labor under invincible ignorance of our holy religion, and who, zealously observing the natural law and its precepts engraven by God in the hearts of all, and who, prepared to obey God, lead an honest and upright life, are able, *by the powerful workings of God's light and grace,* to attain eternal life." [18]

This means that God, in His mercy, will find a way of enabling the man who is invincibly ignorant of the Church and who follows the natural law to achieve his salvation. But Pius IX nowhere says that this can be done without the Catholic Faith. On the contrary, he explicitly says, a few lines later, that it is a "Catholic dogma that no one can be saved outside the Catholic Church." [19] Thus, God will find the way to enable that man to save his soul, and this way will be the Catholic Faith and the Catholic Church.

What is more, in the very sentence which the liberals quote to support their false doctrine, Pius IX says that God will enable that man to attain eternal life, not by keeping him in his ignorance of the Faith, but *by the workings of His light and grace.* God must give sanctifying grace to a person before that person can be saved, and He never gives sanctifying grace apart from or even before the Catholic Faith. It is by enlightening the intellect that God gives us His Faith. Thus to say that God gives *His light* to a person is the same as to say that He gives His Faith to that person. Thus we speak of the "light of Faith."

As a matter of fact, St. Thomas teaches not only that faith and light go together, but that light is the effect of the Catholic faith. In his *Commentary on St. John,* Chapter 12, St. Thomas says: "Illumination therefore is the effect of faith: 'That whosoever believeth in Me may not remain in darkness.' 'May not remain in darkness', namely, the darkness of ignorance, of infidelity and of perpetual damnation...And nevertheless unless they are converted to Christ they shall be led to the darkness of perpetual damnation. 'He that believeth not the Son, the wrath of God abideth on him.'" [20]

Let us repeat here what St. Alphonsus Liguori said: Our first vocation is to the Catholic faith (whose effect is the illumination – light of the soul), which is followed by our vocation to grace.[21]

2. Are There Two Kinds of Membership in the Church?

"Secondly," says Father Donnelly, "baptism of desire confers membership in the Church 'in voto.'" In Part III of this article I shall consider the question of Baptism and what Father Donnelly calls "Baptism of Desire." For the moment, let us examine whether there is any such thing as "membership in the Church 'in voto.'"

A man cannot be more or less a member of the Church. He either is a Catholic, or he is not a Catholic, for the Catholic Church is the Mystical Body of Christ. This means that it is a body in the real sense of the word, and not in a metaphorical sense. Like any other real body, therefore, no member of it can be more or less a part of it. The same soul animates it all, and if a member is separated from the body, it is cut off from it, and is no longer animated by the soul, hence it has no life in it.

Let us ask, therefore, who can be called a member of the Church in any sense? No one can be called a member of the Church in any sense who does not confess the truths of the Faith, does not partake of the Sacraments, and does not submit to the infallible authority of the Supreme Pontiff.

St. Robert Bellarmine, S.J., says that "the one and true Church is the congregation of men bound together by the profession of the same

Christian faith, and by the communion of the same Sacraments, under the rule of the legitimate pastors, and especially of the one Vicar of Christ on earth, the Roman Pontiff." [22]

St. Peter Canisius, S.J., Doctor of the Universal Church, asks in his *Catechism:* "Who is to be called a Christian?" He answers: "He who confesses the salutary doctrine of Jesus Christ, true God and true Man, *in His Church.* Hence, he who is truly a Christian condemns and detests thoroughly all cults and sects which are found outside the doctrine and Church of Christ, everywhere, and among all peoples, as for example, the Jewish, the Mohammedan, and the heretical cults and sects; and he firmly assents to the same doctrine of Christ." [23]

Pope Pius XI says in his encyclical *Mortalium Animos,* "No one is found in the one Church of Christ, and no one perseveres in it, unless he acknowledges and accepts obediently the supreme authority of St. Peter and his legitimate successors." [24]

One wonders what are the sources for Father Donnelly S.J.'s strange doctrine? His sources are other liberal theologians, one of whom, Father Caperan, he quotes, and another, Father Bainvel, S.J., whose work he does not name explicitly. Let us give a few examples:

In the third chapter of his book, *Is there Salvation Outside the Catholic Church?* Father Bainvel examines some solutions given by other liberals to what they call a "contradiction" in Catholic dogmas. These solutions, "good faith, the soul of the Church, the invisible Church, the necessity of precept," he finds inadequate and against the teachings of the Church.[25] But in the next chapter, he proposes *his own* solution!

"The solution of the problem lies in the fact that we can be members of the Church in two ways, externally (visibly) and internally (invisibly)." [26] Father Bainvel claims that he learned this point from St. Thomas: "This solution is by no means new, for it was advocated by the old theologians, especially by St. Thomas." [27] And he refers the reader to the *Summa,* part III, q. 68, a.2, and q. 73, a.3. The reader, may we say, will find no such thing in either Question 68 or Question 73, Part III of the *Summa Theologica* of St. Thomas. Nor anywhere else in St. Thomas will the reader find mention of a person being a member of the Church *invisibly.*

Later in the same book, Father Bainvel says: "This distinction between union with the Church *in act* and union *in desire* dates far back into Christian antiquity," and he gives a quotation from St. Ambrose.[28] Again the amazed reader finds no mention of this odd doctrine in St. Ambrose, who is speaking, in this instance – as was St. Thomas in the two articles mentioned above – of the reception of Sanctifying Grace in relation to the sacraments and *not* of invisible membership in the Church or membership of desire.

But this is not the worst! Not only does Bainvel say that affiliation with the Church can be in desire and invisible, but he goes as far as to say that it can even be *unconscious,* when there is no desire at all of joining the Church! He says, "Souls affiliated with the Church *unconsciously* are united to her by invisible ties, for they are affiliated with her internally, by an *implicit desire,* which God is pleased to regard as equivalent to external membership." [29]

This is the end of all Christianity and all sanity.

Now Caperan, one of Father Donnelly's main authorities, says the same thing in the following two quotations: "When, by reason of invincible ignorance, incorporation into Catholic society is not realized in fact, even an implicit desire to be so incorporated takes the place of actual incorporation." [30]

And again, Caperan says, "Concerning the necessity of Baptism and the necessity of membership in the Church, an implicit desire which is included in the general will to do God's will is sufficient." [31]

It is clear that liberal theologians are teaching that there are two churches, the one visible (having a visible head, the Pope, and visible sacraments), and the other invisible and spiritual. Membership in the invisible church is obtained merely by "righteousness and sincerity." Some of the liberal theologians, like Karl Adam for instance, achieve the separation by saying that some men can belong to the "body of the Church," while others belong only to the "soul of the Church." Other liberal theologians, like Bainvel and Caperan, while claiming to be dissatisfied with the solution of men of Adam's school, bring about the same division by saying that some men can belong to the true Church visibly, and others invisibly, and even unconsciously.

This destroys one of the most central doctrines of the Church, for the Church has always taught that she is a visible society and the only kind of membership in her must necessarily be a visible and external one. St. Robert Bellarmine teaches that no one can be a member of the Church who is not *visibly* affiliated with the one *visible* society founded by Christ, subject to the authority of His vicar, the Roman Pontiff. To quote St. Robert Bellarmine: "The Church is a society, not of Angels, nor of souls, but of men. But it cannot be called a society of men, unless it consist in external and visible signs; for it is not a society unless they who are called members acknowledge themselves to be so, but men cannot acknowledge themselves to be members unless the bonds of the society be external and visible. And this is confirmed by those custom of all human societies; for in an army, in a city, in a kingdom, and other similar societies men would not be enrolled otherwise than by visible signs. Whence Augustine in Book 19 *Against Fautus,* Chapter 11, says: 'Men cannot assemble in the name of any religion, whether it be true or false, unless they be bound together by some fellowship of visible signs or sacraments.'" [32]

This shows clearly St. Robert Bellarmine's teaching on the subject. Let no one, therefore, misunderstand St. Robert's statement in another chapter of the same work when he says that catechumens are not in the Church in fact, but *in voto*.[33] This in no way states that there are two ways of being members of the Church, in fact and *in voto*. It simply means that catechumens have the explicit intention of coming into the Church and of becoming members of the Church, which membership they do not at all have at the moment. St. Robert Bellarmine proves conclusively in various places that catechumens are *not* members of the Church in any sense.[34] For example, after giving his definition of the Church, St. Robert says that catechumens are excluded from this definition because they do not have communion of the sacraments.[35]

3. Can a Person Who Remains Separated from the Church Be Saved?

Father Donnelly says, "He (Pius IX) likewise teaches in the same place that *only* those who are 'contumaciter' and 'pertinaciter' divided from the Church cannot be saved as long as this condition exists."

In saying this, Father Donnelly gives us the impression that those who know the Catholic Church and the Catholic Faith can remain outside the Church either innocently and with a good excuse, or obstinately and without excuse, and that only the latter cannot attain eternal salvation. This is against Catholic doctrine. *No* one can refuse to enter the Church and be saved. When Pope Pius IX mentions those who obstinately remain separated from the Church, he does not contrast them with those who innocently remain separated, but with those who never heard about the Catholic Faith. What he says is that *those who are ignorant of the Church* because they never heard of it, if they have faithfully kept the natural law implanted in their hearts by God, can, with His help, come to the knowledge of the Catholic Church, in which alone they can be saved. But, on the other hand, *those who know* about the Catholic Church and refuse to enter her will perish.[36] It is to emphasize the heinousness of their refusal that Pope Pius IX calls it contumacious and obstinate, not to distinguish between it and some other hypothetical kind of refusal which would *not* be obstinate.

Moreover, it is open heresy to say that *only* those who are contumaciously and obstinately divided from the Church cannot be saved. How about babies who die unbaptized, for example? Are they contumaciously and obstinately separated from the Church? Or will Father Donnelly affirm that unbaptized babies are not condemned? However, there is no end to the surprises which one can find in the heretical writings of the liberals.

Further on in his paper, Father Donnelly writes, concerning the same problem of the salvation of those who are separated from the Church, "It is quite one thing to maintain that Protestants or pagans are just as favorably situated with regard to salvation as Catholics, and quite another thing to maintain that they are in bad faith and are to be spurned because they do not submit to a distorted interpretation of Catholic doctrine."

In other words, Father Donnelly is saying (and this is a favorite liberal theme) that although it is not as easy for Protestants and pagans to get into heaven as it is for Catholics, we cannot say that it is impossible for them to get into heaven. We have shown in many places in this article that the contention that a Protestant or pagan can attain eternal salvation while remaining outside the Catholic Church is false. We profess with the whole Catholic tradition that the Catholic Church is *the* way to salvation. Does Father Donnelly mean to say that there are many ways to salvation, and of these the Catholic Church is the *easy* way?

Liberalism is a blasphemy against the Incarnation of the Son of God. If there are other ways than the Catholic Church, whether they be easier or harder, the result is that Christ's Incarnation and death were in vain. Our liberal teachers of doctrine have stopped teaching Christ Crucified, and they are teaching the natural law, morality, good faith, sincerity, and the like. St. Paul warned us against such blasphemy: "If justice be by the law, then Christ died in vain." (Gal. 2,21.) And again, "And I, brethren, if I yet preach circumcision, why do I yet suffer persecution? Then is the scandal of the cross made void." (Gal. 5,11.)

4. *Are Protestants Formal Heretics?*

Very closely connected with this question of obstinately refusing to join the Catholic Church is the following statement of Father Donnelly: "As for that spirit of hostility manifested in the scarcely veiled assumption that Protestants are to be convicted of bad faith, and henceforth to be treated as formal heretics, etc..."

Does Father Donnelly mean to say that a Protestant who refuses to believe in the truths of the Catholic Faith and to acknowledge the infallibility and supremacy of the Church is only in *material* heresy? Let us examine the teaching of the Church and of the Doctors on this point.

St. Augustine says, "If any there are who defend their opinion, though it be false and perverse, without obstinate fervor, and who seek the truth with all solicitude, ready to correct their opinion when they have found the truth, they are not at all to be accused of heresy." [37] And St. Thomas adds, "namely because they do not have a choice contradicting the doctrine of the Church." [38]

Only a faithful Catholic who obeys the Church and is ready to correct his opinions according to her admonitions can be in error in this sense, without being a heretic. This we call *material* heresy. A man who is in material heresy does not intend to contradict the authority and teachings of the Church. On the other hand, a man who does not intend in the least to follow the teachings of the Catholic Church and to be corrected by her cannot be called a material heretic. It is clear, therefore, that Protestants are not material heretics. Are they, then, *formal* heretics? What is a formal heretic?

St. Augustine says, "A heretic is one who either devises or follows false and new opinions." [39] It is not necessary to tell Father Donnelly that the teachings and opinions of Protestants fall under this last designation, and that Protestants, therefore, hold heresy *formally*. Of course, if Father Donnelly is referring to those millions of former Protestants who are neither baptized nor call themselves Christians, then we would agree that they are not formal heretics, but pagans.[40] In either case, however, heretic or pagan, they cannot be saved unless they come to the Holy, Roman, Catholic Church.

5. *Pope Pius IX's Real Teaching with Regard to the Salvation of Non-Catholics*

Father Donnelly's great concern in his paper is that Catholics shall not judge Protestants religiously, or suggest to Protestants that they should become Catholics in order to be saved. If this is the way Father Donnelly feels about the matter (which certainly is not the way any

Christian apostle or teacher ever felt), why does he not make this a separate issue? Even if we were to be "nice" to Protestants in Father Donnelly's sense, namely even if we were to be completely disinterested in their eternal salvation, does that mean that we should change the doctrines of the Church concerning salvation and the necessary means of salvation?

For example, Father Donnelly says: "Pius IX likewise forbids unconditionally any manifestation by Catholics of a spirit of enmity toward those outside the Catholic Church. 'But let the children of the Catholic Church *in no way whatsoever* be hostile to those who are not one with us in faith and love...' (Denz. 1678)."

Does this mean, as Father Donnelly wants to give us the impression, that Pope Pius IX is asking Catholics not to show those who are outside the Church any indignation on matters of doctrine, and not to tell them that they must become Catholics if they wish to be saved? Father Donnelly claims that this is the meaning of Pius IX in the above quotation. Let us point out that had Father Donnelly completed the sentence of the Pope, the message revealed would have been *a completely contrary one.*

Here is the full quotation:

"But let the children of the Catholic Church in no way be hostile to those who are not joined with us in the bonds of the same faith and of charity, yea rather, let them always strive to attend upon them and to help them in all the duties of Christian charity, whether they be poor or sick or afflicted with any other calamities, and *above all let them strive to snatch them away from the darkness in which they lie miserably, and lead them back to the Catholic truth and to the most loving Mother the Church,* who never ceases to extend Her maternal arms lovingly to them and to call them back to her bosom, *so that being grounded and made firm in faith, hope and charity, and being 'fruitful in every good work'* (Col. 1, 10), *they may attain eternal salvation."* [41]

Can a more deliberate misrepresentation of a Pope's utterance be found than Father Donnelly's?

Again: we could also ask Father Donnelly not to take the trouble of underlining sentences in his quotations, because they always turn to his disadvantage. For example, in one of the passages which Father Donnelly quotes from Pius IX, the emphasized phrase proves *our* point, and not Father Donnelly's! This is the passage: "But let us, so long as here on earth we are weighed down by this mortal body which dulls the soul, hold firmly to our Catholic doctrine: 'one God, one faith, one baptism;' *to try and probe deeper is criminal..."* [42]

320 THEY FOUGHT THE GOOD FIGHT

What does this mean? To try and probe deeper than *what* is criminal? Deeper than the Catholic doctrine: "one God, one faith, one baptism!" *Who* is probing deeper than this doctrine? Is it the man who confesses *one God, one faith,* (the Catholic Faith), and *one baptism* (the gate to the Catholic Church), as the necessary means for salvation? Is it not, rather, the liberal, who goes around dispensing the name of *faith* to any arbitrary and false opinion and the name of *baptism* to any feeling or sentiment, however anti-Christian?

6. *Concerning the Question of Ignorance*

We come, in this section, to the journalistic authorities used by Father Donnelly. Do we need to remind Father Donnelly that a dogmatic issue cannot be decided by quoting a few sentences from a Pope when he had no intention of defining? This is not real loyalty to the Holy Father, nor is it fair to use him in this manner.

Father Donnelly writes: "More explicitly Pius XI said: 'The limits of vincible or of invincible error are among the most difficult to define, even for the most penetrating intellect. Only God, who is TRUTH, who is ALL TRUTH, who calls every creature to the TRUTH, who gives the means according to His measure to arrive at the TRUTH, only God can with certainty define the limit between vincible and invincible ignorance.' (Allocution published in the *L'Osservatore Romano,* 31 January 1938.)"

First, why are we not told by Father Donnelly that this allocution was addressed to scientists, and was dealing primarily with their problems and not with theological questions? However, there are passages in the same allocution where the Pope *does* speak of theological matters (which Father Donnelly does not quote), concerning the inexcusability of those who should know God who do not know Him, and concerning the necessity of the Catholic Faith for salvation. Here they are:

Pope Pius XI says (speaking of scientists), "May not that terrible vision recur to any of them, that terrible vision which, though for a moment, the Apostle of the Gentiles had: namely, that every high intelligence of this kind ought to become deeply interested in the pursuit of the whole truth, so that it might not happen that an intelligence created by God, illuminated by God, would stop at the creature and would not rise to the Creator. To such an intelligence ought to be applied that great, grave and logical condemnation mentioned by the Apostle himself in these terrible words: 'ita ut sine inexcusabiles' (so that they are inexcusable); as if to say that they could not have an excuse not to have known the Maker, the Creator, after having known His work, His creature." [43]

Likewise, in the same allocution, Pius XI says: "These words which the Divine Master says and repeats are applicable to the Faith: 'You are the light of the world...Neither do men light a candle and put it under a bushel, but upon a candle-stick, that it may shine to all that are in the house.' These words are directed to give, above all, the mission, the preaching, the teaching of the Faith: the teaching of *those truths which are indispensable for all,* even for those to whom to speak of the necessity of science becomes a cruel mockery because they neither have nor will have a predisposition for it, and yet *they are in need of the truth,* of that essential truth which Hertz and Marconi acknowledged, together with all those who throughout the world saw the work of the Creator, the truth which resolved the mystery of the world: *the truth of the Faith.*" [44]

It does not seem from these two excerpts that Pius XI is not judging those who do not come to the knowledge of the Truth, or that he says that the Faith is not indispensable for all men.

But this is not all. The same Pope, in his encyclical *Mortalium Animos,* rebukes those Catholics who try to promote love and unity between the faithful and those outside the Church without trying to convert the latter to the true Faith without which they cannot be saved.

Pius XI says, "When the question of promoting unity among Christians is under consideration many are easily deceived by the semblance of good. 'Is it not right,' it is said repeatedly, 'indeed is it not the duty of all who call upon Christ's name to cease mutual recriminations and join together in ties of mutual charity? For who would dare to say that he loves Christ when he will not strive to his utmost to attain that which Christ prayed for to His Father when He asked that His disciples might *be one?* And did not Christ Himself wish His disciples to bear the sign and be distinguished by the characteristic that they love one another: *By this shall all men know that you are my disciples, if you have love for one another?* 'Would', they add, 'that all Christians were one, that they might drive out the evil of irreligion which every day spreads more widely and threatens to overturn the Gospel.'" [45]

Pope Pius XI answers these misrepresentations: "All remember how John, the very Apostle of Charity, who in his Gospel seems to have opened the secrets of the Most Sacred Heart of Jesus and who always inculcated in the minds of his disciples the new commandment, *Love ye one another,* and wholly forbidden them to have relations with those who did not profess entire and uncorrupted the teachings of Christ. *If any man cometh to you and bring not this doctrine, receive him not into your house nor say to him, God speed you.* Since charity is founded in whole and sincere faith, the disciples of Christ must be united by the bond of unity in faith and by it as the chief bond." [46]

So much for this point. Again, Father Donnelly makes use of an allocution delivered in 1927 by Pope Pius XI to substantiate his own theory about the "judgment of others." It is with reference to Our Lord's words from the Cross, "Father, forgive them for they know not what they do." Father Donnelly implies that Pope Pius XI in this allocution is teaching that Our Lord's words from the Cross proclaim the innocence of His crucifiers because of their ignorance!

This distortion of the words of Our Blessed Lord at the most solemn and sad moment of His life, as He is dying for the *sins* of men, is but one of the instances the liberal theologians use from Sacred Scripture to illustrate their perverse teaching. I will list some other passages they use in this way:

> I Cor. 2,8: For if they had known it, they would never have crucified the Lord of glory.

> John, 16,2: They will put you out of the synagogues: yea, the hour cometh, that whosoever killeth you, will think that he doth a service to God.

> I Tim. 1,13: Who before was a blasphemer, and a persecutor, and contumelious. But I obtained the mercy of God, because I did it ignorantly in unbelief.

These texts do not mean what the liberals interpret them to mean. As a rule, the liberal interpretation of these texts is identical with Abelard's which interpretation was condemned. We shall give Abelard's statement, and St. Bernard's answer to this theory of innocence through ignorance.

The following is Abelard's heretical teaching: "...about the Jews who crucified Christ and the others who, persecuting the martyrs, thought they were doing a service to God, ...we answer that those simple Jews indeed were not acting against their conscience, but rather were persecuting Christ out of zeal for their law; nor did they think they were doing evil, and therefore they did not sin; nor were some of them condemned on account of this, but for preceeding sins, in punishment for which they fell into this blindness. And among them were those elect for whom Christ prayed saying: 'Father, forgive them, for they know not what they do (Luke 23,24)'. Nor did He pray that *this* sin be remitted to them, for this was not a sin, but rather *preceeding* sins." [47]

St. Bernard, in Chapter 4 of his *Epistle to Hugh of St. Victor,* says: "Perhaps he who asserts that one cannot sin through ignorance never prays for his ignorances, but rather laughs at the prophet who prays and says, 'The sins of my youth and my ignorances do not remember' (Ps. 24,7). Perhaps he even reproves God Who requires satisfaction for the *sin of ignorance,* and do one of those things which by the law of the Lord are forbidden, and being guilty of sin, understand his iniquity, he shall offer of the flocks a ram without blemish to the priest, according to the measure and estimation of the sin, and the priest shall pray for him, because he did it ignorantly: and it shall be forgiven him, because by mistake he trespassed against the Lord.' (Lev. 5,17-19.)

"If ignorance is never a sin, why is it said in the *Epistle to the Hebrews* that the high priest entered alone once a year into the second tabernacle, not without blood, which he offers for his own and the people's *ignorance?* (Heb. 9,7.) If the sin of ignorance is no sin, therefore Saul did not sin, who persecuted the Church of God, because he did this indeed ignorantly, remaining in incredulity. Therefore he did well in that he was a blasphemer, and a persecutor, and contumelious, – in that he was breathing threats and slaughter against the disciples of Jesus, – thereby being more abundantly a zealous imitator of the traditions of his fathers (Gal. 1, 13-14)! If ignorance is never a sin, then he should not have said, 'I obtained the *mercy* of God' (I Tim. 1, 13), but, rather, 'I received my *reward,*' for certainly if ignorance renders a man free from sin, then in addition emulation makes him worthy of reward.

"*If,* I say, *one never sins through ignorance,* what then do we hold against those who killed the Apostles, since indeed they did not know that to kill them was evil, but, rather, by doing this, they thought they were doing a service to God? (Jn. 16, 2.) *Then also in vain did our Saviour on the Cross pray for those who crucified Him,* since indeed as He Himself testifies, they were ignorant of what they were doing (Lk. 23, 24), and therefore they did not sin at all! For neither is it allowed in any way to suspect that the Lord Jesus was lying, Who openly bore witness that they did not know what they were doing, nor should one suspect that the Apostle, emulating his flesh, could have lied as a man when he said, 'For if they had known it, they would never have crucified the Lord of glory.' (I Cor. 2,8.) Is it not sufficiently clear from these passages in what a great darkness of ignorance lies the man who does not know that one can sometimes sin through ignorance?" [48]

Is ignorance *never* a sin? Why is it that people are ignorant of the Truth? St. Alphonsus Liguori, Doctor of the Church, asks the same question. "But why is it, then, that all men have not known it and that even at this day so many are *ignorant* of it? This is the reason: 'The light is come into the world, and men loved darkness rather than the light' (Jn. 3,19). They have not known Him, and they do not know Him, because they do not *want* to know Him, loving rather the darkness of sin than the light of grace." [49]

St. John Chrysostom, Doctor of the Church, also tells us: "Thus see how, speaking of the Jews, Our Lord deprives them of all excuse: 'If I had not come and spoken to them, they would not have sin', and Paul again, 'But I say: Have they not heard? Yes, verily, their sound hath gone forth into all the earth.' For there is excuse when there is no one to tell a man, but when the watchman sits there, having this as the business of his life, there is not excuse any longer...Whether you go among the Indians you shall hear this, whether into Spain, or to the very ends of the earth, there is no one without the hearing, *except it be of his own neglect.*" [50]

Concerning the "inculpability" of the ignorant Jews who crucified Our Lord, the following proposition of Abelard's was condemned by the Council of Sens in 1141.

(*It is error to say with Abelard*) 10. "That those who crucified Christ, being ignorant, did not sin, and that whatever is done through ignorance is not to be ascribed to sin." [51]

Moreover, concerning the "innocence" of St. Paul as he was persecuting the Church, the following proposition of John Hus was condemned by the Ecumenical Council of Constance:

(*It is error to say with Hus*) 2. "Paul was never a member of the devil, although he did some acts similar to the acts of those who malign the Church." [52]

I know from personal experience that these doctrines of Abelard and Hus are being taught in one of the Catholic colleges of this part of the country.

Now to return to the allocution of Pius XI in 1927 which Father Donnelly used in his paper, – this is the way he quotes it to make his point: "Sad are these conditions, it is true, but nevertheless they provide some consolation, because the greater the ignorance – and who can ever presume to judge a person's good faith except God? – the less the responsibility. So true is this that Jesus Himself sought, as it were, His last consolation in the fact of ignorance, when He cried out from the

Cross to the Father: 'Pardon them, because they know not what they do.' (Allocution of Pius XI, January 11, 1927; *L'Osservatore Romano* of this date.)"

If this translation of Pope Pius XI's allocution is to be trusted, we can be sure that the Pope did not mean by it what Father Donnelly claims that he did. Although we know that in this allocution the Holy Father was not speaking *ex cathedra,* yet it would be presumptuous to assume that he was teaching heresy, for in the light of the evidence already given it would be heretical to hold that the Jews who crucified Our Lord were not guilty of sin because of ignorance. We wish that liberals would be more careful in the way in which they quote our Popes, or else they will be attributing heretical utterances to the successors of St. Peter, who are the guardians of the Faith.

PART III

BAPTISM

1. *Baptism is Absolutely Necessary for Salvation*

Finally we come to the question of baptism and of its necessity for salvation. In his paper, Father Donnelly does not commit himself openly to any statement about the necessity or lack of necessity of baptism for salvation, as he never commits himself openly about anything. But it is easy to see what he holds on the question from the texts he quotes and the way in which he arranges these texts, as also from the irrelevant comments he makes on the impossibility of judging the subjective state of Protestants. It is rather remarkable to watch a professor of dogmatic theology waste his logic and his scholarship in defending the sincerity of heretics, as if the admission of sincerity or lack of sincerity in a person had anything to do with the possibility of being saved without the Catholic Faith outside the Catholic Church.

The same thing happens concerning baptism. After quoting the Council of Trent which says that baptism or at least "the desire of it" is necessary for justification, Father Donnelly goes on to discuss the inculpability, good faith and sincerity of those outside the Church. It is very clear that, hiding behind the authority of an Ecumenical Council, Father Donnelly claims to be defending orthodox doctrine, but in fact he destroys the whole import of the Council he quotes.

Father Donnelly says that "sanctifying grace and, consequently, a title to the Beatific Vision, are conferred by baptism of desire." But what does he mean by "baptism of desire?" By misquoting Pius XI, as I have shown, Father Donnelly openly teaches that a person who is totally ignorant of the truths of the Faith and of the Catholic Church can be justified and attain eternal salvation while remaining in his ignorance until death. But Father Donnelly also says that on the authority of the Council of Trent at least a desire for baptism is necessary for justification. Therefore, it is clear that Father Donnelly believes that a person can have a desire for baptism while being *totally ignorant* of the Church, of the Catholic Faith, and of baptism of water.

Further, Father Donnelly believes that a man can be justified and be saved who "does not believe explicitly in the Catholic Church, and does not accept all the revealed truths proposed by her for belief." But again he says, on the authority of the Council of Trent, that at least a desire for baptism is necessary for justification. It is clear, therefore, that Father Donnelly believes that a person can have baptism of desire, or more correctly a desire for baptism, which would confer sanctifying grace on him, while *rejecting* the Church and the truths proposed by her for belief.

Again, Father Donnelly claims that Pope Pius XI teaches "that *only those* who are 'contumaciter' and 'pertinaciter' divided from the Church cannot be saved as long as this condition exists." Let us repeat, Father Donnelly inserts this word "only" into the Pope's statement, we must infer that Father Donnelly holds the following: Among those who hear of the Catholic Church and her baptism, only those who contumaciously and obstinately refuse the Catholic Church and her baptism will *not* be saved. The remainder – who refuse, but not contumaciously and obstinately, – *will* be justified and saved. But once more, since at least baptism of desire is necessary for justification, it is clear that, according to Father Donnelly, a person can have baptism of desire *while rejecting* baptism of water!

Let us keep in mind these three doctrines of Father Donnelly's: (1) that a person can be said to have a desire for baptism while being *totally ignorant* of the Catholic Faith and ignorant of the baptism of water; (2) that a person can be said to have a desire for baptism while knowing the Catholic Church and the Catholic Faith and *refusing* both; (3) that a person can be said to have a desire for baptism while knowing the baptism of water and *refusing* to receive it.

Before showing that these doctrines are heretical, let us see what the Church, in her definitions, in her tradition and her teachings, says about the necessity of baptism, for salvation.

Our Lord said to Nicodemus: "Amen I say to you, unless a man be born again of water and the Holy Ghost, he cannot enter into the kingdom of God." (John 3,5.)

St. John Chrysostom says, commenting on this text: "Bewail the infidels, bewail those who in nothing differ from the infidels, who died without illumination, without baptism; those are truly worthy of lamentations, those truly worthy of tears; they are outside of the kingdom, along with those who who are subject to punishment, along with the damned. 'Amen I say to you, unless a man be born again of water and the Holy Ghost, he cannot enter the kingdom of God.'" [1]

In a homily on the *Acts of the Apostles* the same Chrysostom says: "What do you suppose is my anguish when I hear that any person has been taken away unbaptized, while I reflect upon the intolerable punishments of that life, the inexorable doom!" [2]

Speaking on the dignity of the priesthood St. John Chrysostom again says: "For it is manifest folly to despise so great a ministry, without which we could obtain neither salvation nor the good things that have been promised. For as no man can enter into the kingdom of heaven, unless he be born of water and the Holy Ghost; and except he eat the flesh of the Lord, and drink His Blood, he shall be excluded from everlasting life; and as all these things are ministered only by the consecrated hands of priests, how could anyone without them either escape the fire of hell or obtain the crown that is prepared?" [3]

St. Ambrose says: "The Church is redeemed by the precious Blood of Christ. Therefore, whoever should believe, whether Jew or Greek, must know how to circumcise himself from sins, that he might be able to be saved;...for no one ascends into the kingdom of heaven except by the sacrament of baptism." [4]

Pope St. Leo the Great says: "The souls of men, before they are breathed into their bodies, were not; nor would they be breathed into a body by anyone except by God the Maker, Who created both them and the bodies; and since by the transgression of the first man the whole progeny of the human race is vitiated, no one can be freed from the condition of the old man except by the sacrament of the baptism of Christ." [5]

Tertullian says in his treatise *On Baptism:* "From that great pronouncement of Our Lord, Who said: 'Unless a man be born again of water and the Holy Ghost, he does not have life', it is prescribed that salvation comes to no one without baptism." [6]

St. Thomas Aquinas says, commenting on the Apostles Creed, "For just as a man cannot live in the flesh unless he is born in the flesh, even so a man cannot have the spiritual life of grace unless he be born again spiritually. This regeneration is effected by Baptism: 'unless a man be born again of water and the Holy Ghost, he cannot enter the kingdom of God.'" [7]

In a profession of faith prescribed to the Orientals, Pope Benedict XIV says: "Likewise baptism is necessary for salvation for every human creature.[8] The Coucil of Trent anathematized anyone who would say that baptism is not absolutely necessary for salvation for every human creature: or if anyone should say: Canon 5. "If any one shall say that baptism is free, that is, not necessary for salvation, let him be anathema." [9]

St. Thomas Aquinas, in his treatise on the Sacraments, says: "It is manifest that all are bound to receive baptism, and that without it there cannot be salvation for men." [10]

St. Robert Bellarmine says the same in his treatise on the Sacrament of Baptism. He had to refute the heretics of his time, the Waldensians, the Zwinglians, the Lutherans, the Calvinists, and the followers of Wyclif. The first question he proves is that baptism is absolutely necessary for salvation.[11] In speaking of this, he says, "There was once the heresy of the Pelagians, saying that baptism was not necessary for the remission of original sin but only for the attainment of the kingdom of heaven, as Augustine testifies in Chapter 69 of his book on heresies. But our heretics, more audacious than the Pelagians, deny that baptism is necessary, not only for the remission of sin but also for the attainment of the kingdom of heaven." [12]

St. Robert Bellarmine then goes on to say that this same heresy is the heresy of Wyclif, Zwingli and Calvin.[13] And may we repeat, heresy being monotonously the same, the error St. Robert was fighting against is today once more being held by people who call themselves Catholics, and these same Catholics are, in our time, actually sharing the heresy of the Protestant heresiarchs. It must be a case of the greatest distress for this glorious Doctor of the Church, St. Robert Bellarmine, to see that some professors of theology in his own Society are teaching the very heresies which he combatted all his life.

But to return to our subject, modern liberals would say that Baptism is not absolutely necessary for salvation because it would not be just to punish all those who are not baptized, as it would not be just to punish all those who do not accept and join His Church. Therefore, they conclude on the authority of their own reasonings, "God must have innumerable other ways of saving those who are not baptized or who are baptized and join some heretical or schismatical sect. For no one can deny that there are innumerable non-Catholics who are sincere and ready to obey God in everything. God cannot punish eternally a person who is not baptized or is not a Catholic if this is not his fault."

According to this false and presumptuous reasoning, they arbitrarily postulate the existence of other means for saving all those non-Catholics, means other than the Church and her sacraments. According to them, such things as invincible ignorance, sincerity, readiness to do God's will, and so on, can confer sanctifying grace on a person who is ignorant or unwilling to receive the sacraments of the Church and affilation with her. Bainvel teaches this openly, and also Father Donnelly, who teaches that a person ignorant of the Church, or a heretic who refuses to become a Catholic, can be justified and receive sanctifying grace without the means ordained by God. This is what makes them speak of the Church and Baptism as the *"ordinary* means instituted by God for salvation."* Thus Bainvel says: "It is indeed the order desired by God, the rule He lays down, that all shall be saved within the Church. The exceptional cases, be they ever so numerous – and they are less numerous than appears at first sight – are outside the Divine intention because of the fault of the human will, and are supplied by God with an extraordinary economy, a special Providence granted in the measure of necessity." [14]

The question, may we say, is not how numerous the exceptions are, but whether we have a right to assume that there *are* any exceptions at all, in other words, to assume that God has any other plans for salvation besides the Church and Baptism. Is not Father Bainvel guilty of rationalization here – that is, guilty of an attempt to subject revelation to his own reasoning?

St. Augustine and St. Robert Bellarmine answer for us by saying that the eternal damnation of those outside the Church and of the unbaptized might seem to be unjust; but this is only because the ways of the justice of God are hidden to us in this life, but when they will be revealed to us in the Beatific Vision, we shall see how very just is the damnation of the unbaptized.[15] "However," says St. Robert, "those who imagine that there is another remedy besides baptism, openly contradict the Gospel, the Councils, the Fathers, and the consensus of the Universal Church." [16]

The heretics and liberal Catholics of Bellarmine's time were especially trying to invent other means of salvation for unbaptized babies. "If baptism is necessary for salvation," they would say, "then innumerable infants would perish without being guilty, which seems to be against God's justice." St. Robert answers saying: "Even though children are not baptized without being guilty thereof, yet they do not perish without any guilt on their part, since they have original sin." [17]

The same arguments are brought forth nowadays in relation to adults, because the liberals of this day would not dare openly contradict what has already been clearly defined about children, namely that they cannot be saved without actual baptism. But what St. Robert says about children applies to adults as well, for, even though some of them could die unbaptized because they never heard of Christ, and hence without being guilty of this ignorance, yet these will perish eternally because they have original sin and because of their actual sins, as St. Thomas unmistakably teaches in the *Summa*.[18] On the other hand, those who heard of Christ and do not join His Church and receive baptism, will perish because of their refusal, which is the sin of infidelity, the most serious of all sins, as St. Thomas says.[19]

But it is pride that incites the liberals to their foolish reasonings. For, as St. Robert says, they do seem to know that the care and protection of all men belongs to God much more than to them, "and Christ well knew, when He asserted that baptism was necessary (John 3) that many would be deprived of this remedy without any fault of their own, and it would be most easy for God, if He wished, to provide baptism for all children, *as He provides it for all His elect...* or those whom God predestined, to them He provides most efficaciously the means of salvation." [20]

The only remedy against original sin is baptism, and all those whom God predestined to salvation, He draws them to this remedy. All the children who die unbaptized and all the adults who die ignorant of baptism, or who, having been drawn to it by God's Providence, refuse it, are not predestinate but will perish eternally.

As a matter of fact, the absolute necessity of baptism for salvation was always recognized so strongly, that some of the Fathers of the Church went as far as to affirm that all those who die unbaptized, even babies, are punished in eternal fire.

For example, St. Fulgentius says in his *De Fide ad Petrum:* "Hold most firmly and do not doubt at all, that not only men who already have the use of reason, but even children who either begin in their mother's wombs and die there, or who, being already born of their mothers, pass from this world without the sacrament of holy baptism, which is given in the Name of the Father and of the Son and of the Holy Ghost, will be punished with the torment of everlasting fire." [21] St. Augustine says the same in his *De Anima et eius Origine.*[22]

But as St. Bonaventure says in his *Breviloquium:* "Lastly, because the lack of that justice in those who are now born is not the result of any choice of their own will, or of any actual delectation, it is not fitting that there should be punishment of the senses in hell after this life for original sin because divine justice which is always accompanied by an overflowing mercy punishes us not beyond what is merited but rather short of that. We must believe that blessed Augustine knew this though his words on the surface seem to sound otherwise because of contempt for the Pelagian error which granted them a different kind of happiness. So that Augustine might lead them back to a middle position, he turned more easily to the other extreme." [23]

In those ages of strong faith, baptism was known to be so important that the holy Fathers were not afraid to go even a little farther in their orthodox affirmations in order to destroy the hateful heresies that surrounded them.

2. *Is Baptism by Itself Sufficient for Salvation?*

When is baptism valid? (1) When water is used, (2) when the proper words are used: "I baptize you in the name of the Father and of the Son and of the Holy Ghost," (3) if the person baptizing has the intention of doing what Christ intended, and (4) in the case of an adult being baptized, if the person baptized has the intention of receiving baptism. For, as Pope Innocent III said, "But he who never consents but entirely contradicts, receives neither the *res* nor the character of the sacrament." [24] St. Thomas also says, "It must be said that if the intention of receiving the sacrament is lacking in an adult, he should be rebaptized." [25]

Now that we have shown that baptism is necessary for salvation, we may ask, – is valid baptism sufficient for salvation? And we answer, for children, yes, but for adults, no. What more is required of an adult besides baptism for salvation? Two more things are required: (1) the Catholic Fatith, since "without Faith it is impossible to please God," (Heb. 11,6) and (2) membership in the Catholic Church under the authority of the Roman Pontiff, since "outside the Church there is no salvation" and since, as St. Thomas says in his treatise *Against the Errors of the Greeks,* "to be subject to the Roman Pontiff is necessary for salvation." [26]

1. Concerning the first of these requirements, namely, Faith, St. Thomas in his treatise on baptism asks the question whether faith is necessary for baptism so that sanctifying grace be conferred on the soul by the sacrament. The Angelic Doctor answers that in order to receive sanctifying grace through baptism "right faith is of necessity required for baptism; since, as it is said in *Rom.* III, 22, 'the justice of God is by

faith in Jesus Christ.'" [27] The Council of Trent speaks of the "Sacrament of Baptism, which is the 'Sacrament of Faith,' without which faith there can be no justification for anyone." [28]

Thus baptism can be valid even if the subject who receives it does not confess the Catholic Faith, *but it cannot be profitable for salvation if the subject is an adult.*

2. Likewise, all those who receive baptism without the explicit intention of becoming members of the Catholic Church under the authority of the Roman Pontiff will receive a valid sacrament but not the effects of the sacrament, namely, sanctifying grace and salvation, except if they are children.

St. Alphonsus Liguori says in his treatise *On the Commandments and the Sacraments:* "We must believe that the Roman Catholic Church is the only true Church. Hence they who are out of our Church, or separated, cannot be saved, except infants who die after baptism." [29] But this is not an exception. Children who are baptized are real members of the Church, even if their parents and the minister who baptizes them are not Catholics. Every child validly baptized is a Catholic, and every adult who is validly baptized and who confesses the Catholic Faith with the intention of joining the Catholic Church is a Catholic.

This is the definition St. Robert Bellarmine gives of the Catholic Church: "The Church is one only and not two and this one and true Church is the congregation of men bound together by the profession of the same Christian Faith, and by the communion of the same sacraments, under the rule of the legitimate pastors, and especially of the one Vicar of Christ on earth, the Roman Pontiff." [30] All those, therefore, who do not profess the Catholic Faith, or who do not participate in the sacraments of the Church or who do not submit to the authority of the Roman Pontiff, are not members of the Church and therefore cannot be saved.

Does this mean that every adult who is baptized outside the Catholic Church, or every baptized child who grows up and follows the heretical sect of his parents cannot be saved? Yes, unless before he dies he repents and joins the Catholic Church. Let us see what the Fathers and Doctors of the Church have to say on this point.

St Fulgentius says: "Whether in the Catholic Church or in any heretical or schismatical church, if anyone receives the sacrament of baptism in the Name of the Father and of the Son and of the Holy Ghost, he receives the integral sacrament; but salvation, which is the power of the sacrament, he will not have, if he has received the same sacrament outside the Catholic Church. Thus therefore, he must return to the Church, not that he might receive the sacrament of baptism anew, which no one ought to repeat in any baptized man, but that, being now in Catholic society, he might receive eternal life, which can never, in any way, be obtained by one who, with the sacrament of baptism, would remain a stranger to the Catholic Church." [31]

Again St. Fulgentius says: "Hold most firmly, and do not doubt at all, that the sacrament of baptism can be, not only in the Catholic Church, but also among the heretics who baptize in the Name of the Father and of the Son and of the Holy Ghost, but that *outside the Catholic Church it cannot profit.* Nay rather, as in the Church salvation is conferred by the sacrament of baptism to those who believe rightly, so to those baptized outside the Church, if they do not return to the Church, destruction is completely fulfilled by the same baptism. For, the unity of this Ecclesiastical society is of such value for salvation, that he is not saved by baptism to whom it has not been given where it ought to have been given." [32]

Again: "Hold most firmly, and do not doubt at all, that everyone baptized outside the Catholic Church cannot be made partaker of eternal life, if before the end of this earthly life, he does not return to the Catholic Church and become incorporated with it." [33]

The same St. Fulgentius says: "Hold most firmly, and do not doubt at all, that not only all the pagans, but also all the Jews, and all the heretics and schismatics who end the present life outside the Catholic Church, will go into the eternal fire, 'which was prepared for the devil and his angels' (Mt. 25,41)." [34]

St. Augustine says in his commentary on St. John: "And yet it may be that one may have baptism apart from the dove" (i.e. the Catholic Church), "but, that baptism apart from the dove should do him good, is impossible." [35] Speaking of the heretic or schismatic St. Augustine says: "I, says he, have baptism. You have it, but that baptism without charity profits you nothing, because without charity you are nothing...*For you did have baptism to destruction,* outside (the Church); if you shall have it within, it begins to profit you to salvation." [36]

St. Bonaventure says in his *Breviloquium:* "Because outside of the unity of faith and love which makes us sons and members of the Church, no one can be saved, hence if the sacraments are received outside the Church, they are not effective for salvation, although they are true sacraments. However, they can become useful if one returns to Holy Mother the Church, the only Spouse of Christ, whose sons alone Christ the Spouse deems worthy of eternal inheritance." [37]

St. Augustine, in his *Baptism against the Donatists,* Bk.4, says: "The Church compared to Paradise indicates to us that certain men are able to receive baptism even outside of Her, but that no one is able either to grasp or to retain the salvation of beatitude outside of Her.

"For even the rivers from the font of Paradise, as the Scripture testifies, flowed widely outside. They are remembered by name and it is known to all through what lands they flowed and that they existed neither in Mesopotomia nor in Egypt, in which those rivers flowed. So it is that, though the water of Paradise is outside of Paradise, there is no beatitude except within Paradise.

"So the Baptism of the Church can exist outside of the Church but the gift of a blessed life is not found except within the Church which was founded on a rock and received the keys of binding and loosing. She is the one that keeps and possesses every power of Her Spouse and Lord, and through this conjugal power She can also bring forth sons from the handmaids, who, if they be not proud, shall be called into their share of inheritance. If, however, they are proud, they shall remain without.

"Because we fight for the honor and unity of the Church, let us not concede to the heretics what we know to be false, but rather let us teach them by arguments that they cannot attain salvation through unity unless they come to that same unity. For the water of the Church is faithful and salutary and holy for those who use it well. *But outside of the Church no one can use it well.*" [38]

In the same book St. Augustine says: "Therefore we are right in censuring anathematizing, abhorring and abominating the perversity of heart shown by heretics; yet it does not follow that they do not have the sacrament of the Gospel, because they have not what makes it avail." [39]

We do not deny that baptism can be validly administered outside the Church, if all the conditions for its validity are fulfilled. But we deny that it can confer sanctifying grace and a title to the Beatific Vision if one does not intend to join the Church while receiving it. We say with the whole tradition of the Church that a non-Catholic can receive baptism outside the Church, but not sanctification.

Now, let us be sure that everything is perfectly clear. We have seen (1) that for one who has not the intention of being baptized, baptism is *not valid;* (2) if one has the intention of being baptized *but does not confess the Catholic Faith,* his baptism is valid BUT it does not confer sanctification and salvation.

Therefore, if this is true of real baptism, how can the so-called "baptism of desire" of Father Donnelly confer sanctification and salvation when the man has neither the required explicit intention of receiving the baptism of water nor confessed the Catholic Faith?

We confess with the Catholic Church, and with the whole Christian tradition, that it is absolutely impossible to attain salvation outside the Catholic Church. As we have shown, we mean by this what the Church herself means: (1) that no adult can be saved if he does not, whether through ignorance or obstinacy, explicitly confess the Catholic Faith; (2) that no adult can be saved who dies ignorant of the Catholic Church, or who, having known the Church refuses to become one of her members; (3) that no adult can be saved who dies ignorant of baptism or who, having heard of it, refuses to receive it; (4) that no adult can be saved who is baptized into a heretical or schismatical church, unless before he dies he joins the Catholic Church; (5) that no adult can be saved if he does not explicitly confess the Catholic Faith, or if he denies one truth of the Faith, or if he does not submit fully to the authority of the Roman Pontiff; (6) and that no child who dies unbaptized can be saved.

Therefore, it is impossible for a man to be saved if he holds other beliefs than those of the Catholic Church, if he belongs to any other religious community than the Catholic Church, and if he does not receive the baptism instituted by Christ.

St. Robert Bellarmine, who defends very strongly the doctrine that outside the Church there can be no salvation for anyone, says that he means by the Catholic Church "the congregation of men bound together by the profession of the same Christian Faith, and by the communion of the same sacraments, under the rule of the legitimate pastors, and especially of the one Vicar of Christ on earth, the Roman Pontiff." [40]

But if those who are outside the Church cannot attain salvation, is there a way of determining exactly who is a member of the Church and who is not? Bellarmine answers: "From this definition it can be easily gathered what men belong to the Church and what men do not. For there are three parts of this definition: the profession of the true Faith, the communion of the Sacraments, and the subjection to the legitimate Pastor, the Roman Pontiff. By reason of the first part are excluded all infidels, as much those who have never been in the Church, like the Jews, Turks and Pagans; as those who have been and have fallen away, like heretics and apostates. By reason of the second, are excluded catechumens and excommunicates, because the former are not to be admitted to the communion of the sacraments, the latter have been cut off from it. By reason of the third, are excluded schismatics, who have faith and the sacraments, but are not subject to the lawful pastor, and therefore they profess the Faith outside, and receive the Sacraments outside. However all others are included, even if they be reprobate, sinful and wicked." [41]

In his *Compendium of Christian Doctrine,* Bellarmine says: "I believe that for the good Christians there is eternal life full of every happiness and free from every sort of evil; as, on the contrary, for the infidels and for the bad Christians there is eternal death full of every misery and deprived of every good." [42]

St. Peter Canisius says in his *Catechism,* speaking of the Catholic Church: "Outside of this communion (as outside of the Ark of Noah) there is absolutely no salvation for mortals: not to Jews or Pagans, who never received the faith of the Church; not to heretics who, having received it, forsook or corrupted it; not to schismatics who left the peace and unity of the Church; finally neither to excommunicates who for any other serious cause deserved to be put away and separated from the body of the Church, like pernicious members...For the rule of Cyprian and Augustine is certain: He will not have God for his Father who would not have the Church for his Mother." [43]

Pope Boniface VIII, in his Bull *Unam Sanctam,* says: "Urged by faith, we are obliged to believe and to hold that the Church is one, holy, catholic, and also apostolic. We firmly believe in her, and we confess absolutely that outside her there is neither salvation nor the remission of sins, as the Spouse in the Canticles (VI,8) proclaims: 'One is my dove, my perfect one. She is the only one of her mother, the chosen of her that bore her,' who represents one mystical body, whose head is Christ, and the head of Christ is God. In her there is one Lord, one faith, one baptism. There was indeed at the deluge only one ark of Noah, prefiguring the One Church, which Ark, having been finished to a single cubit, had only one pilot and guide, i.e. Noah, outside of which, as we read, all that subsisted on the earth was destroyed." [44]

Origen said in one of his homilies: "If anyone from this people wants to be saved, let him come to this house, in which is the Blood of Christ in sign of redemption...Let no one therefore persuade himself, let not one deceive himself: outside of this house, that is outside of the Church, no one is saved; for, if anyone should go out of it, he is guilty of his own death." [45]

St. Cyprian in his treatise *On the Unity of the Catholic Church* says: "...Our Lord said: 'I and the Father are one.' And again it is written about the Father and the Son and the Holy Spirit; 'And these three are one.' And does anyone believe that this unity coming from the divine power, and joined by heavenly sacraments, can be torn apart in the Church and separated by the division of opposing wills? Whoever does not hold this unity, does not hold the law of God, does not hold the faith of the Father and of the Son, does not hold life and salvation." [46]

Speaking to the Philadelphians, St. Ignatius of Antioch says: "Do not err, my brethern: If anyone follow a maker of schism, 'he shall not possess the kingdom of heaven' (I Cor. 6,9-10). If anyone walk in a foreign doctrine, he does not communicate with the Passion." [47]

St. Irenaeus says in his *Treatise against Heretics:* "In the Church God has set apostles, prophets, doctors' (I Cor. 12,28), and all the remaining operation of the Spirit, of which are not partakers all those who do not hasten to come into the Church, but defraud themselves of life, by an evil determination and a worse operation. For where the Church is, there is also the Spirit of God; and where the Spirit of God is, there is the Church and every grace; for the Spirit is truth." [48]

Let us listen to Pope Pius XI who, Fr. Donnelly says, believes that there can be salvation outside the Catholic Church: "No one is found in the one Church of Christ and no one perseveres in it unless he acknowledges and accepts obediently the supreme authority of St. Peter and his legitimate successors. Did not the very ancestors of those who are entangled in the errors of Photius and the Protestants obey the Roman Bishop as the high shepherd of souls?

"Let them listen to Lactantius crying: 'It is only the Catholic Church that retains the true worship. She is the fountain of truth, she is the abode of faith, she is the temple of God; if anyone does not enter her or if anyone shall depart from her, he is a stranger to the hope of life and salvation. Let not one deceive himself, therefore, by continuous disputations. Life and salvation are in the balance, which if not looked to carefully and diligently, will be lost and destroyed.'" [49]

St. Fulgentius says, concerning all those who are outside the Catholic Church, whether baptized or not: "Hold most firmly and do not doubt at all, that not only all the pagans, but also all the Jews, and all the heretics and schismatics who end the present life outside the Catholic Chuch, will go into the eternal fire, 'which was prepared for the devil and his angels' (Mt. 25,41)." [50]

Finally, the Council of Florence, under Pope Eugene IV, decreed in the Bull *Cantate Domino:* "The most holy Roman Church firmly believes, professes and preaches, that *none of those existing outside the Catholic Church, not only pagans, but also Jews and heretics and schismatics, can have a share in life eternal;* but that they will go into the eternal fire, 'which was prepared for the devil and his angels,' unless before death they become affiliated with Her; and that so important is the unity of this ecclesiastical body that only those remaining within this unity can profit by the sacraments of the Church unto salvation, and they alone can receive an eternal recompense for their fasts, their almsgiving, their other works of Christian piety, and the duties of a Christian soldier. No one, let his almsgiving be as great as it *may, no one even if he pour out his blood for the name of Christ, can be saved, unless he remain within the bosom and the unity of the Catholic Church."* [51]

3. *"Baptism of Blood" and "Baptism of the Spirit"*

(a) *Introduction.* But let us come now to what Father Donnelly and the other liberal theologians call "baptism of desire." Is there anything in Catholic tradition to warrant this phrase and its use by liberals?

As I have already said, the expression "baptism of desire" is a mistranslation of the Latin expressions: "baptismus Flaminis" and "baptismus in voto" or "votum baptismi." The first of these expressions (baptismus Flaminis) means, as St. Thomas explains in the *Summa,* Part III, Question 66, Article 11, "baptism of the Holy Spirit," which is a far cry from the interpretation which the modern liberal puts on this phrase, as I will show. The other two expressions, (baptismus in voto and votum baptismi) make use of the word *votum,* which means *will, intention, purpose,* and can therefore be translated as: "baptism in purpose" of "will for baptism."

What do the Fathers and Doctors teach concerning this question of baptism *in voto* or of baptism of the Spirit?

First let us quote St. Ambrose on the efficacy of baptism: "And thus you have read that *three* testimonies in baptism *are one, water, blood and the Spirit;* since, if you remove one of these, the sacrament of baptism does not stay. For what is water without the Cross of Christ? A common element, without any effect of sacrament. Nor again is the mystery of regeneration without water; for 'unless a man be born again of water and the Holy Ghost, he cannot enter into the kingdom of God.' Now a catechumen also believes in the Cross of Our Lord Jesus Christ, by which he also signs himself, but unless he be baptized in the Name of the Father and of the Son and of the Holy Ghost he cannot receive remission of his sins, nor can he receive the gift of spiritual grace." [52]

Likewise, St. Thomas says: "The baptism of water has its efficacy from the passion of Christ, to which someone conforms himself through baptism, and ultimately from the Holy Spirit as from a first cause." [53]

Elswhere in the *Summa,* St. Thomas explains this: "A sacrament in causing grace works after the manner of an instrument. Now an instrument is twofold; the one, separate, as a stick, for instance the other, united, as a hand. Moreover, the separate instrument is moved by means of the united instrument, as a stick by the hand. Now the principal efficient cause of grace is God himself, in comparison with Whom Christ's humanity is as a united instrument, whereas the sacrament is as a separate instrument." [54]

We see, therefore, that sanctification is primarily *caused* by the Three Divine Persons and is the *work* of the Holy Spirit by appropriation. It is, however, achieved in us through Christ's Passion as a primary instrument, and through water as a secondary instrument. All three, namely, the Spirit, the blood of Christ, and water are, consequently, indispensable, and no one can be sanctified if one of the three is missing.

(b) *Meaning of "Baptism of Blood" and "Baptism of the Spirit."*

Now the word *baptism,* which comes from the Greek, means *washing.* Every time a person passes out of the state of sin (whether original or actual), he is said to be washed, or cleansed. The first sacrament of the Church is a general washing, and is therefore called baptism. But even a baptized person can fall back into sin, though not original sin. The only way for this person to come back to the state of grace is through another purification or washing.

It is in prefiguration of these washings from sin that the Jews had to have so many ablutions, especially before their meals. We also are asked to wash before our Eucharistic meals. But *this* washing is not the renewal of the sacrament of baptism, which cannot be repeated. It is, rather, a washing from actual sin only, not from original sin. This is why Our Lord insisted on washing the Apostles' feet before He instituted the Sacrament of the Holy Eucharist. Jesus came first to Peter who refused to see his God and his Master descend so low as to wash his feet. But Jesus answered: "If I wash thee not, thou shalt have no part with me." Frightened lest he should lose his beloved Master's friendship, Peter said, "Lord, not my feet, but also my hands and my head." And Jesus said to him, "He that is washed, needeth not but to wash his feet, but is clean wholly." [55]

This indeed signifies the sacrament of penance which is a certain washing, but a washing only of that in us that touches the earth; for he that is washed wholly by baptism needs only to have his feet washed. Says St. Augustine, "And every day, therefore, is he who intercedes for us washing our feet...For 'if,' as it is written, 'we confess our sins, He is faithful and just, to forgive us our sins, and to cleanse us from all iniquity,' that is, even to our feet wherewith we walk on the earth." [56]

Therefore every washing whereby the Holy Spirit comes to inhabit the soul can be called a baptism, a cleansing, although we do not necessarily mean the real sacrament of baptism. Every time the sacrament of penance is administered a certain washing or baptism is administered, but it is not a baptism of water, but rather a *baptism of the Holy Spirit.* Likewise, when a Catholic is about to be martyred and is unable to receive the sacrament of penance for the remission of his sins, his martyrdom itself effects this remission, and can thus be called a kind of washing or baptism, a *baptism of blood.*

St. Thomas says the same thing about these two baptisms, the baptism of blood and the baptism of the Spirit: "But those who live after baptism in this mortal life are not able to ascend to such a height of perfection that the inordinate motions of sensuality may not still rise up from earthly affections; and therefore it is necessary that they wash their feet, either by martyrdom, which is the *baptism of blood* (baptismus sanguinis), or by penance, which is the *baptism of the Spirit* (baptismus Flaminis), in order that they might be saved." [57]

But how about an unbaptized person? Could these two kinds of baptism be received by persons who have not been actually baptized with water? And if these sacraments could be received by them (baptism of blood and baptism of the Spirit, that is), would they supply the place of baptism of water, so that the persons who received them could attain salvation without being baptized with water? Let us see what the Fathers and the Doctors of the Church have to say about this:

(c) *Baptism of Blood.*

St. Cyril of Jerusalem says about baptism of blood: "If anyone does not receive baptism, he does not have salvation, with the exception of the martyrs alone, who even without water receive the kingdom." [58]

St. Fulgentius says: "From the time when Our Saviour said, 'unless a man be born again of water and the Holy Ghost, he cannot enter into the kingdom of God' (John 3,5), no one, without the sacrament of baptism, can receive the kingdom of heaven or life eternal, except those who, without baptism, *shed their blood for Christ in the Catholic Church.*[59]

St. Augustine says in his *City of God:* "For whoever being not yet regenerate, dies for confessing Christ, is freed of his sin as well as if he had received the sacrament of baptism. For he Who said: 'Unless a man be born again of water and the Holy Ghost, he cannot enter into the kingdom of God,' elsewhere says about the martyrs, 'Everyone therefore that shall confess me before men, I will confess him before My Father Who is in Heaven;' and again: 'He that shall lose his life for My sake shall find it.' Whereupon it is that 'Precious in the sight of the Lord is the death of His saints.' For what is more dear than the death wherein all the wickedness of a man is abolished and his good augmented?" [60]

St. Robert Bellarmine says: "Martyrdom is rightly called, and is, a certain baptism." [61]

Martyrdom for the Name of Christ can therefore supply the place of baptism of water, and this both for adults and children, – witness the Holy Innocents who were killed for the sake of Christ.*

When *can* martyrdom supply the place of baptism? Can a man who knows that he is going to be killed for confessing Christ and who on this account refuses or neglects the baptism of water because martyrdom is a perfect substitute, can such a man be saved? Or can a man who dies for confessing Christ while remaining in an heretical or schismatical sect be saved? Or again, is there any way in which a man can be saved by the baptism of blood if he is ignorant of Christ and His Church?

Martyrdom is a substitute for the baptism of water only in case of a catechumen who has the Catholic Faith and confesses Christ and His Church, and who, because of his apprehension by pagans or heretics, is unable to receive the baptism of water. Thus St. Augustine, in the *City of God,* says that these martyrs will be saved "because they willed rather to die in confessing Christ than to deny Him." [62] Therefore, martyrdom can replace Baptism only in the case of a man who cannot receive the Sacrament of Baptism *because* he is dying for Christ.

Thus it is clear that even a catechumen who dies confessing Christ cannot be saved if he refuses the baptism of water, or if he does not try to receive it, knowing that he is going to be martyred.

Moreover, it is not enough to confess Christ in order to have the baptism of Blood. One needs also to confess His Church and to be dying as a Catholic, although prevented by martyrdom from receiving the baptism of water. Thus, St. Fulgentius says that no one can be saved without the baptism of water, "except for those who, without baptism, *shed their blood for Christ in the Catholic Church.*" [63]

---

* Father Feeney was later to criticize the Holy Innocents and the Good Thief (although many of the Fathers use them), as examples of Baptism of Blood, because they died before the foundation of the Catholic Church at Pentecost and therefore before the sacrament of Baptism became obligatory. It is interesting that St. Augustine who at one time had used the Good Thief as an example of Baptism of Blood, later retracted this opinion, though Father Feeney would have said, for the wrong reason. "In his *Retractationes* (Bk. 2, Chp.44) Augustine finds the example of the thief inappropriate because 'it is uncertain whether he had been baptized.'" Theisen, Abbot Jerome, OSB., *The Ultimate Church and the Promise of Salvation,* St. John's University Press, Collegeville, Minnesota, 1976, p.15, n.46.

Further, St. Paul said, in his first Epistle to the Corinthians (13,3): "And if I should distribute all my goods to feed the poor, and if I should deliver my body to be burned, and have not charity, it profiteth me nothing." This does not mean (and St. Robert Bellarmine in his treatise on Baptism clearly proves it)[64] that a martyr needs to have *perfect* charity before he is martyred. Imperfect charity is sufficient, since martyrdom itself would confer perfect charity on the martyr. But it means that unless a man is dying for Christ *in His Church,* he cannot be saved. For, as St. Thomas shows, separation from the Body of the Church and from the authority of the Vicar of Christ on earth is a sin against charity.[65]

This is why the Council of Florence, on the authority of St. Paul, decreed: "No one, let his almsgiving be as great as it may, *no one even if he pour out his blood for the name of Christ, can be saved, unless he remain within the bosom and the unity of the Catholic Church.*" [66]

Therefore Bellarmine rightly concludes that salvation can be attained by "Those who are killed for Christ *in the confession of the true Faith, and in the unity of the Church. For heretics and schismatics cannot be martyrs,* since they place an obstacle to the grace of God by their sin of infidelity and schism, in which they actually persevere." [67]

And St. Cyprian in his book on the *Unity of the Church* writes: "If such (heretics or schismatics) should even suffer martyrdom for the name of Christ, they would not expiate their crime. There can be no such thing as a martyr out of the church. Though they should be thrown into the fire, or be exposed to the fury of wild beasts, such a death will never be esteemed a crown of their faith and constancy, but rather a punishment of their perfidy. Such a man may be put to death but cannot be crowned. – If the schismatic should suffer out of the church of Christ, he will never thence become entitled to the recompense which none can claim who are not in it. There is but one God, one Christ, one church, one faith, one entire body of Christian people. – Whatever shall be separated from the fountain of life, can have no life remaining in it, after having lost all communication with its vital principle." [68]

Hence also, a man who is ignorant of Christ and His Church (whether culpably or not) cannot possibly receive the baptism of blood, since an open confession of the true Faith and of the true Church is indispensable for martyrdom.

(d) *Baptism of the Holy Spirit.*

1st question: Can Sanctifying Grace Precede the Reception of a Sacrament?

Let us come now to the third kind of baptism, namely the baptism of the Holy Spirit. And first it must be noted that the Holy Spirit cannot possibly effect sanctification in a man apart from any sacrament or visible sign. Thus, before the coming of Christ, sanctification came to men by means of circumcision, sacrifice and the other sacraments of the Old Law. Since the coming of the Messiah sanctification comes by means of the sacraments of the Church, which are seven in number.

The first of these sacraments, without which no other sacrament can be received, is baptism. And baptism is invalid for an adult if he does not have the explicit purpose of receiving it, and unprofitable if he does not explicitly confess Christ and His Church. This is why baptism is called "The sacrament of faith." Therefore without faith it is impossible to receive sanctifying grace from any of the seven sacraments, which are the only channels of grace.

The explicit intention to receive the sacrament, faith in Christ and His Church, are therefore necessary on the part of an adult for the reception of sanctifying grace. But they are not enough. Actual reception of the sacrament is also needed this is why St. Ambrose says: "A catechumen also believes in the Cross of Our Lord Jesus, by which he also signs himself; but unless he be baptized in the Name of the Father and of the Son and of the Holy Ghost, he cannot receive remission of his sins, nor can he receive the gift of spiritual grace." [69]

But there could be a case when a man, together with the explicit intention of receiving a sacrament, and with the profession of the Catholic Faith and of the Catholic Church, would make an act of *perfect charity,* even before the actual reception of the sacrament. In that case the man can receive sanctifying grace before the sacrament, *if* he firmly intends to receive the sacrament at the earliest possible opportunity. This is true for example about penance. Thus St. Thomas says:

"If anyone has *perfect contrition* before the absolution of the priest, he obtains the remission of his sins, by the fact that he intends to subject himself to the keys of the Church, *without which intent there is no real contrition.*

"But if the contrition sufficient for remission is not full beforehand the remission of the guilt is obtained in the absolution itself, unless he puts an obstacle to the Holy Spirit." [70]

The same happens in all the other sacraments, *if a perfect act of charity is made,* together with an act of Faith and a *firm purpose of receiving the sacrament.* In the case of baptism too, if the catechumen to be baptized can make an act of perfect charity, remission of his sins can precede the actual reception of baptism, provided explicit faith and an *explicit intent to receive baptism* are not lacking. St. Thomas says:

"For it happens that some adults before they come to the sacrament of baptism *in act,* having it *in intent* (in voto), obtain remission of their sins, and are baptized by the baptism of the Spirit (baptismo Flaminis); and yet, baptism which follows, effects the remission of sins, as far as its part goes, although in him in whom they are already remitted, it does not have this opportunity, but obtains only an augmentation of grace.

"But if an adult is not perfectly disposed before baptism to obtain remission of his sins, he obtains this remission by the power of baptism, in the very act of being baptized, unless he place deceivingly an obstacle to the Holy Spirit." [71]

But who can presume to affirm about any man that he has received sanctifying grace before the actual reception of a sacrament, seeing that it is impossible to know whether or not he was able to make a perfect act of love? And yet this is what the liberals do all the time. They can even *name* people who had sanctifying grace before their baptism! They can even name people who had it even while rejecting explicitly some truths of the Catholic Faith and without intending to come to the Church! Here is an example of such an arrogant attitude: (in a letter recently received by one of our staff from a liberal theologian) "*Surely,* Chesterton and Newman had grace before their conversions, *even though they rejected certain Catholic doctrines.*" Nothing can be more opposed to the Catholic Faith than a statement of this kind.

In the same way, Caperan, Director of the Grand Seminaire of Toulouse, who is Father Donnelly's main authority, says, "Without any doubt, the action of grace does not stop at the frontiers of Catholicism; its radiance extends on all sides, as far as there is a soul to save." [72]

There is no doubt that in Father Donnelly's mind, too, people who are totally ignorant of the Catholic Faith and people who know the Church and refuse to join her can have sanctifying grace, independently of the Sacraments, of the Faith, and therefore of perfect contrition. Not only is it impossible for such people to have sanctifying grace as long as they are thus visibly separated from the Church but even in the case of catechumens who have the Catholic Faith and a real intent of receiving baptism, there is no way of telling whether they have perfect charity or not, except if it is revealed by God, as in the case of Cornelius, in *Acts* 10. For, as St. Augustine says, "Cornelius even before his baptism, was filled with the Holy Spirit." [73] This reception of the Holy Spirit in anticipation of the baptism of water is called *baptism of the Spirit,* or *baptism in voto.*

This is what the Council of Trent was teaching when it said (as Fr. Donnelly well knows) that the *justification* of the unbaptized may be described "as the transfer from that state in which a man is born as the son of the first Adam, to the state of grace and adoption of the sons of God, through the second Adam, Jesus Christ Our Saviour; and this transfer indeed, after the promulgation of the Gospel, cannot be accomplished without the water of regeneration *or the will for it* (aut eius voto), as it is written: 'Unless a man be born again of water and the Holy Ghost, he cannot enter into the kingdom of God.'"[74]

Let us remind Fr. Donnelly that the same Council of Trent to which he is appealing teaches unmistakeably that this justification comes from Jesus Christ and only to those who believe in Him according to the true Faith, as the Apostle says (Rom. 3,23-26): "For all have sinned, and do need the glory of God, being justified freely by His grace, through the redemption that is in Christ Jesus, Whom God hath proposed to be a propitiation, *through faith in His Blood,* to the showing of His justice, for the remission of former sins,...that He Himself may be just, *and the justifier of him, who is of the faith of Jesus Christ.*" (Cf. Denz. 794.)

Again the same Council of Trent says: "Indeed, since the Apostle said that man is justified by *faith* and *freely,* these words must be understood in that sense, which the perpetual consensus of the Catholic Church held and expressed, namely that *we are thus said to be justified by faith,* since 'faith is the beginning of human salvation,' *the foundation and root of every justification, 'without which it is impossible to please God' and to come to the fellowship of His children.*"[75]

Justification, therefore, and sanctifying grace, can come to a person before the actual reception of the sacrament of baptism, provided explicit faith in Christ, explicit purpose to receive the sacrament and to join the Catholic Church, and perfect charity are not lacking.

This is certainly not the way Fr. Donnelly interprets the paragraph he quotes from the Council of Trent; for it is clear that he holds that a man who is ignorant of Christ and His Church, or a man who refuses to accept both, can be justified by some kind of feeling of righteousness which can be called *baptism of desire.* It is also clear that Father Donnelly in quoting the Council of Trent was confusing *justification* with *salvation.* The Council of Trent in this text was defining justification and not salvation. Everyone knows that a man justified is not yet saved, but has to fulfill certain other conditions for salvation.

2nd Question: Is Sanctifying Grace When Received Before Baptism Sufficient for Salvation?

Is, then, the reception of sanctifying grace through baptism of the Spirit a real substitute for baptism of water, so that a man like Cornelius did not need baptism and could have been saved without it?

Are there two ways of belonging to the Church, one through baptism of water and the other through baptism *in voto,* so that the one would be sufficient without the other for salvation?

St. Augustine who, in his treatise *On Baptism Against the Donatists* asks us "not to depreciate a man's righteousness should it begin to exist before he joined the Church, as the righteouness of Cornelius began to exist before he was in the Christian community," also says in the same sentence that this righteouness "was not thought worthless, or the angel would not have said to him, 'Thy alms have been accepted and thy prayers have been heard'; *nor did it yet suffice for his gaining the kingdom of heaven, or he would not have been told to send for Peter,"* [76] in order to be baptized by him.

It is clear therefore that Cornelius, who was already in the state of sanctifying grace even before the actual reception of baptism, would not have been saved if he had not sent for Peter to be baptized by him, or if, having sent for him, he had refused to be baptized with water. St. Augustine says, "Cornelius would have been guilty of contempt for so holy a sacrament if, even after he had received the Holy Ghost, he had refused to be baptized." [77]

St. Robert Bellarmine says the same thing, especially on the authority of St. Augustine: "Further, Augustine, in his Epistle 57 to Dardanus, in Book I *Of the Predestination of the Saints,* Chapter 7; in Book I, Question 2, *To Simplician;* in Book I, Chapter 8, *On Baptism;* and in Book IV, Chapter 21 of the same, says that Cornelius the Centurion, although he was praised in Scriptures, was not yet such that he could have been saved, unless he became incorporated in the Church through the Sacrament of Baptism." [78]

To repeat, then, sanctifying grace can be received ahead of the Sacrament of Baptism, and in that case it is sufficient for *justification,* but this does not mean that it is sufficient for *salvation* if the actual Sacrament of Baptism is not received. Cornelius and his friends received sanctifying grace and the Holy Spirit even before the actual reception of Baptism. They were speaking with tongues, like the Apostles at Pentecost. The water of Baptism would have seemed totally superfluous for them, and yet they could not have been saved without it. That is why, as St. Augustine adds, "they were baptized, and for this action we have the authority of an Apostle as a warrant." [79] Again, St. John the Baptist was born in the state of sanctifying grace, and yet he had to be baptized by the baptism of Christ before he died, for as St. John Chrysosotom says (Homily 4 on Matthew), "Since, when John said, 'I ought to be baptized by thee,' Christ answered, 'Suffer it to be so *now,'* it follows that afterwards Christ did baptize John." [80] Likewise St. Jerome says, commenting on Matthew 3:13, that as Christ was baptized in water by John, so John had to be baptized by Christ in water and the Holy Spirit.[81]

The catechumen who confesses the Catholic Faith and has perfect charity and the intention of joining the Church can therefore receive sanctifying grace before the actual reception of Baptism. It is in this sense that St. Augustine (as quoted by St. Robert Bellarmine) says that such a catechumen may be said to be of the soul of the Church (because the theological virtues and the Gifts of the Holy Ghost are the vivifying principle in the Church).[82] But as we have shown in Part II of this article, this does not mean that there are two kinds of membership, one in the soul and one in the body, for in the same chapter St. Robert Bellarmine says clearly that catechumens are not members of the Church, because they do not have communion of the sacraments.[83] Likewise, St. Augustine in his treatise *On Baptism Against the Donatists,* which we quoted, says that Cornelius received sanctifying grace previous to baptism, "before he was *joined* to the Church," [84] – namely, before he was a *member* of the Church.

Membership in the Church is necessary for salvation, as we have shown. We have also shown that sanctifying grace can be received before Baptism, but in that case it does not confer membership in the Church. Therefore, even though a man can be justified before the actual reception of Baptism, as the Council of Trent says, this does not mean, as Father Donnelly wrongly concludes, that this justification is sufficient for the man's salvation.

3rd Question: Is There Any Case When Baptism of the Holy Spirit Without Actual Reception of Baptism of Water Can Be Sufficient for Salvation?

Now that we have considered the defined truths which must be believed, namely, the absolute necessity of the Catholic Faith, the absolute necessity of membership in the Catholic Church, the absolute necessity of submission to the Roman Pontiff, the absolute necessity of baptism of water, for salvation, there remains but one point to examine; that is, whether there is any case where a man can be saved without actually receiving the water of baptism on his head.

At this point we have to depart from *infallibly defined dogma* and must rely on the teachings of the Fathers and Doctors because it has never so far been defined that any human being can be saved who was not actually baptized, except for those who lived before the coming of Our Lord, and except for the martyrs.

What is the teaching of the Fathers and the Doctors? Some Fathers deny that there is *any* case in which a man could be saved without the actual reception of the water of baptism (with the exception of the martyrs alone).* But most of them agree in saying that there *is* one case, and only one case, when a man could be saved without having been actually baptized with water. It is the case of a *catechumen* who confesses the Catholic Faith, who is sorry for his past sins, who is burning with desire to be baptized and to join the Catholic Church, under the authority of the Roman Pontiff, but who, having been kept without baptism by the Church until he has been fully instructed, is overtaken by death suddenly and is incapable of receiving baptism. Such a catechumen, it is believed, can be saved, if he makes an act of perfect charity.[85]

In answer to our third question, therefore, we shall say that according to the majority of the Fathers and Doctors, baptism of the Holy Spirit, without the actual reception of Baptism of water, can be sufficient for salvation if the following five conditions are fulfilled:

First, that person must have the Catholic Faith. (We have already proved that no one can be saved without the Catholic Faith, and that not even the Sacrament of Baptism can be profitable for salvation if the subject who receives it does not confess the Catholic Faith.)

Second, he must have an explicit will or desire to receive the Sacrament of Baptism. For example, St. Bernard says that he must have an "entire yearning for the sacrament of Jesus." [86]

Third, he must have perfect charity. For St. Robert Bellarmine says that only *"perfect conversion* can be called baptism of the Spirit, and this includes true contrition and charity." [87] St. Augustine says that he must have "faith and conversion of the heart." [88] St. Thomas says that, as in the case of the Sacrament of Penance, so also in the Sacrament of Baptism, if sanctifying grace is to be received previous to the Sacrament, a perfect act of charity is necessary, for "if an adult is not perfectly disposed before baptism to obtain remission of his sins, he obtains this

---

* Abbot Jerome Theisen, OSB. in his *The Ultimate Church and the Promise of Salvation* states that neither St. John Chrysostom nor any of the Cappadocian Fathers thought that salvation was possible for a catechumen overtaken by death before the actual reception of the sacrament. (Theisen, Abbot Jerome, OSB., *The Ultimate Church and the Promise of Salvation,* St. John's University Press, Collegeville, Minnesota, 1976, p.12, n.35.) This was also the later opinion of Father Feeney as we shall see in his lecture, "The Waters of Salvation," which is contained in its entirety in Appendix III.

remission by the power of baptism, in the very act of being baptized." [89]
St. Bernard says that "right faith, God-fearing hope and sincere charity"
must be present.[90]

Fourth, he must have an explicit will to join the Catholic Church, –
for, as we have shown, not even actual Baptism is profitable for
salvation if it is received outside the Catholic Church (except for babies)
and without an explicit will to join the Church. Much less, therefore,
does baptism *in voto* profit for salvation if it does not include an explicit
will to join the Catholic Church.

Fifth, he must be dying and although yearning for the Baptism of
Water is unable to receive it because of an absolute impossibility, not
because of a contempt for it. Thus St. Augustine says that baptism of the
Spirit or perfect conversion to God, "may indeed be found when Baptism
has not yet been received, but never when it has been despised. For it
should never in any way be called a conversion of the heart to God when
the sacrament of God has been despised." [91] In the same way St.
Bernard says that since the time of the promulgation of the Gospel
"whoever refuses now to be baptized, after the remedy of baptism has
been made accessible to all everywhere, adds of his own accord a sin of
pride to the general original stain, carrying within himself a double
cause of the most just damnation if he happens to leave the body in the
same state." [92] Also, St. Thomas says, "It is necessary, in order that a
man might enter into the kingdom of God, that he approach the baptism
of water *actually (in re),* as it is in all those who are baptized; or *in voto,*
as it is in the *martyrs* and *the catechumens who were hindered by death
before they could fulfill their intent* (votum); or in *figure,* as in the
ancient Fathers," – that is, in those before Christ.[93]

Now that we have shown in what sense a person who has the desire
for baptism can be saved, let us enumerate again Father Donnelly's
three doctrines which we listed at the beginning of Part III, namely, (1)
that a person can be said to have desire for Baptism while being *totally
ignorant* of the Catholic Faith and ignorant of the Baptism of water; (2)
that a person can be said to have a desire for Baptism while knowing the
Catholic Church and the Catholic Faith and *refusing* both; (3) that a
person can be said to have a desire for Baptism while knowing the
Baptism of water and *refusing it.* From the evidence we have presented
it must be clear that these doctrines are erroneous and cannot be held.

CONCLUSION

Modern liberalism, which makes membership in the Catholic Church unnecessary for salvation, undermines something more than the dogma that there is no salvation outside the Catholic Church. In postulating the existence of an Invisible Church, or in suggesting that membership in the Visible Church can be invisible and purely internal, liberals are actually, whether they realize it or not, endangering the doctrine of the Incarnation. The whole point of the Incarnation is that the Person of the Word assumed human flesh in order to redeem us from our sins as Man, by dying on the Cross, and in order to institute a visible society with a visible head and visible sacraments, in which society every man must be visibly incorporated if he wishes to be saved.

Our salvation, therefore, is Jesus Christ, the Incarnate God, who took His flesh from the Blessed Virgin Mary. The Church prevents us from falsely emphasizing the spiritual and invisible, as divorced from the sensible and visible, by keeping constantly before us in infinite repetition the prayer which ushered in the Incarnation, "the Lord is with thee; blessed art thou among women and *blessed is the fruit of thy womb.*" The Son of God did not will our salvation to be achieved apart from His Humanity and, consequently, apart from His visibility.

As Mary was the gate through which our God came to us on earth, so she is the gate through which we go to Him in eternity. She is the great Mediatrix of all Graces. Now, just as no man can be saved outside the Catholic Church, so, St. Grignion de Montfort says, no man can be saved without Mary. This is what the great Apostle of Our Lady says:

"The learned and pious Suarez, of the Society of Jesus, the erudite and devout Justus Lipsius, doctor of Louvain, and many others have proved invincibly, from the sentiments of the Fathers, among others, St. Augustine, St. Ephrem, deacon of Edessa, St. Cyril of Jerusalem, St. Germanus of Constantinople, St. John Damascene, St. Anselm, St. Bernard, St. Bernardine, St. Thomas and St. Bonaventure, that devotion to our most Blessed Virgin is necessary to salvation, and that (even in the opinion of Oecolampadius and some other heretics) it is an infallible mark of reprobation to have no esteem and love for the holy Virgin; while on the other hand, it is an infallible mark of predestination to be entirely and truly devoted to her.

"The figures and words of the Old and New Testaments prove this. The sentiments and the examples of the saints confirm it. Reason and experience teach and demonstrate it. Even the devil and his crew, constrained by the force of truth, have often been obliged to avow it in spite of themselves. Among all the passages of the holy Fathers and Doctors, of which I have made an ample collection in order to prove this truth, I shall for brevity's sake quote but one: 'To be devout to you, O Holy Virgin,' says St. John Damascene, 'is an arm of salvation which God gives to those whom He wishes to save.'"[1]

To conclude, therefore, may we say that in the modern liberal presentation of the Church's doctrine concerning salvation outside the Church there are contained THE FOLLOWING ERRORS:

1. One can be saved outside the Church.
2. One can be saved without having the Catholic Faith.
3. Baptism is not necessary for salvation.
4. To confess the supremacy and infallibility of the Roman Church and of the Roman Pontiff is not necessary for salvation.
5. One can be saved without submitting personally to the authority of the Roman Pontiff.
6. Ignorance of Christ and His Church excuses one from all fault and confers justification and salvation.
7. One can be saved who dies ignorant of Christ and His Church.
8. One can be saved who dies hating Christ and His Church.
9. God, of His Supreme Goodness and Mercy, would not permit anyone to be punished eternally unless he had incurred the guilt of voluntary sin.
10. A man is sure of his salvation once he is justified.
11. One can be saved by merely an implicit desire for Baptism.
12. There are two Churches, the one visible, the other invisible.
13. There are two kinds of membership in the Church.
14. Membership in the Church can be invisible or even unconscious.
15. To know and love the Blessed Virgin is not necessary for salvation.

We feel that nothing short of an infallible pronouncement on the matter by our Holy Father will put an end to these heretical teachings, which are seriously injuring the Faith of Catholics. Therefore, prostrate at the feet of His Holiness, Pope Pius XII, and knowing that no one can be saved outside of the Church of which he is the visible head, nor without that Faith of which he is the protector, nor without personal submission to him, the Vicar of Christ on earth, we humbly present this paper, and beseech His Holiness to crush the erroneous teachings listed above and to fulfill Christ's promise to Peter, that through him and his successors the gates of hell shall not prevail against His Church.

INDEX OF NOTES

PART I

1. J. Bainvel, S.J., *Is There Salvation Outside the Catholic Church?* Authorized English Translation by J.L. Weidenhan, S.T.L. 2nd Ed., Ch. V, p. 43.
2. Pope Pius IX, Allocution *Singulari Quadam,* 9 Dec. 1854 (See Denzinger *Enchiridion Symbolorum,* 1647).
3. Bainvel, *Op. cit., Ch. III, p. 26.*
4. *Pius IX, Singulari Quadam,* Denz. 1647.
5. Pius IX, Encyclical *Quanto Conficiamur,* 10 Aug. 1863, Denz. 1677.
6. Pope Innocent III, Epist. *Maiores Ecclesiae Causas,* 1201, Denz. 410.
7. St. Bonaventure, *Breviloquium,* Part III, Ch. V, n. 2.
8. Bainvel, *Op. cit.,* Ch. II, pp. 10-11.

PART II

1. St. Thomas Aquinas, *Summa Theologica,* Part II-II, qu. 2, a.3.
2. St. Thomas Aquinas, *Op. cit.,* id. a. 5.
3. *Ibid. In Corp.*
4. St. Thomas Aquinas, *Op. cit.,* Part II.II, qu. 2,a. 3.
5. *Id.,* a. 8.
6. *Id.,* a. 6.
7. St. Thomas Aquinas, *Op. Cit.,* Part II-II, qu. 5, a. 3.
8. *Ibid., Ibid., In Corp.*
9. St. Alphonsus Liguori, *Instruction on the Commandments and Sacraments,* Part I, Ch. I, Sect. I "On Faith." n. 6.
10. St. Thomas Aquinas, *Collationes De Pater Noster, et Credo in Deum,* Exposition of the Apostles' Creed, First Article.
11. Council of Trent, Sess. VI, Ch. 8, Denz. 801.
12. St. Robert Bellarmine. *Doctrina Christiana.* Introduction.
13. St. Alphonsus Liguori, *The Incarnation, Birth and Infancy of Jesus Christ.* Meditation for the Feast of the Epiphany. (English translation of the Ascetical Works of St. Alphonsus, vol. 4, p. 286).
14. Pope Pius XI, *Encyclical Mortalium Animos.*
15. Pius IX, *Singulari Quadam,* Denz. 1645.
16. Pope Innocent XI, *Errores varii de rebus moralibus* (4 March, 1679), n. 64. Denz. 1214.
17. Council of Constance, Sess, VII, *Errors of John Wycliff,* n. 41, Denz. 621.
18. Pius IX, *Quanto Conficiamur,* Denz. 1677.
19. *Ibid.*
20. St. Thomas Aquinas, *Commentary on the Gospel of St. John,* Ch. XII, Lect. VIII, n. 6.
21. St. Alphonsus Liguori, *The Incarnation, etc.,* Cf. note 13.
22. St. Robert Bellarmine, *On the Church Militant,* (Latin Ed. Venice, 1721) Bk. III, Ch. II, (Tom. 2, p. 53D).
23. St. Peter Canisius, *Catechism,* First Question.

24. Pius XI, Enc. *Mortalium animos.*
25. Bainvel, *Op. cit.,* Ch. III, pp. 25ss.
26. *Id* Ch. IV, p. 37.
27. *Ibid.*
28. Bainvel, *Op. cit.,* Ch. VI, p. 54.
29. *Ibid.*
30. Rev. Louis Caperan, *Le Probleme du salut des Infideles* (new ed., Toulouse, 1934). Vol.II, p.102.
31. Louis Caperan, *Union Missionaire du Clerge* (October, 1945 and January, 1946) article entitled, "La mission de l'Eglise et les missions dans le plan providential du salut."
32. St. Robert Bellarmine, *On the Church Militant,* Bk. III, Ch. XII (Tom. 2, p. 71 D-E).
33. *Id.* Bk. III, Ch. II, (p.54B).
34. *Id.* Bk. III, Ch. III, (p. 54 D, D, A, B) – Also: Bellarmine, *On Penance,* Bk. II, Ch. XIV (Tom. 3, p. 525B).
35. Bellarmine, *On the Church Militant,* Bk. III, Ch. II, (Tom. 2, p.53E)
36. Pius IX, *Quanto Conficiamur,* Denz. 1677.
37. St. Augustine, Epist. XLIII *Ad Glorium, Eleusium, Felicem Grammaticos et caeteros,* Ch. I (J.P. Migne, *Patrologiae Cursus Completus,* Series Latina, Vol. 33, p. 160.
38. St. Thomas Aquinas, *Summa Theologica,* Part II-II, qu. 11, a. 2, ad 3.
39. *Id.,*a. 1, S.C.
40. St. Thomas Aquinas, *Op. cit.* Part II-II, qu. 10, a. 5, *In Corp.*
41. Pius IX, *Quanto Conficiamur,* Denz. 1678.
42. Pius IX, *Singulari Quadam,* Denz. 1647.
43. *L'Osservatore Romano,* 31 January, 1938.
44. *Ibid.*
45. Pius XI, *Mortalium Animos.*
46. *Ibid.*
47. St. Bernard, Epist. CXC., *Capitula Haeresum Petri Abaelardi,* Cap. XI, (Migne, Vol 182).
48. St. Bernard, Epist. LXXVII, to Hugh of St. Victor. *De Baptismo, etc.,* Cap. IV (Migne P.L. Vol. 182).
49. St. Alphonsus Liguori, *The Incarnation, etc.,* (Cf. note 13) Meditation VIII for the Novena of Christmas (Ascetical Works, Vol 4, p. 33).
50. St. John Chrysostom, *Homilies on the Acts of the Apostles,* Homil. V, n. 4, Chrysostom, Vol. 9, part 1, p. 55A-B).
51. Council of Sens, 1140 or 1141, *Errors of Peter Abelard,* n. 10, Denz. 377.
52. Council of Constance, Sess. XV, 1415, *Errors of John Hus,* n. 2, Denz. 628.

PART III

1. St. John Chrysostom, *Homilies on the Epistle to the Philippians,* Homil. III, n. 4.
2. St. John Chrysostom, *Homilies on the Acts of the Apostles,* Homil I, n. 8, (Greek and Latin edition, Vol 9, part 1, p. 15 C-D.)
3. St. John Chrysostom, *On the Priesthood,* Bk. III, n. 6.

4. St. Ambrose, *De Abraham,* Bk. II, Ch. XI, n. 79.

5. Pope St. Leo the Great, *Epistle XV,* n. 10.

6. Tertullian, *On Baptism,* XII. (See Rouet de Journal, S.J., *Enchiridion Patristicum,* 306).

7. St. Thomas Aquinas, *Collationes De Pater, etc.,* Exposition of the Apostles Creed, Tenth article.

8. Pope Benedict XIV, *Profession of Faith prescribed to the Orientals,* constit. *Nuper ad nos* Denz. 1470.

9. Council of Trent, Sess. VII, March 1547, *Canons on the Sacrament of Baptism,* Can. 5, Denz. 861.

10. St. Thomas Aquinas, *Summa Theologica,* Part III, qu. 68, a. 1, *In Corp.*

11. St. Robert Bellarmine, *On the Sacrament of Baptism,* Bk. I Ch. IV, (Tom. 3, pp.115-118).

12. *Id.* (p. 115A).

13. *Id.* (p. 115B).

14. Bainvel, *Op. cit.,*Ch. V, p.43.

15. St. Robert Bellarmine, *On the Sacrament of Baptism,* Bk. I, Ch. IV, (Tom. 3, p. 118A-B).

16. *Id.* (p. 118B).

17. *Ibid.*

18. St. Thomas Aquinas, *Summa Theologica,* Part II-II, qu. 10,a. 1, *In Corp.*

19. *Id.* a. 3.

20. St. Robert Bellarmine, *On the Sacrament of Baptism,* Bk. I, Ch. IV, (Tom. 3, p. 118B-C).

21. St. Fulgentius, *De Fide, ad Petrum,* Ch XXVII, n. 68.

22. St. Augustine, *De Anima et eius Origine,* Bk. IV, Ch. XI, n. 16.

23. St. Bonaventure, *Breviloquium,* Part III, Ch. V, n. 6.

24. Pope Innocent III, Epist. *Maiores Ecclesiae Causas,* 1201, Denz. 411.

25. St. Thomas Aquinas, *Summa Theologica,* Part III, qu. 68,a. 7, ad 2.

26. St. Thomas Aquinas, *Contra Errores Graecorum,* In Titulo, "Quod ad eum (Petrum) pertinet determinare quae sunt Fidei."

27. St. Thomas Aquinas, *Summa Theologica,* Part III, qu. 68, a. 8, *In Corp.*

28. Council of Trent, Sess. VI, Ch. 7, Denz. 799.

29. St. Alphonsus Liguori, *Instructions on the Commandments and Sacraments,* Part I, Sect. I "On Faith," n. 10.

30. St. Robert Bellarmine, *On the Church Militant,* Bk. III,Ch. II, (Tom 2, p. 53D).

31. St. Fulgentius, *De Fide, ad Petrum,* Ch. III, n. 41.

32. *Id.*Ch. XXXVI, n. 77.

33. *Id.* Ch. XXXVII, n. 78.

34. *Id.* Ch. XXXVIII, n. 79.

35. St. Augustine, *Commentary on the Gospel of St. John,* Tract. VI, n.13.

36. *Id.* Tract. VI, n. 14.

37. St. Bonaventure, *Breviloquium,* Part VI, Ch. V, n. 4.

38. St. Augustine, *On Baptism against the Donatists,* Bk, IV, Ch. I (n. 1) – Ch. II (n. 2).

39. *Id.* Bk. IV, Ch. XXV, n. 32.

40. St. Robert Bellarmine, *On the Church Militant,* Bk. III, Ch. II, (Tom. 2, p.53D).

41. *Id.* p. 53 D-E.

42. St. Robert Bellarmine, *Compendium of Christian Doctrine,* Exposition of the Apostles Creed, Twelth Article.

43. St. Peter Canisius, *Exposition of the Apostles' Creed,* Ninth Article, "Communion of Saints."

44. Pope Boniface VIII, Bull *Unam sanctam,* Nov. 18, 1302, Denz. 468.

45. Origin, *In Jesu Nave homiliae* Hom. III, n. 5.

46. St. Cyprian, *On the Unity of the Catholic Church,* VI, Journal 557.

47. St. Ignatius of Antioch, *St. Ignatius of Antioch, Epistle to the Philadelphians,* Ch. III, n. 2.

48. St. Irenaeus, *Adversus Haereses,* Bk. III, Ch. XXIV, n. 1.

49. Pope Pius XI, Enc. *Mortalium Animos.*

50. St. Fulgentius, *De Fide, ad Petrum,* Ch. XXXVIII, n. 79.

51. Council of Florence, "Decree for the Jacobites," Pope Eugene IV, Bull *Cantate Domino,* Denz. 714.

52. St. Ambrose, *De Mysteriis,* Ch. IV, n. 20.

53. St. Thomas Aquinas, *Summa Theologica,* Part III, qu. 66, a. 11, *In Corp.* Cf. also a. 12, *In Corp.*

54. *Id.* qu. 62. a. 5, *In Corp.*

55. Gospel according to St. John, XIII, 5-10.

56. St. Augustine, *Commentary on the Gospel of St. John,* Tract LVI, n. 4.

57. St. Thomas Aquinas, *Commentary on the the Gospel of St. John,* Ch. XIII, Lect. II, n. 8.

58. St. Cyril of Jerusalem, *Catecheses,* Cat. III, c. 10.

59. St. Fulgentius, *De Fide ad Petrum,* Ch. III, n. 41.

60. St. Augustine, *The City of God,* Bk. XIII, Ch. VII.

61. St. Robert Bellarmine, *On the Sacrament of Baptism,* Bk. I, Ch. VI, (Tom. 3, p. 120A).

62. St. Augustine, *The City of God,* Bk. XIII, Ch. VII.

63. St. Fulgentius, *De Fide, ad Petrum,* Ch. III, n. 41.

64. St. Robert Bellarmine, *On the Sacrament of Baptism,* Bk. I, Ch. VI, (Tom. 3, p. 121 E, A, B, C,).

65. St. Thomas Aquinas, *Summa Theologica,* Part II-II, qu.39, a. 1, *In Corp.*

66. Council of Florence, "Decree for the Jacobites," Pope Eugene IV, Bull *Cantate Domino.* Denz. 714.

67. St. Robert Bellarmine, *On the Sacrament of Baptism,* Bk. I, Ch. VI, (Tom. 3, p. 121 A-B).

68. St. Cyprian, *On the Unity of the Church,* cf. Pope Pelagius II, Ep. 2 to the schismatical bishops of Istria, Denz. 247, and Migne, P.L. 4, 511.

69. St. Ambrose, *De Mysteriis,* Ch. IV, n. 20.

70. St. Thomas Aquinas, *Commentary on the Gospel of St. John,* Ch. XI, Lect. VI, n. 6.

71. *Ibid.*

72. Louis Caperan, *Le Probleme du Salut des Infideles,* Vol. II, p. 102.

73. St. Augustine, *On Baptism Against the Donatists,* Bk. IV., Ch. XXI, n. 28.

74. Council of Trent, Sess. VI, Ch. 4, Denz. 796.

75. *Id.* Sess. VI, Ch. VIII, Denz. 801.

76. St. Augustine, *On Baptism Against the Donatists,* Bk. IV, Ch. XXI, n. 28.

77. *Ibid.*

78. St. Robert Bellarmine, *On the Sacrament of Penance,* Bk. II, Ch. XIV, (Tom. 3, p. 526C).

79. St. Augustine, *On Baptism Against the Donatists,* Bk. IV, Ch. XXII, n. 29.

80. St. John Chrysostom, *Eruditi Commentarii in Evangelium Matthaei,* Homil. IV, (Migne, P.G. 56, 658).
81. St. Jerome, *On Matthew* Bk.II, Commentary on Matthew III, 13, (Migne, P.L. 26, 31).
82. St. Robert Bellarmine, *On the Church Militant,* Bk. III, Ch. II (Tom. II, p. 54B).
83. *Id.* (p.53E).
84. St. Augustine. *On Baptism Against the Donatists.* Bk. IV. Ch. XXI, n. 28.
85. St. Ambrose, *De obitu Valentiniani,* n. 51-53; St. Augustine, *On Baptism Against the Donatists,* Bk. IV; Innocent II, Ep. *Apostolicam Sedem* (*Denz. 388*); *Innocent III, Ep. Debitum Pastoralis Officii* (Denz. 413); St. Thomas Aquinas, *Summa Theologica,* Part III, qu. 68, a. 2, *In Corp.;* St. Bernard, Ep. *to Hugh of St. Victor; St. Robert Bellarmine, On the Sacrament of Baptism,* Bk. I, Ch. VI, (Tom. 3, p. 121C).
86. St. Bernard, *Epistle to Hugh of St. Victor,* Ch. II, n. 8.
87. St. Robert Bellarmine, *On the Sacrament of Baptism,* Bk. I, Ch. VI, (Tom. 3, p. 121C).
88. St. Augustine, *On Baptism Against the Donatists,* Bk. IV, Ch. XXII, n. 29.
89. St. Thomas Aquinas, *On St. John,* Ch. XI, Lect. VI, N. 6.
90. St. Bernard, *Epistle of Hugh of St. Victor,* Ch. II, n. 6.
91. St. Augustine, *On Baptism Against the Donatists,* Bk. IV, Ch. XXV, n. 32.
92. St. Bernard, *Epistle to Hugh of St. Victor,* Ch. II, n. 6.
93. St. Thomas Aquinas, *On St. John,* Ch. III, Lect. I, n. 4.

CONCLUSION

1. St. Louis Marie Grignion de Montfort, *True Devotion to the Blessed Virgin,* (Fourth English Edition, Ottawa-Eastview, Ontario, 1941,) Part I, Ch. I, Art. II, Cons. II, n. 1, p. 29.

APPENDIX II

LETTER OF THE HOLY OFFICE
TO THE ARCHBISHOP OF BOSTON

(Protocol Number 122/49), August 8, 1949

INTRODUCTION

Father Feeney, as we have seen from his correspondence with Rome, thought that the Letter of the Holy Office to the Archbishop of Boston was heretical at least in its simple and obvious interpretation. We saw in Part I that the *Worcester Telegram* of September 2, 1949 ran the following headline: "VATICAN RULES AGAINST HUB DISSIDENTS, Holds No Salvation Outside Church Doctrine *to Be False.*" But this was not just the popular interpretation of non-theologians, but that of professional theologians as well, and Fr. Karl Rahner, SJ. would later use it as the launching pad for his infamous "Anonymous Christianity" and his claim of universal salvation. Father Rahner writes:

> "...There can be, and actually are, individuals who are justified in the grace of God, who attain to super-natural salvation in God's sight (and, moreover, to Christ as well), yet who do not belong to the Church or to Christendom as a visible historical reality as a result of having been touched by the preaching of the gospel in any concrete 'this worldly' sense at any point in their lives. No truly theological demonstration of this thesis can be supplied here from scripture or tradition. Such a demonstration would not be easy to make, because the optimism of universal salvation entailed in this thesis has only gradually become clear and asserted itself in the conscious faith concerning salvation for unbaptized catechumens in Ambrose, through the doctrine of *baptismus flaminis* and the *votum ecclesiae* in the Middle Ages and at the Council of Trent, down to the explicit teaching in the writings of Pius XII to the effect that even a merely implicit *votum* for the Church and baptism can suffice...
>
> It was declared at the Second Vatican Council that atheists too are not excluded from this possibility of salvation, though here the distinctions between positive and negative atheism, between atheism of greater or lesser duration, usually accepted up to that point were not applied at the Second Vatican Council. The only necessary condition which is rec-

ognized here is the necessity of faithfulness and obedience to the individual's own personal conscience. This optimism concerning salvation appears to me one of the most noteworthy results of the Second Vatican Council. For when we consider the officially received theology concerning all these questions, which was more or less traditional right down to the Second Vatican Council, we can only wonder how few controversies arose during the Council with regard to these assertions of optimism concerning salvation, and wonder too at how little opposition the conservative wing of the Council brought to bear on this point, how all this took place without any setting of the stage or any great stir even though this doctrine marked a far more decisive phase in the development of the Church's conscious awareness of her faith than, for instance, the doctrine of collegiality in the Church, the relationship between scripture and tradition, the acceptance of the new exegesis, etc."

Rahner, Fr. Karl, SJ., "Problem of the 'Anonymous Christian,'" *Theological Investigations,* Volume XVI, The Seabury Press, New York, 1976, pp.283,284.

But I think this somewhat ambiguous *Letter* is also susceptible of an orthodox interpretation. The *Letter* was issued in 1949 but not published in full until after the issuance of the encyclical *Humani Generis* in 1950 which complained that "some reduce to a meaningless formula the necessity of belonging to the True Church in order to gain salvation," which is of course exactly what the *Worcester Telegram* and Father Rahner were doing. But it is especially in the light of the Dogmatic Constitution on the Church (*Lumen Gentium*) of Vatican Council II that allows us to give a proper interpretation of the *Letter.*

The two paragraphs in the *Letter* which Father Feeney found especially objectionable were:

12. That one may obtain eternal salvation, it is not always required that he be incorporated into the Church actually as a member, but it is necessary that at least he be united to her by desire and longing.

13. However, this desire need not always be explicit, as it is in catechumens; but when a person is involved in invincible ignorance, God accepts also an implicit desire, so called because it is included in that good disposition of soul whereby a person wishes his will to be conformed to the will of God.

A reference to the "Letter of the Holy Office to the Archbishop of Boston" appears in an official footnote to *Lumen Gentium* (2,16). The Letter however is not mentioned in the *relatio*, the official report which accompanied the *schema*, so it was evidently just appended by one of the *periti* who composed the *schema*. The relevant passage of *Lumen Gentium* reads:

Those also can attain to everlasting salvation who through no fault of their own do not know the gospel of Christ or His Church, yet sincerely seek God, and moved by grace strive by their deeds to do His will as it is known to them through the dictates of conscience.[59]

The Documents of Vatican II, Abbot, Fr. Walter M., SJ., (General Editor), America Press, New York, 1966, p.35; n.59 Cf. *Letter of Holy Office to the Archbishop of Boston*, Denz. 3869-72.

This passage of *Lumen Gentium* is similar to the *Letter* but with one significant difference. The phrase "implicit desire" (*votum implicitum*) which was so objectionable to Father Feeney has been dropped. Abbot Jerome Theisen, OSB. comments on this ommission:

The suppression of *votum implicitum* is probably due to disenchantment with the term, especially since it was used indiscriminately to describe the situation of both separated Christians and the "unevangelized" in their diverse relations to the Roman Catholic Church.

Theisen, Abbot Jerome, OSB., *The Ultimate Church and the Promise of Salvation*, St. John's University Press, Collegeville, Minnesota, 1976, p.57.

The relevant passage from *Lumen Gentium* continues:

> ...Nor does divine Providence deny the help neces-
> sary for salvation to those who without blame on
> their part, have not yet arrived at an explicit knowl-
> edge of God, but who strive to live a good life, thanks
> to His grace. Whatever goodness or truth is found
> among them is looked upon by the Church as a
> *preparation for the Gospel* (my emphasis, TMS). She
> regards such qualities as given by Him who
> enlightens all men so that they may finally have life.
> Abbot, *Op. cit.,* p.35.

So a person of goodwill who is involved in invincible ignorance and
has an implicit desire to be joined to the Church, may indeed be saved,
but *not where he is.* Whatever of truth or goodness is found in such a
person is looked upon by the Church as a *preparation for the gospel,* and,
as *Lumen Gentium* continues, it is to such persons that the Church "to
promote the glory of God and *procure the salvation of all such men*
(emphasis mine), and mindful of the command of the Lord, "Preach the
gospel to every creature" (Mk. 16:16),...painstakingly fosters her missionary work. (*Idem,* p.35.)

THE BOSTON PILOT

Saturday, September 6, 1952

The Supreme Congregation of the Holy Office has examined again the problem of Father Leonard Feeney and St. Benedict Center. Having studied carefully the publications issued by the Center, and having considered all the circumstances of this case, the Sacred Congregation has ordered me to publish, in its entirety, the letter which the same Congregation sent to me on the 8th of August, 1949. The Supreme Pontiff, His Holiness, Pope Pius XII, has given full approval to this decision. In due obedience, therefore, we publish, in its entirety, the Latin text of the letter as received from the Holy Office with an English translation of the same approved by the Holy See.

Given at Boston, Massachusetts,
the 4th day of September, A.D. 1952.

Walter J. Furlong,
    Chancellor

Richard J. Cushing
Archbishop of Boston

. . . .

From the Headquarters of the Holy Office
August 8, 1949

Protocol Number 122/49

Your Excellency:

1. This Supreme Sacred Congregation has followed very attentively the rise and the course of the grave controversy stirred up by certain associates of "St. Benedict Center" and "Boston College" in regard to the interpretation of the axiom: "Outside the Church there is no salvation."

2. After having examined all the documents that are necessary or useful in this matter, among them information from your Chancery, as well as appeals and reports in which the associates of "St. Benedict Center" explain their opinions and complaints, and also many other documents pertinent to the controversy, officially collected, the same

Sacred Congregation is convinced that the unfortuanate controversy arose from the fact the axiom, "outside the Church there is no salvation," was not correctly understood and weighed, and that the same controversy was rendered more bitter by serious disturbance of discipline arising from the fact that some of the associates of the institution mentioned above refused reverence and obedience to legitimate authorities.

3. Accordingly, the most Eminent and Most Reverend Cardinals of this Supreme Congregation, in a plenary session held on Wednesday, July 27, 1949, decreed, and the August Pontiff in an audience on the following Thursday, July 28, 1949, deigned to give his approval, that the following explanations pertinent to the doctrine, and also that invitations and exhortations relevant to discipline be given:

4. We are bound by divine and Catholic faith to believe all those things which are contained in the word of God, whether it be Scripture or Tradition, and are proposed by the Church to be believed as divinely revealed, not only through solemn judgment but also through the ordinary and universal teaching office (Denzinger, n. 1792).

5. Now, among those things which the Church has always preached and will never cease to preach is contained also that infallible statement by which we are taught there is no salvation outside the Church.

6. However, this dogma must be understood in that sense in which the Church herself understands it. For, it was not to private judgments that our Saviour gave the teaching authority of the Church.

7. Now, in the first place, the Church teaches that in this matter there is question of a most strict command of Jesus Christ. For he explicitly enjoined on His apostles to teach all nations to observe all things whatsoever He himself had commanded (Matt. 28:19-20).

8. Now, among the commandments of Christ, that one holds not the least place by which we are commanded to be incorporated by baptism into the Mystical Body of Christ, which is the Church, and to remain united to Christ and to His Vicar, through whom He Himself in a visible manner governs the Church on earth.

9. Therefore, no one will be saved who, knowing the Church to have been divinely established by Christ, nevertheless refuses to submit to the Church or withholds obedience from the Roman Pontiff, the Vicar of Christ on earth.

10. Not only did the Saviour command that all nations should enter the Church, but He also decreed the Church to be a means of salvation without which no one can enter the kingdom of eternal glory.

11. In his infinite mercy God has willed that the effects, necessary for one to be saved, of those helps to salvation which are directed toward man's final end, not by intrinsic necessity, but only by divine institution, can also be obtained in certain circumstances when those helps are used only in desire and longing. This we see clearly stated in the Sacred Council of Trent, both in reference to the sacrament of regeneration and in reference to the sacrament of penance (Denzinger n. 797, 807).

12. The same in its own degree must be asserted of the Church, in as far as she is the general help to salvation. Therefore, that one may obtain eternal salvation, it is not always required that he be incorporated into the Church actually as a member, but it is necessary that at least he be united to her by desire and longing.

13. However, this desire need not always be explicit, as it is in catechumens; but when a person is involved in invincible ignorance, God accepts also an implicit desire, so called because it is included in that good disposition of soul whereby a person wishes his will to be conformed to the will of God.[1]

14. These things are clearly taught in that dogmatic letter which was issued by the Sovereign Pontiff, Pope Pius XII, on June 29, 1943, *On the Mystical Body of Jesus Christ.* (AAS, Vol. 35, an. 1943, p. 193 ff.) For in this letter the Sovereign Pontiff clearly distinguishes between those who are actually incorporated into the Church as members, and those who are united to the Church only by desire.

[1] I can't resist commenting that if this passage is understood in the way the *Worcester Telegram* and Father Rahner understood it, it also would have involved the condemnation of Orestes Brownson. We saw that Brownson had written in *The Great Question:*

> Their approach to the Church is explicit, not constructive, to be inferred only from a certain vague and indefinite longing for the truth and unity in general, predicable in fact, we should suppose, of nearly all men; for no man ever clings to falsehood and division, believing them to be such. Their desire for truth and unity is explicit. Their faith is the Catholic faith; the unity they will is Catholic unity; the Church at whose door they knock is the Catholic Church; the sacraments they solicit, they solicit from the hands of her legitimate priest. They are in effect Catholics, and though not *re et proprie* [properly and in fact] in the church nobody ever dreams of so understanding the article out of the church no one can be saved, as to exclude them from salvation.
>
> "The Great Question," *Brownson's Quarterly Review* (October 1847), pp.564,565.

15. Discussing the members of which the Mystical Body is composed here on earth, the same august Pontiff says: "Actually only those are to be included as members of the Church who have been baptized and profess the true faith, and who have not been so unfortunate as to separate themselves from the unity of the Body, or been excluded by legitimate authority for grave faults committed."

16. Toward the end of this same encyclical letter, when most affectionately inviting to unity those who do not belong to the body of the Catholic Church; he mentions those who "are related to the Mystical Body of the Redeemer by a certain unconscious yearning and desire," and these he by no means excludes from eternal salvation, but on the other hand states that they are in a condition "in which they cannot be sure of their salvation" since "they still remain deprived of those many heavenly gifts and helps which can only be enjoyed in the Catholic Church" (AAS, loc. cit. 243).

17. With these wise words he reproves both those who exclude from eternal salvation all united to the Church only by implicit desire, and those who falsely assert that men can be saved equally well in every religion (cf. Pope Pius IX, Allocution *Singulari quadam,* in Denzinger, nn. 1641, ff. also Pope Pius IX, in the encyclical letter, *Quanto conficiamur moerere,* in Denzinger, n. 1677).

But it would be hard to believe that the *Letter* would involve a condemnation of Brownson, since as we saw, the article "The Great Question" was supervised by Bishop Fitzpatrick, and Brownson had the complete endorsement of all the bishops in attendance at the Seventh Provincial Council of Baltimore, plus a letter of encouragement from Pope Pius IX. We may speculate then how Brownson would have responded had he read in the Letter of the Holy Office "...that one may obtain eternal salvation, it is not always required that he be incorporated into the Church actually as a member, but it is necessary that at least he be united to her by desire and longing." I feel sure that he would have replied in the words of "The Great Question":

> That those in societies alien to the church, invincibly ignorant of the church, if they correspond to the graces they receive, and persevere, will be saved, we do not doubt, but *not where they are* [emphasis mine, TMS], or without being brought to the church. They are sheep in the prescience of God Catholics, but sheep not yet gathered into the fold. "Other sheep I have," says our blessed Lord, "that are not of this fold. THEM ALSO I MUST BRING; THEY SHALL HEAR MY VOICE; and there shall be made one fold and one shepherd." This is conclusive; and that these must be brought, and enter the fold which is the church in this life, St. Augustine expressly teaches.
> "The Great Question," pp.558,559.

18. But it must not be thought that any kind of desire of entering the Church suffices that one may be saved. It is necessary that the desire by which one is related to the Church be animated by perfect charity. Nor can an implicit desire produce its effect, unless a person has supernatural faith: "For he who comes to God must believe that God exists and is a rewarder of those who seek Him." (Hebrews 11:6.) The Council of Trent declares (Session VI, chap. 8): "Faith is the beginning of man's salvation, the foundation and root of all justification, without which it is impossible to please God and attain to the fellowship of His children." (Denzinger, n. 801.)

19. From what has been said it is evident that those things which are proposed in the periodical *From the Housetops,* fascicle 3, as the genuine teaching of the Catholic Church are far from being such and are very harmful both to those within the Church and those without.

20. From these declarations which pertain to doctrine certain conclusions follow which regard discipline and conduct, and which cannot be unknown to those who vigorously defend the necessity by which all are bound of belonging to the true Church and of submitting to the authority of the Roman Pontiff and of the Bishops "whom the Holy Ghost has placed...to rule the Church." (Acts, 20:28.)

21. Hence, one cannot understand how the St. Benedict Center can consistently claim to be a Catholic school and wish to be accounted such, and yet not conform to the prescriptions of Canons 1381 and 1382 of the *Code of Canon Law,* and continue to exist as a source of discord and rebellion against ecclesiastical authority and as a source of the disturbance of many consciences.

22. Furthermore, it is beyond understanding how a member of a religious institute, namely Father Feeney, presents himself as a "Defender of the Faith," and at the same time does not hesitate to attack the catechetical instruction proposed by lawful authorities, and has not even feared to incur grave sanctions threatened by the sacred canons because of his serious violations of his duty as a religious, a priest and an ordinary member of the Church.

23. Finally, it is in no wise to be tolerated that certain Catholics shall claim for themselves the right to publish a periodical for the purpose of spreading theological doctrines, without the permission of competent Church authority, called the "imprimatur," which is prescribed by the sacred canons.

24. Therefore, let them who in grave peril are ranged against the

Church, seriously bear in mind that after "Rome has spoken" they cannot be excused even by reasons of good faith. Certainly, their bond and duty of obedience toward the Church is much graver than that of those who as yet are related to the Church "only by an unconscious desire." Let them realize that they are children of the Church, lovingly nourished by her with the milk of doctrine and the sacraments, and hence, having heard the clear voice of their Mother, they cannot be excused from culpable ignorance, and therefore to them apply without any restriction that principle: submission to the Catholic Church and to the Sovereign Pontiff is required as necessary for salvation.

In sending this letter, I declare my profound esteem, and remain,
Your Excellency's most devoted,
F. Cardinal Marchetti-Selvaggiani

A. Ottaviani, Assessor

To His Excellency
Most Reverend Richard James Cushing
Archbishop of Boston

. . . .

As the Spiritual Shepherd of the Archdiocese of Boston, my heart goes out in love to Father Feeney and to those who have been misled by false ideas. It is my fervent hope that now, after the Supreme Authority of the Church has spoken, Father Feeney and all his followers will prove themselves to be loyal children of the Church and of our Holy Father, Pope Pius XII.

I invite all the faithful to join with me in this prayer.

Richard J. Cushing
Archbishop of Boston.[2]

---

[2] Again this document is not in the *Acta Apostolicae Sedis,* but appeared for the first time in the 1963 edition of Denzinger (3866-3873), presumably included by Fr. Karl Rahner, SJ. who was the editor through 1962. Father Rahner gives as his source for this document, not the *Acta,* as is usual, but *The American Ecclesiastical Review,* October, 1952, which is highly unusual.

APPENDIX III
"The Waters of Salvation"
by
Father Feeney
from *Bread of Life,* 1952.

INTRODUCTION

As Frank Sheed said, Father Feeney "was condemned but not answered." His case from the Solemn Magisterium of the Church is very impressive. It is *de fide* from the Fourth Lateran Council (Denz. 430), the Bull *Unam Sanctam* (Denz. 469), and the Council of Florence (Denz. 714), that membership in the Church and submission to the Holy Father are necessary for salvation. It is also *de fide* from the Council of Trent (Denz. 861) that baptism is necessary for salvation.

However there is nothing from the Solemn Magisterium regarding the possibility of salvation by Baptism of Desire, so on this subject we must turn to the teachings of the Fathers.

As I mentioned before, Father Feeney supervised and gave his final approval to "Reply to a Liberal" by Raymond Karam, a work which attempted to set forth the teaching of St. Thomas Aquinas on salvation. St. Thomas, as we have seen, allowed one apparent exception to the absolute necessity of the sacrament of baptism for salvation – the case of a catechumen, who had the faith and perfect charity, yet was overtaken by death before the actual reception of the sacrament. Father Feeney gradually came to feel that since the liberals usually began with the catechumen, and then branched out to include practically every other category of non-Catholic, that the catechumen was a loophole that should be plugged up. To begin with he thought that St. Thomas' teaching on the catechumen had a very flimsy base – St. Ambrose's sermon on the death of the emperor Valentinian. He thought that Valentinian certainly must have been baptized, as all catechumens were when in danger of death, and that St. Ambrose knew this and would have been horrified at the interpretation put on his words.

Furthermore, the doctrine of the necessity of the Church for salvation was not under attack in St. Thomas' time, and he felt that if it had been, St. Thomas would have written differently. But the necessity of the Church for salvation was under attack in St. Augustine's time by the Pelagians who taught that a man could be saved by natural virtue alone. St. Augustine did not think that a catechumen who was overtaken by death before the actual reception of the sacrament of baptism could be saved, and Father Feeney gradually adopted this opinion as his own.

Let me quote a few excerpts on this point from a wonderful book on St. Augustine, *Augustine the Bishop* by F. Van der Meer:

"This whole evil [a catechumen delaying his baptism] was one with which Augustine never wearied in doing battle. Even the anniversary of his consecration found him in a fighting mood. I care naught, he cried out on this occasion, that today of all days you expect to hear something pleasant from me. I must warn you in the words of Holy Scripture: 'Defer it not from day to day, for his wrath shall come on a sudden.' God knows that I tremble in my *cathedra* myself when I hear those words. I must not, I cannot, be silent. I am compelled to preach to you on this matter and 'to make you fearful, being myself full of fear.' [97] How dangerous, he says, is every delay! How many rascals are saved by being baptized on their deathbeds? And how many earnest catechumens die unbaptized? – which, for Augustine is equivalent to saying they are lost forever.[98] He compares the carefree condition of mind that such people often display with the dread sleeping-sickness of an old man, who keeps on saying, 'Let me sleep,' although the doctor keeps warning those around him that sleep is the one thing he must not do. And do not make it a reproach to me, he continues, that I disturb your peace of mind. How can I comfort you when the threat comes from God himself? For I am but the steward, not the father of the house.[99] You say, 'I will do it later, I will do it tomorrow. Why do you frighten us? Have we not been promised forgiveness?' Yes, forgiveness is promised you, but it has not been promised to you that you shall see tomorrow.'...

Even in doubtful cases Augustine always advised baptism. If anyone is seriously ill and is not capable of learning the *symbolum* (creed) by heart, he is to be questioned article by article and can then simply answer, 'Yes.' If there is occasion for haste, he need not even be asked whether he still bears anybody hatred or have any similar question put to him.[18] But is it not a disgraceful thing that a man should receive baptism in this fashion through his own fault and have to answer the questions, so to speak, at the gallop?[19] And how many die before they can be baptized, sometimes after a lifelong catechumenate?

'Yes, beloved, when people get ill, they send some-body round to the church or have themselves carried there in person; then they are baptized and renewed and it will be for their good.' [20] Better late than never. If one comes to a catechumen and finds him already unconscious he should be baptized, although, so Augustine tells, most people are afraid of doing this because it is written, 'Throw not that which is holy before the dogs.' Although one does not know in such a case whether the person in question truly consents, it is nevertheless better to baptize a person against his will than to deny baptism to a person who desires it, and that is all the more true in cases where there is no absolute certainty but the degree of probability that baptism is actually desired is high – a curious example of Augustine's probabilism. He would quite readily baptize a man who was *in extremis,* though he had been living with a divorced woman and refused, while he had his health, to mend his ways. If such a person recovered, however, he had to abide by the general rules laid down for those baptized, and was made to put his matrimonial affairs in order.[21] His great anxiety was to let no-one die unbaptized. We should remember that he was quite unable to con-ceive of a pious catechumen's being saved if he died a sudden death and was not baptized at the time." [1]

So while Father Feeney gradually adopted St. Augustine's opinion that a catechumen overtaken by death before the actual reception of Baptism could not be saved, it should be emphasized that he was not condemned for this opinion, but for the opinion of St. Thomas Aquinas, as expressed in "Reply to a Liberal," namely that a catechumen with faith and perfect charity could be saved if overtaken by death before the

---

[1] Van der Meer, F., *Augustine the Bishop,* translated by Brian Battershaw and G.R. Lamb, Sheed and Ward, New York, 1961, p.150, n.97 Frangipane, *Sancti Aurelii Augustini Hipponensis, Sermones* X; n.98 *Sermones,* 27,6; n.99 Frangipane, *Op. cit.,* 2,8b-9; n.18 *De Fide et Operibus, Liber Unus,* 6,8,9; n.19 *De Baptisme* 1,13,21; n.20 *Sermones* 393; n.21 *De Conjugiis Adulterinis, Libri Duo* 1,26,33 and 28,35.

actual reception of the sacrament of Baptism. "Reply to a Liberal" appeared in 1949 and the Letter of the Holy Office to the Archbishop of Boston was also sent in 1949. *Bread of Life* from which the following lecture "The Waters of Salvation" is taken, did not appear until 1952.

The newspaper reporters would often ask Father Feeney "what would you do if the Pope came out and defines that there is salvation outside the Church?" Father Feeney would reply, "but the Pope couldn't do that." "Why not," they would ask, "he's the Pope, isn't he?" Father Feeney would say, "God can't contradict Himself; the Holy Ghost would prevent him." The reporters would fall silent, but I suspect remained unconvinced.

Father Feeney's opinion on the absolute necessity of Baptism for salvation, which developed only after his condemnation, was never the subject of reporter's questions. But if a reporter had asked, "what would you do if the Pope said that a catechumen who had faith and charity, but died before the reception of Baptism, could be saved?" Father Feeney, I am sure, would have answered, "I would submit immediately." Father Feeney always considered his position on Baptism of Desire an opinion, an opinion which he shared with some great saints, such as St. Augustine, but only an opinion. That is why he sent copies of *Bread of Life* in which the following lecture "The Waters of Salvation" is contained, to the Holy Father and to every Cardinal; he was submitting his opinion to the judgment of the Church.

It might seem today that the subject of Baptism of Desire is a dead issue, but many, even good Catholics, are now saying that aborted babies can be saved by Baptism of Desire – the desire being on the part of the parents or of the Church. It seems to me that this will only encourage abortion. If a poor girl in trouble is wondering if she should have an abortion, and some one tells her that her baby will be saved by Baptism of Desire, this could push her over the brink. It certainly seems that there is an urgent need of an authoritative magisterial pronouncement on Baptism of Desire, and on the closely related problem of the Limbo of the Unregenerate. This would also present a perfect opportunity to deal with the unanswered questions raised by Father Feeney.

Galileo had to wait for three hundred years for his eventual exoneration by the Church. The question of a geocentric versus a heliocentric universe however, was not a particularly pressing matter. But the questions raised by Father Feeney couldn't be more urgent; they are a matter of eternal life or eternal death.

The Waters of Salvation

The Catholic Faith in the United States of America is always academically ascribed to the *Baltimore Catechism.*

The *Baltimore Catechism* was confected at the Third Plenary Council of Baltimore, by a group of American Bishops under the control and influence of James Cardinal Gibbons, Archbishop of Baltimore. James Cardinal Gibbons was a Catholic prelate who did not hesitate to get up before a Methodist congregation in a Methodist Church, and give a supposedly Catholic sermon while reading from a Protestant Bible!

Cardinal Gibbons was not a great theologian. He was a controller of theological thought. I hesitate to call him an opportunist, because there may be times when a priest might brilliantly take advantage of a situation, for Our Lord's sake. But when a Catholic prelate becomes *all* opportunistic, and is interested in teaching what doctrines of the Church would be most to the liking of his hearers or what general summary of the Church's history – as in the Baltimore Cardinal's book, *The Faith of Our Fathers* – will be least offensive to his new-found neighbors, then I think opportunism is serious defect.

Cardinal Gibbons' main ambition was to show that Catholicism was good Americanism. It is for that reason he went out of his way to take such metaphorical expressions in theology as "Baptism of Desire" and "Baptism of Blood" and put them side by side with *Baptism of Water.* As a consequence, every little Catholic child in a Catholic school, from the time of Cardinal Gibbons on, has been required to say, in answer to the question, "How many kinds of Baptism are there?": "There are *three* kinds of Baptism: Baptism of Water, Baptism of Desire, and Baptism of Blood."

That is heresy! There is only *one* Baptism, just as there is only one Lord and one Faith. (Eph. 4:5.) Council of Vienne explicitly defines that this one Baptism, which is administered by Water, is the one which must be faithfully confessed by all.

The Council of Trent, in its second Canon on the subject of Baptism, declares, with the majestic authority of the Church:

> If anyone shall say that true and natural water is
> not of necessity in Baptism, and therefore shall turn
> those words of Our Lord, Jesus Christ, "unless one be
> born again of water and the Holy Spirit" (John 3:5),
> into some metaphor, *let him be anathema.*[1]

---

[1] The Council of Trent is condemning the Protestant teaching that any liquid which could be used for bathing was valid matter for baptism (Luther, *Table Talk,* cf. Pallavicini, *History of the Council of Trent,* IX, 7). Father Feeney here is merely

Therefore, I repeat, metaphorical water is forbidden under pain of heresy. And what is "Baptism of Desire," as the Liberals teach it, but metaphorical water dishonestly substituting itself for the innocent requirement of Christ?

The same heretical theology that turned Baptism of Water into *any dry desire one might have in the general direction of Heaven,* has also turned *one Lord,* into *one's personal sincerity,* and *one Faith* into the *light of invincible ignorance!*

And, by the way, speaking of the *Baltimore Catechism,* even its most ardent supporters are forced to admit that shortly after the publication of the *Baltimore Catechism,* various editions with word meanings, explanatory notes, and even with different arrangements, came forth – so that, by testimony of all Catholic theologians in America, there is a considerable diversity in the books that go by the name of the *Baltimore Catechism.* Yet the *Baltimore Catechism* is always referred to in a singular apostrophe, as though it had the dignity of the Gospel itself.

A catechism is as good as the man who wrote it. If the *Baltimore Catechism* is so good, why do they revise it and revise it and revise it?

The crucial point, then, at which heresy entered the Catholic Church in the United States and backwashed to the dying Faith of Europe and the rest of the world, was through the teaching of the doctrine known as "Baptism of Desire," in the *Baltimore Catechism.*[2]

As I have explained to you many times, neither "Baptism of Desire" nor "Baptism of Blood" should truly be called *Baptism.* Neither is a sacrament of the Church. Neither was instituted by Jesus Christ. No one can receive any of the other sacraments by reason of having received these so-called "Baptisms." *Baptism of Water* is the initial requirement for the reception of all the other sacraments.

---

accomodating the phrase "metaphorical water" to apply to Baptism of Desire. He never claimed that the Council of Trent condemned Baptism of Desire.

[2] The catechisms of St. Robert Bellarmine and of St. Peter Canisius contain no mention of Baptism of Desire, nor did the first American catechism composed by St. John Neuman, the fourth Bishop of Philadelphia. His catechism simply states:

Question 3.	*Why is Baptism the most necessary Sacrament?*
Answer.	Because without Baptism no one can be saved.
Question 4.	*Why can we not be saved without Baptism?*
Answer.	Because we are cleansed from original sin only by Baptism.

Neuman, Saint John Nepomucene, *Small Catechism of the Catholic Religion,* Baltimore, 1884, p.31; republished by Saint Benedict Center. Box 142, Still River, Massachusetts, 1982.

Did Jesus really mean *water* to be essential for the Baptism He instituted? He did. When He started His public life Jesus came down and stood in the water, in the River Jordan, where John was baptizing. He wanted, thereby, to let us know what *Baptism* was to mean in the Catholic Church forevermore. *Baptizing* forever means *pouring water* on you, or *sprinkling you with water,* or *dipping you in water.*

As John the Baptist was baptizing Jesus, John said to Him, "I ought to be baptized by thee, and comest thou to me?" Then Jesus said, "Suffer it to be so now. For so it becometh us to fulfill all justice." (Matt. 3:14,15.)

Unfulfilled justice is the state of justification. Fulfilled justice is the state of salvation. What Jesus is saying to us, at His own baptism by John in the river Jordan, is that justification is now being turned into salvation with the aid of water.

Jesus goes so far as to praise and belittle John the Baptist in terms of this very rite of baptism. He says of John the Baptist, "Amen I say to you, there hath not risen among them that are born of women a greater than John the Baptist: yet he that is the lesser in the kingdom of Heaven is greater than he. (Matt. 11:11.) John the Baptist's greatness came from being admitted into the kingdom of Christ in salvation.

If Jesus was baptized with water to fulfill all justice, how shall *we* have justice fulfilled in us without baptism of Water?

There are only three birthdays commemorated by the Church in the liturgical year. All other saints in Heaven are commemorated on the days of their death. The three birthdays the Catholic Church celebrates are those of Jesus, Mary and John the Baptist. The crown of these three birthdays, of course, is the birth of Christ, the born One, Who was for the rebirth of the world.

The eighth of September is the most beautiful human birthday in the whole year. It is the birthday of Mary, the Mother of God. June twenty-fourth is the birthday of the most beautiful sheerly human boy that could be. It is the birthday of Saint John the Baptist, who was sanctified in his mother's womb, when Mary, with Jesus in her womb, visited Elizabeth.

Mary gave birth to Jesus. John the Baptist baptized Him. Baptism is a virginal birth, and Jesus' birth was for a virginal Baptism. Birth and Baptism go together in Christian regeneration, and in Christian salvation. Natural birth is belittled in terms of baptismal birth. Jesus calls Baptism, "being born again of water and the Holy Ghost."

If in admiration of the power of water in Baptism, you are going to ask me, "How do you expect water to do so much?", I cannot answer you. I would never ask water to do so much. I would never think that. But Jesus has asked water to do so much! As a matter of fact He gives the components of our foundational Sacrament – one of earth and one of Heaven – even though you might think it irreverent, Jesus mentions the water first and the Holy Ghost second! "Unless a man be born again of water and the Holy Ghost, he cannot enter into the Kingdom of God." (John 3:5.) That is how important water is!

Without Baptism of Water, you never can receive any of the other sacraments. All the Apostles had to be baptized. They were not in the state of mortal sin. But, they had to be baptized. From this need we can see the difference between justification and salvation.

I have told you this many times: Were I not to have been baptized by water, my ordination to the priesthood would be invalid. Suppose I never knew I had not been baptized? Well, I would never know I was not a priest. That is how important Baptism of Water is.

Can you not have Holy Orders of Desire? No! Are the Sacraments being tampered with in the United States today? Yes! Is the Faith practically gone? Yes!

When the Holy Ghost came down at Pentecost and flooded the first Christians with light, probably many made perfect acts of love. Why did Saint Peter add Baptism of Water? Why did he say, "Do penance, and be baptized every one of you!" (Acts 2:38.) Why did he undertake to baptize three thousand people in one day?

Why, as we learn in the Acts of the Apostles, was St. Paul struck down by a blinding light and told to go over to Damascus and have water poured on his head? Why was Cornelius at Caesarea told to send for Peter, and why was Saint Philip transported to Gaza to baptize the Ethiopian eunuch? Why were these baptizings necessary? Why all this "waste" of water and energy?

Why did Saint Martin of Tours raise a catechumen from the dead, and baptize him? Why did the North American martyrs come over here, if unbaptized Indians could make perfect acts of love? The Indians poured scalding hot water on one of the North American martyrs, St. John de Brébeuf, by way of ridiculing the Baptism of Water he was preaching. Why did the Church allow this torture to be provoked, if the waters of Baptism are non-essential to Indian salvation?

Q. What does "Baptism of Desire" mean?

A. It means the belief in the necessity of Baptism of Water for salvation, and a full intent to receive it.

Q. Can "Baptism of Desire" save you?

A. Never.

Q. Could "Baptism of Desire" save you if you really believed it could?

A. It could not.

Q. Could it possibly suffice for you to pass into a state of justification?

A. It could.

Q. If you got into the state of justification with the aid of "Baptism of Desire," and then failed to receive Baptism of Water, could you be saved?

A. Never.[3]

Actually, no one who has not been baptized can stay in the state of Christian justification very long, because he does not have the sacramental helps to keep justification alive. So, if he were in the state of justification, it would be only for a day or two, maybe three. If we who are Catholics have a hard enough job to keep in the state of sanctifying grace, with all the prayers and sacramental helps we have, good God!

[3] I can't emphasize enough that this isn't just Father Feeney's personal opinion, but also that of many of the Doctors of the Church. For example, St. Gregory Nazianzen says:

> "...If you were able to judge a man who intends to commit murder solely by his *intention,* and without any *act* of murder, then you could likewise reckon as baptized one who *desired* Baptism without having *received* Baptism. But since you cannot do the former, how can you do the latter? I cannot see it! If you prefer, we will put it this way; if, in your opinion, *desire* has equal power with *actual* Baptism, then make the same judgement in regard to glory. You would then be satisfied to desire glory, as though that longing itself were glory. Do you suffer any damage by not attaining the actual glory as long as you have a desire for it?"
> St. Gregory Nazianzen, "Oration on the Holy Lights," *Patrologiae Graece* 36, 40:23. (Cf. Jurgens, W.A., *The Faith of the Early Fathers,* Volume II, The Liturgical Press, Collegeville, Minnesota, 1970, p.37 [1012].)

how is anyone without them going to stay in the state of a perfect act of love of God? It is a blasphemy to say one could!

What induces this perfect act of love which is required to make "Baptism of Desire" effective for justification? And *is* it a perfect act of love of God? A perfect act of love of what God? Jesus Christ? No man cometh to the Father, but by Me," Jesus said. (John 14:6.)

These are the questions we must ask ourselves when offered a choice between the Sacrament of salvation and our own sanctimoniousness. No one can make a perfect act of love of God without Jesus and His Blessed Mother and His divine special graces. We, who have been baptized and have received Holy Communion, are very much in doubt as to whether we can make a perfect act of love of God! We hope for it, and pray for it! This man the Catholic Liberals talk about seems to be outfitted to make a perfect act of love of God without any of the sacraments! Not only are the Liberals getting rid of Baptism; they are getting rid of the whole sacramental order.

The Council of Trent, when treating of the Sacraments, anathematizes in most solemn canons those who say: (1) that the Sacraments of the New Law are not necessary for salvation; (2) that one can even get into a state of justification without at least a resolve to receive them; (3) that they are all of equal dignity and necessity; (4) that their purpose is mere support of Faith.

You do not have Faith by saying you have Faith! You do not have love by saying you have love! YOU cannot love God if you do not love Jesus. And you cannot love Jesus if you do not know Him through His great gifts, His Sacraments. If you do not know Him, I defy you to make a perfect act of love. You are calling it perfect love, and at the same time you are refusing that which poured out of the heart of Jesus: Blood and water. You are refusing the Blood of the Eucharist and the water of Baptism. To call that love is a blasphemy!

You have to know substantially everything about the Faith, to make a perfect act of love. Imagine being able to make a perfect act of love without knowing the Blessed Eucharist, or the Blessed Mother, or the forgiveness of sins!

This is the way the situation is now discussed in American seminaries:

"A man makes a perfect act of love. He is in the state of justification."

"How soon does he have to be baptized?"

"Within a reasonable period."

"What is a reasonable period?"

"Whatever the priest appoints."

"What would be a reasonable period to appoint?"

"Well, the candidate would have to be well instructed. In some countries, like Africa, for instance, a catechumen is instructed for three or four years. Poor, simple, untutored people have to be taught."

"Suppose one of these catechumens dies before being baptized?"

That is where the seminary professor runs out of answers, and has to make up confused ones, with the assistance of the *Baltimore Catechism, The Catholic Encyclopedia,* and a few articles by some hitherto brilliant unknowns in the *American Ecclesiastical Review.*

The paragraph in *The Catholic Encyclopedia* on the allowability of "Baptism of Desire" is one of the most sneaky pieces of surreptitious theology ever placed in print. It was written by Rev. William H. Fanning, S.J., professor of Church History at Saint Louis University, who pretends to tell you in the entire article on Baptism, that Baptism of Water is necessary for salvation, but gives you the Liberal escape you were looking for, by reason of his interpretation of a phrase in a sermon delivered by Saint Ambrose, the Bishop of Milan, on the death of a catechumen, the Emperor Valentianian II.

Saint Ambrose, in his sermon, declared of Valentinian: "Did he not obtain the grace which he desired? Did he not obtain what he asked for? Certainly, he obtained it, because he asked for it."

Any simple and loving Catholic would understand Saint Ambrose to have meant by this comfort, that he hoped Valentinian had been baptized by somebody, even though he (Saint Ambrose) did not know who it was, and even though there was no official record of it. Because if the grace Valentinian desired was something other than Baptism of Water, why call him a catechumen?

Is a catechumen one who desires other graces than the grace of Baptism of Water? And did one of his instructors in the Faith declare to Valentinian that in case he died before being baptized with water, he was still sure to be saved? And did he tell Valentinian that in case he did die before being baptized, Ambrose, Bishop of Milan, would get up in the pulpit and assure his bereaved friends that Baptism of Water, in the case of Valentinian II, had suddenly become unnecessary?

Personally, I think the three sentences of Saint Ambrose quoted by Father Fanning are unfortunate, if only for the fact that they can be turned to such a purpose. But if Father Fanning were sincere in wanting to know what chances for salvation, according to Saint Ambrose, a catechumen has who has not yet received Baptism of Water, and dies before he does receive it, Father Fanning would have quoted this clear-cut theaching on the subject from the writings of Saint Ambrose in his treatise, *De Mysteriis* (Ch. IV, no. 20):

> ...Nor again is there any mystery of regeneration without water, *for except a man be born anew of water and of the Spirit he cannot enter the Kingdom of God.* (John 3:5.) But even a catechumen believes in the cross of the Lord Jesus, wherewith he also is signed; but unless he is baptized *in the name of the Father, and of the Son, and of the Holy Ghost,* he cannot receive the remission of sins nor imbibe the gift of spiritual grace.

Notice that Saint Ambrose did not add, concerning this catechumen, "unless he dies in the meantime." This is what he should have added if what Father Fanning says about Saint Ambrose is true.

Father Migne, one of the greatest authorities on patrology in the Catholic Church, positively denies that Saint Ambrose ever held the opinion attributed to him concerning the salvation without Baptism of Water of the Emperor Valentinian (*Patrologia Latina,* Vol. XVI, p. 412, n. 19).[4]

If anyone should wish to add, concerning the catechumen who dies before receiving Baptism, that though he did not receive Baptism of Water, he did receive "Baptism of Desire," I doubt if such a one would dare to call the "Baptism of Desire" a sacrament. And Saint Ambrose knowing that "Baptism of Desire" is not a sacrament, was holy and clear enough to say:

> ...For no one ascends into the Kingdom of Heaven except by the Sacrament of Baptism. (*De Abraham,* Bk. II, ch. XI, no. 79.)

Saint Ambrose also declares:

---

[4] This note of Father Migne reads:

> "From among the Catholic Fathers perhaps no one insists more than Ambrose on the absolute necessity of receiving Baptism, in various places, but especially in Book II *De Abraham,* cap. 11, num. 84; Sermon 2 *In Psal.,* cxviii, num. 14, and the book *De mysteriis,* cap. 4, num. 20."
> *Patrologiae Latinae,* Tomus XVI, S. Ambrosius, pp.1428,1429, n.38.

> One is the baptism which the Church administers, the baptism of water and the Holy Ghost, with which catechumens need to be baptized. (*Exposition on Psalm 118*, s. 3, p. 18.)

I myself would say, my dear children, that a catechumen who dies before Baptism, is *punished*. The notion now is that he is rewarded! He is a great hero. What a holy man! That is a queer morbidity, is it not?

But let us return again to the "perfect act of love" which is supposed to accompany "Baptism of Desire" so as to make it be the substitute for Baptism of Water. How a man knows he has made a perfect act of love of God, I do not know! The Liberals always seem to know that he has. Without the Sacraments, we cannot determine for certain what is the value of our private acts. It is by way of discouraging this sanctificational self-sufficiency, that the inspired writer of the Book of Ecclesiastes was led to say, "Man knoweth not whether he be worthy of love or hatred." (Eccl. 9:1.)

By the way, the theologians who are so sure of how easy it is for those outside the Faith to make a perfect act of love of God when they (the theologians) are talking about salvation, are very difficult persons for you or me to meet in the confessional box when they are talking about absolution from sins. If *you* said to them, "I made a perfect act of love of God," they would say to you, "How do you know? That is presumption! No man knows whether he is worthy of love or hate!" They only allow the perfect act of love of God when they want to excuse themselves for not evangelizing Protestants and infidels.

With regard to a perfect act of love of God, the same principle applies in Confession, as in Baptism. If you commit a mortal sin and make a perfect act of love of God, the sin is forgiven. But you must mention this sin in your next Confession. If you do not, you return to the state of mortal sin. Everyone admits that.

Suppose I went to Confession and said, "Bless me, Father, for I have sinned. But I am not going to tell you my sins, I committed many mortal sins, but I made perfect acts of love."

"You had better tell me your sins!" the priest would say.

"Does not a perfect act of love forgive sins?"

"It does for an ignorant native, but not for you!"

That does not sound right, now does it?

In case any theologians, more anxious to be correct than true, – to be cautious rather than courageous, – should, at this point, offer me the difficulty: If a man in the state of mortal sin can get out of it by a perfect act of love of God, provided he *intends* to receive the Sacrament of Penance, why cannot a man in the state of original sin get out of it if he *intends* to receive the Sacrament of Baptism? My answer is, that I am not defending and never intended to defend the confession of one's sins by a *necessity of means,* for salvation. It is necessary by the *necessity of precept.* Baptism is necessary by the necessity of means *and* precept, together.

All these cautious theologians, all these truth skippers, know this as well as I do. But they pretend not to have learned it, when they are trying to teach me the Liberal value of "Baptism of Desire"; when they are trying to teach me the Sacrament of Baptism not as Christ instituted it, but as they have manufactured innovations to go with what Christ instituted.

Perhaps, before I go on, I should explain what *necessity of means* and *necessity of precept* are, in simple terms. That I will do.

If you do not receive Baptism of Water, you cannot be saved, whether you were guilty or not for not having received it. If it was not your fault that you did not receive it, then you just do not go to Heaven. You are lacking something required for Heaven. You did not add your own positive rejection of the requirement so as to give you a *positive* deficiency. Yours is a permanent lack of something required for eternal salvation.

The little baby who dies without Baptism, cannot go to Heaven. He has never committed a mortal sin. But he lacks the entrance requirement for Heaven. He will not be punished for having rejected Baptism. He will not be accused by God of having committed a mortal sin. He will go to the essential Hell (Limbo) which is the loss of the Beatific Vision. But he will not go to the Hell of fire where one is positively punished for what one has positively done.

With regard to the Sacrament of Penance, a man in the state of mortal sin is required to confess that mortal sin. If he should make a perfect act of love in the meantime, that mortal sin is forgiven, but the confessing of it is still required.

If a man should commit a mortal sin, and then elicit a perfect act of love of God, which included the intention to confess his sin, and then later went to Confession and refused to confess the sin he had been forgiven because of the act of perfect love, he would never get that sin back again. But he would get a new sin for failing to confess the old one, and that would be a new mortal sin. And that mortal sin would send him to Hell, if he died in that state.

If a man in the state of mortal sin made a perfect act of love of God, and intended to confess his mortal sin, but died before the priest reached him, he would have died before he received a sacrament which was necessary *by precept,* but not a sacrament which was necessary by the necessity of both *precept* and *means.* Penance is not of its essence a salvational sacrament. It is a sacrament of justification, or rather, of re-justification for those who are baptized. Baptism is the sacrament of justification and salvation alone, if justification has preceded it.

And now let me go back to what is called *necessity of means* in a sacramental requirement. *Necessity of means* means, if you have not got the requirement, it is just too bad for you, whether you are to blame or whether you are not to blame. If you are not to blame, it is just too bad. And if you are to blame, so much the worse!

Necessity of precept means, that if you have not fulfilled a require-ment, and you are not to blame for not fulfilling it, then it is all right, provided you have taken care of it in another way, and provided there *is* another way to take care of it.

If you have fulfilled a Divine precept in another way, you are still required to fulfill it literally in the way Christ prescribed when you can. In case you cannot, there is no need to worry.

Baptism is necessary for salvation by a necessity of means. This necessity is imposed on all men, including infants.

Baptism is necessary for salvation by a necessity of both means and precept for adults, who are not yet baptized.

Unbaptized infants who die go to Limbo. Notice, they do not go to Hell. Also notice, they do not go to Heaven.

Unbaptized adults who die go to Hell. Notice they do not go either to Limbo or to Heaven.

And, just as the necessity of Baptism for salvation is insisted on by the Church, so is the necessity of explicit Faith on the part of any adult who is going to be baptized. Under Pope Clement XI in 1703, when the missionary movement to "ignorant natives" was at its height, all mis-sionaries were explicitly forbidden by the Holy Office to baptize even a barbarian, even if he was dying, unless they elicited from him an explicit act of belief in Jesus Christ. Nor was it enough, declared the Holy Office, for this barbarian to know that God exists and is a remunerator. He must be told all the central mysteries of the Faith that derive from the Blessed Trinity and the Incarnation. The Holy Office also declared that a knowledge of these mysteries was necessary for salvation by a neces-sity of means.[5]

---

[5] The complete text of this document reads:

What I am giving you here, my dear children, is the common man's peek at discursive theology. Can you not now see why discursive theology, all by itself, will not make a saint? Can you not see why there are so many mediocre Doctors of Divinity who know only the technical values of the Faith?

We were not told by Our Lord to speak this kind of theology! We were told by Him to speak authoritatively, to say out what He had commanded us to say – be the conclusions what they may!

I have often told you what a scandal it is for the simple of heart to have to listen to nothing but professional theology preached to them, instead of authoritative theology. God's holy Word is seen not by reason of the clever reasons added to support it but by reason of the authoritative voice, and gesture, and strength, and simplicity, and indignation, and tenderness, and certitude, of the one who preaches it. We might call *this*

> Clement XI, 1700-1721.
> Concerning Truths which Necessarily Must be Explicitly Believed. (Response of the Sacred Office to the Bishop of Quebec, January 25, 1703)
> Whether a minister is bound, before baptism is conferred on an adult, to explain to him all the mysteries of our faith, especially if he is at the point of death, because this might disturb his mind. Or, whether, it is sufficient, if the one at the point of death will promise that when he recovers from the illness, he will take care to be instructed, so that he may put into practice what has been commanded him.
> *Resp.* A promise is not sufficient, but a missionary is bound to explain to an adult, even a dying one who is not entirely incapacitated, the mysteries of faith which are necessary by a necessity of means, as are especially the mysteries of the Trinity and the Incarnation.
> (Response of the Sacred Office, May 10, 1703.)
> Whether it is possible for a crude and uneducated adult, as it might be with a barbarian, to be baptized, if there were given to him only an understanding of God and some of His attributes, especially His justice in rewarding and punishing, according to this remark of the Apostle: "He that cometh to God must believe that he is and that he is a rewarder" (Heb. 11:6), from which it is inferred that a barbarian adult, in a certain case of urgent necessity, can be baptized although he does not believe explicitly in Jesus Christ.
> *Resp.* A missionary should *not* baptize one who does not believe explicitly in the Lord Jesus Christ, but is bound to instruct him about all those matters which are necessary, by a necessity of means, in accordance with the capacity of the one to be baptized. (Denzinger, 2380,2381.)

style of theology I plead for, "Pauline," in the noble sense. Saint Paul would hardly be called a Doctor of Sacred Theology by any savant today, but the Ephesians, and Colossians, and Philippians, and Romans, and Hebrews, (to speak of a few groups) knew he meant what he said because no man could possibly speak with such clarity and courage and authority unless God was speaking through him.

As I give you this grammer-school course in pretentious theological thinking, naturally I expect you, at times, to rebel and to say, "Where is the mercy of God in all this? Are we saved or damned according to theological technicalities?"

If you were to say to me, "Does it not seem odd that unbaptized children should never see the face of God?" I would have to say that it did seem odd, according to *my* standards. I do not know what scheme I would have made for unbaptized children, if I were God.

I only know what covenants God has made. I must seek first the kingdom of God and His justice as He revealed it, and let *Him* add His mercies, by Himself. I am the servant of God, not His counsellor! "*Who hath been His counsellor?*" Isaias inquires in Holy Scripture, in scorn and indignation! (Isa. 40:13.)

It might even be that it were better for a particular child to die before Baptism, and go to Limbo. Perhaps that child, if baptized, might have grown up and committed heinous mortal sins, and be hurled into postitive Hell. I do not know!

God knows, and God is more merciful than I am, and His mercies are not in the least clouded, simply because I seem not to be thinking of them when I am trying to fulfill His justice as He has revealed it.

As between an unbaptized baby in Limbo, and a blasphemy against the Sacrament of Baptism, give me the Limbo baby and let me keep the sacrament of salvation!

Another point which I must make in distinction between the necessity of Baptism and the necessity of the Sacrament of Penance, for our salvation, is this: Baptism is wholly necessary, and the Sacrament of Penance is only provisionally necessary.

You never have to go to confession unless you have committed a mortal sin. Were it to be that you never had committed a mortal sin in your whole life, you would never have needed to go to Confession in your whole life by virtue of any precept. It might be well for you to go to Confession, under this circumstance, by way of counsel, to confess your venial sins, and to help keep you from committing mortal sin, but there is no positive precept requiring anyone who has never committed a mortal sin to go to Confession at any time. With regard to the commandment of the Church by which we are required, under pain of mortal sin, to confess our sins at least once a year: we do not violate this commandment by failing to confess our sins if we have no mortal sins on our soul.

Theoretically, therefore, we could get into Heaven without ever going to Confession – if we never committed a mortal sin. There have been some saints who never committed a mortal sin in their whole lives. If they went to Confession, it was because they wanted to go, not because they were required to go by virtue of precept.

And so, with regard to the commandment to confess our sins once a year, and with regard to the general precept to confess our mortal sins, the proviso must always be added: *in case you have committed a mortal sin.*

With regard to Baptism, the outlook is completely different. We are not told we must be baptized *in case* we are in original sin. It is of the Faith that everyone of us was born in the state of original sin. We come into this world guilty enough, because of our birth, to need the waters of Baptism.

These waters of Baptism are so all-embracing in their necessity that we cannot even presume to go to Confession until this Baptism has been administered. And we are not allowed to tell in Confession any sin committed before we were baptized, because Baptism administered in the case of an adult washes away not only original sin – of which everyone is guilty – but also actual sins, in case there are any on the catechumen's soul.

It is a strange thing that I should have to be at such pains in a country where there are so many Catholic colleges, and so much theological instruction in our seminaries, to have to elaborate and painfully explain this distinction between the necessity of waters of Baptism, and the necessity of the absolution of a priest in the Sacrament of Penance.

Let us suppose that a man has elicited an act of perfect love of God before he has received Baptism. I am very much surprised if such acts of love are either practically possible, or in any sense too likely, at least since the days of Pentecost. I very much suspect acts of love of even being possible, unless the man is font-bound for Baptism as he is making them.

But, let us suppose an act of perfect love has occurred in a man's soul. Can this man be said to be freed from original sin by this perfect act of love of God? He cannot, in the true and full sense. There has not been imprinted on his soul, by reason of this perfect act of love of God, the character which Baptism imprints to seal him as redeemed, and outfit him for the resurrection of the body and life everlasting.

Therefore, I should be inclined to say that this man, by his perfect act of love of God, was freed from *one* of the effects of original sin, namely, the absence of sanctifying grace, but was not freed from the obligation to go on and secure a title to the Beatific Vision.

Even Adam, in the state of original justice, was not entitled to the Beatific Vision. Adam, in the state of sanctifying grace, without original sin, fully sanctified as far as guiltlessness could to, was still required to observe God's command not to eat of the fruit from a forbidden tree – before he could be saved!

It is not justice alone that saves us. It is justice, allied to the positive commands of God!

I will give you one more challenging answer to the muggy theological thinking of our day by our Liberal clergy, and then I promise you, my dear children, I shall go back to thinking about salvation in the ways of love, not just in the ways of logic.

Let us suppose a man receives Baptism for an evil purpose. Let us suppose he receives that Baptism sinfully. Let us suppose he receives that Baptism just to marry a dowager, just to make money, just to have his name written in the Baptismal book under the aegis of Christian protection, as thousands of Jews did in Spain.

As long as that man *intends to receive Baptism,* he is freed from original sin!

Does he go into a state of justification? He does *not.* The intention for which he received Baptism puts him immediately in the state of positive mortal sin. But the fact that he intended to receive Baptism, rids him of original sin. Were he then to go to Confession, the only sin he would be required to confess would be the sin of sacrilegious reception of Baptism, not the sin of having simply received it.

With regard to his other sins, they would have been blotted out forever, without confessing them. He might need now to add the attrition required for the forgiveness of sins, but he would not need to add the confession. And even this malefactor – even this Jew – were he later by Confession, to get into the state of sanctifying grace, would now without further Baptism, be entitled to receive the Blessed Eucharist. No unbaptized person has that right – no matter how justified he is by acts of perfect love – apart from the waters of redemption.

It is an old saying of the Church, and a true one, given us by our Holy Mother in guileless childlike fashion, that the law of praying is the law of believing. Or, as it is put in Latin, *Lex orandi est lex credendi.*

Where better could I learn how the law of praying is the law of believing than in the central structural prayers of the Holy Sacrifice of the Mass? To show you how salvation-minded our Holy Mother the Church is, for those who have passed the catechumen stage and have been admitted through the doors of Baptism into the sanctuary of her love in the Holy Sacrifice of the Mass, here is the way our Holy Mother tells her priest to pray at the Offertory of every Mass, when he is offering the host to the Eternal Father as the bread which is soon to be transubstantiated into the Body of Jesus:

> Receive, O holy Father, almighty and eternal God, this spotless host, which I, Thy unworthy servant, offer unto Thee, my living and true God, for mine own countless sins, offenses, and negligences, and for all here present; as for all faithful Christians living and dead, that it may avail both for my own and their *salvation* unto life everlasting.

Did you notice here, my dear children, the intense salvational purpose of the Mass? Did you notice here how we pray to be included in its election? And did you not also clearly notice those who are excluded?

Here is how the priest, just before the Canon of the Mass, makes his prayer of oblation of the bread and wine, and of himself and of his washed hands:

> Receive, O Holy Trinity, this oblation which we make to Thee in remembrance of the Passion, Resurrection and Ascension of our Lord Jesus Christ, and in honor of Blessed Mary ever Virgin, of Blessed John the Baptist, the holy apostles Peter and Paul, and of all the saints that it may avail to their honor and our *salvation:* and, that they may vouchsafe to intercede for us in heaven, whose memory we celebrate on earth. Through the same Christ our Lord. Amen.

Do you see here who are those who still need to be saved? And do you also see those who are being congratulated for having been saved? And do you notice the Mother, the Precursor, and the key Apostles of Jesus, put in one little group as the pure fruits of the Saviour's life and death? Are we not asking those who have been saved to save us who are still waiting for it?

There is only one Name by which we are saved, and it is the Name of Jesus. It was the Name which the angel told Our Lady and her most chaste spouse, Saint Joseph, that they should give to Jesus, not when He was born, but when He was circumcised – in the "baptism" of the Old Testament.

Briefly, my dear children, let me tell you how to handle this whole difficulty of justification and salvation, as it is presented to us by confused minds who are pretending in our day that their own doubts make for good scholarship, and by this route, for good theology.

Our Lord said, "Unless a man be born of water and the Holy Ghost he cannot enter the Kingdom of Heaven." This water means literally *water,* poured on you, sprinkled on you, or into which you are immersed. Our Lord *can* speak metaphorically, as must everyone who speaks at all, at times. But with regard to *this* water, He is not so speaking. Nothing in His utterance indicates this; nothing in the practice of the Church vouchsafes it; and nothing in the teachings of the Doctors or the definitions of the Popes, the behavior of the Apostles, or the manner of dying of the martyrs, will allow the water Christ refers to, to be other than water of the kind He was immersed in in the River Jordan, when His Father's voice was saying, "This is My Beloved Son, in Whom I am well pleased." (Matt. 3:17.)

When you hear a theologian saying, "I know that was what Christ said, but first we must understand what He means," you know you have a sceptic on your hands, who is blasphemously trying to improve on the utterances of Jesus. He is implicitly telling you that Jesus gave us vague notions as to what Baptism meant, and he (the theologian) is now going to clarify this matter.

He will then say to you, "Well, how were the souls in the Old Testament saved, before Baptism was instituted?"

You must reply to him, "There were no souls saved in the Old Testament. They had to wait in Limbo for the coming of Christ."

He will then say, indignantly, "Well, how were they justified? Was it not without Baptism?"

And you will say, "Obviously, if Baptism had not yet been instituted!"

He will then say, "Well, cannot you be justified in the New Testament without Baptism?"

The answer to this is, "Suppose you can?"

He will then say, "If you die in the state of justification, without yet being baptized, are you not saved?"

You must answer him, "No, you are not. That is your reasoning in the matter. That is not Christ's statement."

And if he persists in saying, "Well, where does one go who dies in the state of justification which has been achieved without Baptism?" –

insist that he does not go to Heaven.

And if he goes on to yell at you angrily, "Where are you going to send him – to *Hell?*", say: "No, I am not going to send him to Hell because I am not the Judge of the living and the dead. I am going to say what Christ said, 'He cannot go into Heaven unless he is baptized by water.'"

It is important to add, "*I* am making an act of Faith. *You* are not. *I* believe in Baptism because Christ revealed it, not because I have also figured it out by my own notions concerning the intrinsic requirements for justification. The reasons for a thing being so, are not the true motives of Faith. Also I believe that the reasons against a thing being so, are not the true defenses of Faith. There is only one true defense for the Catholic Faith, namely: That is not what Christ said."

There is no one about to die in the state of justification whom God cannot secure Baptism for, and indeed, Baptism of Water. The schemes concerning salvation, I leave to the sceptics. The clear truths of salvation, I am preaching to you.

If the Liberal theologians are going to end up by handing me a group of justified people who have not yet been baptized, who have to go to Heaven because they cannot go to Hell, I am going to hand them right back to the Liberal theologians to take care of !

If *I* seem to be cruel in this matter, I ask them what greater form of seeming cruelty could one offer than that of a Catholic mother's unbaptized child who died before the waters of Baptism reached his little head, and whose one reason for not now having the Beatific Vision is because he did not receive the waters of Baptism.

My own little brother was such a child, who died before he could be baptized. I have never believed that he has been saved; because I am trying to seek first the Kingdom of God and His justice, so as to save my own as yet unsaved soul.

Here is a brief catechism line-up, in case you would like to brush up on what I have been saying:

> Q. Can anyone now be saved without Baptism of Water?
> A. No one can be saved without Baptism of Water.
> Q. Are the souls of those who die in the state of justification saved, if they have not received Baptism of Water?
> A. No. They are not saved.
> Q. Where do these souls go if they die in the state of

> justification but have not received Baptism of
> Water?
> A. I do not know.
> Q. Do they go to Hell?
> A. No.
> Q. Do they go to Heaven?
> A. No.
> Q. Are there any such souls?
> A. I do not know! Neither do you!
> Q. What are we to say to those who believe there are
> such souls.
> A. We must say to them that they are making reason
> prevail over Faith, and the laws of probability over
> the Providence of God.

May I pause here to declare that I think, both with regard to the Sacrament of Baptism and the Sacrament of Penance, that the Liberal theologians, when it suits them, are making perfect acts of love of God altogether too easy for a fallen nature like ours.

I am not going to think it as difficult for a Catholic who has fallen into mortal sin but who, through his Faith, remembers his Holy Communions, his Blessed Mother, his past confessions, God's rich forgiveness in the sacraments, to make an act of perfect love, as for a catechumen, who has not yet had the benefit of *one* of God's sanctifying sacraments. But the very fact that the Church requires every mortal sin committed to be confessed, whether one is perfectly sorry for it or not, shows the Church has a maternal suspicion of this perfect act of love of God obtaining forgiveness apart from the Sacrament of forgiveness instituted by Christ.

When I am dying, my dear children, if I tell you I am in the state of mortal sin (and I promise to do so if so it seems to me) do run for a priest, no matter how far you have to run! Do not just kneel down and teach me how to perfectly love without any sanctifying grace in my soul!

If a priest reaches me before I die, know that I have truly received the mercy of God. If the priest does not reach me, then wonder very much whether I have received it or not!

That is all that can be said for our unaided love. It is only when God's own Love in Person comes down and inhabits us that our love can truly be called eternal. And the Holy Spirit is not interested in our love until the waters of regeneration have flowed on us. At the same Baptism where our Saviour was being washed with the waters of the Jordan by

Saint John the Baptist, and where the Father's voice was audible, and was heard saying, "This is My Beloved Son in whom I am well pleased," the Third Person of the Blessed Trinity, the Love of God, become visible as a dove.

Do not think, my dear children, that the waters of the world, which God took such great care in making and arranging in the initial days of creation, were not made for some supreme purpose. They were not made for mere reservoir reasons. They were made for redemptional reasons. They were meant to be the waters of salvation. And that is why, for all the monotonous simplicity that the water has in itself, God the Father has given it such variety and importance.

There is not one place in the world where you could go and say, even to the most ignorant native, "You must be baptized by water and the Holy Ghost," and hear him reply, "What is water?"

Water is the greatest physical need our nature has by way of refreshment. When men lie on the hot sands of the desert, parched and feverish, they do not cry out for money or gold or diamonds or any fantastic forms of food. They cry for water.

Water is somehow the history of the world: in the Flood; in the passage of the Chosen People through the Red Sea; and in all journeys, discoveries and explorations. It is impossible to spoil water, for no matter how much filth you pour into it, you need only drop it on the earth and let it sink into the ground, and it will purify itself and return to you in the spring and fountain, as pure and virginal as it was originally created.

Indescribable as this essentially colorless, odorless, tasteless, and unshaped substance is, God lets it roam through our world in all manners and varieties so as to give interest and color and light to our thoughts and prepare them for the initial overture of salvation. A dehydrated mind cannot function physically, cannot think imaginatively, and cannot be saved in apostolic challenge.

"As the heart panteth after the fountains of water, so my soul panteth after Thee, O God!" (Ps. 41:2.)

Water supplies us with a whole reservoir of thoughts and words so that Christianity shall have a vocabulary which the world could never improve upon. Water is the brook and the well and the spring and the fountain and the pond and the lake and the river and the gulf and the strait and the bay and the sea and the ocean. Yes, and the water is the whirlpool and the eddy and the falls and the torrent and the geyser. It is the surf, foam, breaker, wave, roller, brine, mist, dew. It is hail, snow, frost, slush, and sleet. It is ice, icicle, and iceberg; rainbow, cloud, and steam. The swimmer dives and splashes in it. The sailor travels on it. Water is what makes things damp, wet, and soggy; and it sprinkles the world, laves it, and rinses it, for there is never an end to what it can do.

Water is one of the world's greatest natural mysteries. And when God's only Begotten Son, Jesus Christ, entered our world to talk our language and take us on our own terms, He used as the first instrument of our sanctification that which was most natural for us to know and understand. He saw water all around us and did not despise it. He turned it into the child's Sacrament, the same Jesus who said,"Unless you be converted, and become as little children, you shall not enter into the Kingdom of Heaven." (Matt. 18:3.) He took water and sanctified it with spiritual power. He transformed it into the Sacrament of Baptism, by the union of water and the Holy Ghost.

When Christ died on the Cross, and the centurion pierced His side with a spear, there flowed out blood and water. (John 19:34.) All Christ's blood flowed out for our salvation. A little water followed, to indicate the simple requirement of Baptism. Imagine blood and water ever having any higher meaning in the whole of Holy Scripture than they have as they flow from the Sacred Heart of Jesus.

Saint John, the beloved disciple, was the one who saw this blood and water flow from the heart of Our Saviour after He had died:

> John 19:35. And he that saw it, hath given testimony; and his testimony is true. And he knoweth that he saith true; that you also may believe.

It is the same Beloved Disciple who concludes his beautiful revelation from God known as the Apocalypse, with these words – and so ends the whole of Holy Scripture:

> Apoc.22:1. And he showed me a river of water of life, clear as crystal, proceding from the throne of God and the Lamb...
>
> 11. He that hurteth, let him hurt still: and he that is filthy, let him be filthy still: and he that is just, let him be justified still: and he that is holy, let him be sanctified still...
>
> 14. Blessed are they that wash their robes in the blood of the Lamb: that they may have a right to the tree of life, and may enter in by the gates into the city.

15. Without are dogs, and sorcerers, and unchaste, and murderers, and servers of idols, and every one that loveth and maketh a lie.

16. I Jesus have sent my angel, to testify to you these things in the churches. I am the root and stock of David, the bright and morning star.

17. And the spirit and the bride say: Come. And he that heareth, let him say: Come. And he that thirsteth, let him come: and he that will, let him take the water of life, freely.

18. For I testify to every one that heareth the words of the prophecy of this book: If any man shall add to these things, God shall add unto him the plagues written in this book.

19. And if any man shall take away from the words of the book of this prophecy, God shall take away his part out of the book of life, and out of the holy city, and from these things that are written in this book.

20. He that giveth testimony of these things, saith, Surely I come quickly: Amen. Come Lord Jesus.

21. The grace of our Lord Jesus Christ be with you all. Amen.

WORKS CITED

Abbot, Fr. Walter, S.J. (General Editor), *The Documents of Vatican II*, America Press, New York, 1966.

Broderick, Fr. James, S.J., *Robert Bellarmine*, The Newman Press, Westminster, Maryland, 1961.

Clarke, Catherine Goddard, *The Loyolas and the Cabots*, Ravengate Press, Boston, 1950.

Clarke, Catherine Goddard, *Gate of Heaven*, Ravengate Press, Boston, 1950.

Deedy, John, *Seven American Catholics*, The Thomas More Press, Chicago, 1978.

Feeney, Fr. Leonard, S.J., *The Leonard Feeney Omnibus*, Sheed and Ward, New York, 1943.

Feeney, Fr. Leonard, MICM, *Bread of Life*, Ravengate Press, Boston, 1952.

Jurgens, W.A., *The Faith of the Early Fathers*, Volume II, The Liturgical Press, Collegeville, Minnesota, 1970.

Meer, F. Van der, *Augustine the Bishop*, translated by Brian Battershaw and G. R. Lamb, Sheed and Ward, New York, 1961.

Neuman, St. John Nepomucene, *Small Catechism of the Catholic Religion*, Baltimore 1884, St. Benedict Center, Box 142, Still River, Massachusetts, 1982.

YOU'D BETTER COME QUIETLY

After we have passed the last flaming seraph in the world of angel, what comes next? The Godhead itself?... In the order of nature, yes. In the order of grace, no!

Strangely enough, in the dispensation of Grace, creation restores itself into flesh and blood once more, and we find human nature again at the portal of the Divine Reality. We find it in the form of a girl. Our minds, weary of climbing without pictures to assist us, through the tenuous droves of spirits that lie above us in the nine worlds of angel, are refreshed once more with an imaginative picture of something we know, love and have seen, before we step across the threshold again; with hands and eyes and hair, and a heart; airing her maiden-mother manners at the summit of all creation, constituted Queen of the Universe, with dominion over all angels and all men, more beautiful in her single reality, more pleasing to God, more full of Grace, than all the rest of creation put together. She is "beautiful as the moon, chosen as the sun, mighty as an army set in array." She is the Queen of the Angels. She is the Mother and Queen of Men. She originated on this little planet of ours, pertains to our race, our kind, is related to us not by the angelic ties of love and thought, but by the very fibres of flesh and blood.

She is still a woman, even in this awful majestic status bestowed upon her by God. And she likes compliments. *Tower of Ivory, Mystical Rose, Morning Star*...Such tributes please her.

Her alliance to God is threefold. She is the Daughter of the Father, the Spouse of the Holy Spirit, and the Mother of the Son. She presents all creation with a baby, whose name in eternity is God, and whose name in time is Jesus.

She is the Mother of Divine Grace, powerful in her intercession. She is not God, she is the *Gate to God,* the Gate of Heaven. There is no passing to Eternal Life except through her. She is understanding, innocent, marvelously simple and unsuspicious, tender towards sinners. She takes us each by the hand and leads us to the Beatific Vision, and shares the radiant beauty of Christ's human nature begotten in her womb.

One cannot escape her. One cannot get into Heaven except through the Gate!

"You'd better come through the Gate!" God says to each of us. "Hesitations, incertitudes, nervousness, suspicions, doubts, what good do these do either a man or an angel?

"You'd better come through the Gate...!

"And...YOU'D BETTER COME QUIETLY!"

Fr. Leonard Feeney, "You'd Better Come Quietly,"
The Leonard Feeney Ominibus, Sheed and Ward,
New York, 1943, pp.164,165.

INDEX

pp. 331, 332.
Council of Trent;
justification by faith,
p. 345.
Pope Clement XI; explicit
faith in Trinity and
Incarnation, p. 391.
footnote, pp. 391, 392.

Feeney, Fr. Leonard:
Comparison of Brownson
and Father Feeney, p. 186.
Summary of Case from
1949 to 1972, p. 186.
Their teachings
complement one another,
pp. 186, 187.
Brownson followed St.
Thomas on catechumen,
Father Feeney, St.
Augustine, pp. 186, 187.
*Leonard Feeney: In
Memoriam* by Fr. Avery
Dulles, S.J., pp. 193-199.
St. Benedict Center
founded by Catherine
Clarke, p. 193.
Father Feeney spiritual
director of Center, p. 193.
His oratory described by
Father Dulles, p. 194.
His poetry described by
Father Dulles, p. 195.
His humor described by
Father Dulles, p. 195.
Gift of putting deepest
mysteries of faith in simple
terms, p. 196.
Vocations and Catholic
marriages, p. 197.

No salvation outside
Church, pp. 197, 198.
Did not judge; left non-
Catholics to mercy of God,
p. 198, footnote, p. 198.
Excommunication, p. 198.
Boston Common, p. 198.
Center moves to Still
River, 1958, p. 198, 199.
Reconciliation, 1972, p. 199.
Majority of disciples
reconciled in 1974, p. 199.
Two members ordained to
priesthood, p. 199.
Born in Lynn,
Massachusetts, 1898,
p. 203.
Literary editor of *America,*
p. 203.
Spiritual director of St.
Benedict Center, 1942,
p. 204.
First issue of *From the
Housetops,* p. 204.
"Sentimental Theology" by
Fakhri Maluf, *Housetops,*
September, 1947,
pp. 205-207.
Publicly praised by
Archbishop Cushing at
Center, October, 1947,
pp. 207, 208.
Infant of Prague
procession on Archbishop's
grounds, pp. 208, 209.
Ordered to Holy Cross,
August, 1948, pp. 209, 210.
Discipline versus doctrine,
pp. 210-212.
St. Thomas; superiors not